Telling the Little Secrets

Telling the Little Secrets

American Jewish Writing since the 1980s

Janet Burstein

THE UNIVERSITY OF WISCONSIN PRESS

The University of Wisconsin Press
1930 Monroe Street
Madison, Wisconsin 53711

www.wisc.edu/wisconsinpress/

3 Henrietta Street
London WC2E 8LU, England

5   4   3   2   1

Printed in the United States of America

Library of Congress Cataloging-in-Publication Data
Burstein, Janet.
    Telling the little secrets: American Jewish Writing since the 1980s /
    Janet Burstein.
        p.   cm.
    Includes index.
    ISBN 0-299-21240-8 (cloth: alk. paper)
        1. American literature—Jewish authors—History and criticism.
    2. Judaism and literature—United States—History—20th century.
    3. American literature—20th century—History and criticism.
    4. Jews—United States—Intellectual life.   5. Judaism in literature.
    6. Jews in literature.   I. Title.
    PS153.J4B868   2005
    810.9´8924´0904—dc22   2005005454

TO BOB

It's all different from what you
    think, from what I think,
the flag still waves,
the little secrets are still intact,
they still cast shadows —on this
you live, I live, we live.

Paul Celan,
translated by John Felstiner,
from *The Forward*, 2 June 2000

Contents

Preface   xi

Introduction: The New Wave   3

1   Riddling Identity: The Gates of Roth   14

2   Writing the Pathos of Belatedness:
    Second-Generation Memoirs   25

3   Voice and Mourning in the Aftermath:
    Second Generation Fictions   48

4   Recalling "Home" from Exile:
    Revisiting the Past   76

5   Portnoy's Successors: Gendered Ethnicity
    and the Embodying of Jewish Men   116

6   Becoming Rubies: Engendering Jewish Women   141

7   Midrash as Undertow: Looking Back
    and Moving On   174

    Epilogue: Moving from the Mirror
    to the Window   206

    Notes   209
    Index   249

Preface

Sometimes a sliver of one person's story can open a narrow window onto the culture of her generation. When I began to teach American Jewish literature I started my first course with stories by European Jews—in translation. I knew no Yiddish. My parents had taken care to shield me from it during the time when, as Philip Roth's Eli[1] discovers, everything European seemed somehow dark, threatening to the precarious postwar identities of American Jews. My mother had long been obsessed with the murder of Yiddish-speaking Jews in Europe. But she had turned her despair, and her rage, into devotion to Israel and the rescue of survivors. She studied Hebrew—looking away from the culture Jews had made in Europe, concentrating fiercely through my earliest childhood on the work of building a homeland and gathering into it the Jewish children of murdered parents. She wanted me to look away also. To be "American." But after years of graduate work and teaching as a Victorianist, I decided to offer a course in American Jewish literature. As I studied what immigrants and later Jewish writers had made and were making here, I needed to know what came before them, what cultural ground their work was rooted in. I believed my students needed to know that too. Seeing for the first time this gap in my education, I wondered that I had come so far—without so much.

Retrospect uncovers other avoidances in my preparation and teaching of that first course. I devoted only a tiny space in it to literature of the Holocaust. Like my mother, I probably feared the darkness of those texts and their power to dominate the course. Like a good academic, however, I rationalized their exclusion. To my department I argued that the Holocaust occupied one terrible moment in a very long and rich cultural history—a history punctuated, it was true, by periodic oppressions, but one in which Jews had been mostly active, creators of culture. The "moment" of the Holocaust had transformed them into victims. I said I didn't want students to leave my course in American Jewish literature holding an image of Jews as victims. I never questioned this decision until I began to read—about six years ago—the literature of the second generation. As I confronted in their work the legacy of the Holocaust that persists among us, I wondered again at the gap in awareness that I had now perpetuated in my students.

In these and other familial, personal, and professional turnings away from European Jewry—and what happened to it in our time—one can see a fragment of a pattern that is also collective. This book traces the larger pattern in stories, including those framed as autobiographies and memoirs, which open windows onto the culture of avoidance—and its aftermath—among American Jews. I am particularly interested here in the aftermath, for I belong to it—as both a literary scholar and an American Jewish woman. It seems to me that in the aftermath of loss, one first reaches back. I can see that first gesture in much of my own work. Distanced from the European past, its culture and its violent erasure, by parents who hurled themselves forward after its destruction—into the American and the Zionist future—I took up scholarly work that looked always backward: first to the myths that underlay Western culture, then to the study of Victorian literature that seemed deeply attuned to potentially explosive tensions beneath the surfaces of ordinary life. Only marginally aware of particular stresses in Jewish women's experience because my mother suffered but obscured them, I studied in the aftermath of her deprivations the feminist writings that burgeoned not only within my specialty, Victorian literature, but everywhere in intellectual and Jewish life during the seventies. I have written that part of the aftermath in my earlier book about Jewish mothers and daughters. But from within the growing awareness of my own deprivations, as a Jewish woman turned away from graduate work in Jewish studies, directed instead toward a literary program, I turned toward the study of American Jewish literature. Because my critical lens has been ground partly by the effort to clarify my mother's and my own losses, and partly by the attempt to recuperate them, I suspect that the work of the aftermath includes both the recognition of loss and the effort to move beyond it.

This book proposes to study the work of American Jewish writers since the eighties to discover the ways in which contemporary culture addresses its losses, reconstructs memory of the Jewish past and what happened to it, and moves on. I believe that work is reshaping our sense of our collective experience. Cultural historians are already at work trying to explain the recuperative literary interest in the Jewish past. Some scholars ask, for example, why the complex, multivocal, collective discourse of American Jews waited so long to address and reformulate issues that rise out of the Holocaust. And why this part of the collective past has now become so prominent in contemporary writing. This study attempts not to explain but to clarify that cultural shift by studying the ways in which writers since the eighties have both reflected it and helped it to happen. Aware of their losses, the writers considered here reconfigure issues and assumptions that have vexed American Jews since the time of the immigrants; they reformulate familiar preoccupations; they do important cultural work.

Jane Tompkins has described best, I think, the critical attempt undertaken by this study: to see literary works not just as "objects of interpretation and appraisal," but as "powerful examples of the way a culture thinks about itself."[2] Because literature is one of many discourses that stream through our cultural lives, stories not only reflect and clarify our preoccupations but also serve as "agents of cultural formation."[3] They shape our sense of issues that are alive but often unarticulated in what critics since Lionel Trilling have recognized as the almost inaudible "hum and buzz of implication" that surrounds us all the time. To some extent we breathe and speak and move about in culture like fish in water, unaware of the medium that nourishes, supports, and weighs upon us. Therefore, Tompkins argues, we need to see stories "as doing a certain kind of cultural work within a specific historical situation . . . as providing society with a means of thinking about itself" (200). One can see the thumbprint of this cultural work in writings of the last decades: they return to ethnic issues,[4] they engage with some old and still unresolved problems, and they try to reframe them, finally, in terms of the culture and the loss of European Jewry that came before. Most urgent here is the attempt to see how these efforts inflect the attitudes of American Jews toward longstanding concerns: with our sense of ourselves as gendered, embodied creatures, with the ancient and ongoing Jewish problem of being at home in exile, and with the fashioning of collective memory.

For the most part, I have included in this study American writers who speak as Jews: whose work owns a Jewish past and looks forward to a Jewish future—a simple solution to a very complicated problem—and whose writings were published after nineteen-eighty—an arbitrary yet surprisingly accurate boundary for this long "moment" of cultural turning. I have included novels, short stories, memoirs, and autobiographies but not, until the last chapter, critical essays. I believe—like Cynthia Ozick—that the telling of stories and the writing of critical essays are surely related; both, she has taught us, are hypotheses, fictions "made up in response to an excited imagination."[5] But the need to curtail the number of texts considered within a single study argued against the inclusion of critical essays except for those that seemed to me to reshape the form of the essay itself in an effort to instruct collective memory. As always, my principles of inclusion and exclusion probably say as much about my own critical idiosyncrasies as about the field in general. I lean toward what seems important, deep, and particularly fraught in these decades. I haven't tried to write a cultural or literary history of this period. But I like to think I have chosen texts and subjects that demonstrate clearly the kinds of cultural work that I believe contemporary writings are doing.

Solitary at this desk, I want to summon here the familiar spirits whose presence has sustained the work. Some of them are writers and teachers: wise, generous, and kind friends who read a chapter now and then and told me what was missing or unclear. Thanks especially to Aryeh Lev Stollman, Norma Rosen, David Roskies, Pearl Abraham, Thane Rosenbaum, Sarah Mechlovitz—and two excellent, but nameless, readers for the press. They bear no responsibility for the remaining defects. Karla Simcikova, Josie Cook, and the Drew library staff were the most precious of research resources. Paolo Cucchi, "my" dean, was the most ingenious finder of support for this project. Beloved children, Julie and Mark Burstein, Mark Maben, and David Calle, keep me steady against the pull of the past; blessed grandsons, Zeke and Micah, make me hopeful for the future. My husband, Bob, has taught me through his long illness many things about loss, and love, and memory. Those dear things have probably found their way into the subtext of this book—which is dedicated to him.

Telling the Little Secrets

Introduction

The New Wave

Like a stone that falls into deep water, the extermination of the European Jews caught our attention and then seemed to sink from view. But where it lay, beneath the surface of collective consciousness, it attracted in time the imagination of American Jewish writers—who coaxed it back into visibility. Both its disappearance and its reappearance have become "interesting": subjects of speculation, research, and argument.[1] Cultural historians seem now to be concerned with the reasons why it went unnoticed for so long. Writers have been showing us since the late fifties the cultural consequences of its disappearance. And in the last twenty years an all but obsessive preoccupation with the European past has become not only the subject of much American Jewish writing, but also a pervasive presence—even in works that concentrate on other subjects. Indeed, virtually all the salient issues that perplex American Jews and that figure in their literature after 1980 are bent, wrinkled in some way by either the forgetting or the remembering of what happened in the thirties and forties to the Jews of Europe.

It's not hard to imagine at least one reason why Americans looked away so quickly from the evidence uncovered by liberation of the camps. They had other things to think about. Peter Novick points out that Buchenwald was liberated on April 11; on April 12 President Roosevelt died. Dachau was liberated on April 29; Mussolini was executed a day earlier; Hitler committed suicide a day later. Mauthausen was liberated on May 6; the next day Germany surrendered. Then came the battles of Iwo Jima and Okinawa, followed by the bombings of Hiroshima and Nagasaki, and finally VJ Day. It's hardly surprising that these events chased from the front pages the first pictures—of emaciated, corpse-like men who stood behind barbed wire, their eyes full of horror, despair, and accusation; and of women who sat on the earth peeling potatoes while a mound of tangled, dead bodies spread across the field behind them. Reminders of the dead, and of the damage done to those who still lived, simply faded from general awareness, displaced by other significant images of World War II.

We also know, now, reasons why this initial displacement lasted for so long. Jonathan Freedman explains that American Jews busied themselves after the war with the work of assimilation and "culture making"—apparently unconcerned with their severance from European Jewish culture and, indeed, from European Jews. As first- and second-generation immigrants struggled to infiltrate the cultural industries of postwar America, they made their way into what Freedman calls the Anglo-Saxon "temple of high culture." European Jews appeared to have been irrelevant to this structure. One wonders, though. Maybe as assimilationists entered this temple their buried feelings about the murders and cultural losses made their way into other channels. Maybe we can even discern the ghosts of those feelings in what Freedman describes as the assimilationists' aggressions against and idealizations of the non-Jewish writers they sought to own, to imitate, to revise, and in some cases to subvert.

The losses they were to busy to notice—much less to mourn—were not, however, without consequences for American Jews. In 1959 Philip Roth's "Goodbye, Columbus" showed us the nature of those consequences. His portrayal of the Patimkins highlights one dimension of assimilationist, middle-class American Jewish life in the fifties: its emphasis on materiality and appearances, its reverence for wealth and status—for cashmere sweaters, straight, short noses, and Ivy League credentials—its pretentious moralizing and even deeper irresponsibility. Without analyzing the sources of this emphasis—were they just too busy to mourn? was the busy-ness of getting and spending an avoidance of the work of mourning? were they cushioning their lives materially against spiritual and psychological losses and anxieties too massive to be acknowledged?—Roth juxtaposed in other early stories these features of postwar American Jewish culture with its apparent disregard for the recent European past and its survivors. "Eli, the Fanatic," for example, dramatized the layer of dark memory that threatens would-be assimilationists when a community of religious survivors settles in a newly integrated American suburb. Eli Peck, a nearly assimilated lawyer, eventually moves into that darkness, exchanging clothes as he identifies himself with one of the survivors.

Roth's Zuckerman in *The Ghost Writer* (1979) would take a similar path. The novel invokes the image of Brenda Patimkin's cosmetic surgery to highlight the increasingly fragile, shrill, self-protective insistence of assimilating American Jews on their difference from the Jews of Europe: "We are not the wretched of Belsen!" Nathan Zuckerman shouts: "We are not the victims of that crime! You want to see physical violence done to the Jews of Newark, go to the office of the plastic surgeon where the girls get their noses fixed. That's where the Jewish blood flows in Essex County."[2] Zuckerman's defense will ultimately collapse; he will want to marry the ghost of Anne Frank, a metaphor that corrects the disconnection that had long defended American Jews against fuller awareness of the Holocaust—but had also, one suspects, rendered their lives as Jews sterile and superficial.[3] First the denial of likeness, then the desire to "marry" Anne Frank: in some ways we seem to have lived out Roth's metaphor. Chapter 1 develops more fully his importance to writers of the eighties and after, but here it is sufficient to note that his stories bracket the continuum of American Jewish attitudes toward what had happened in Europe.

In the late fifties and sixties American Jews began to retrieve *Yiddishkeit,* and researchers began to confront the traumatic aftereffects of the Holocaust on survivors—most of whom had gone silent during the years when no one wanted to hear their stories. That work of retrieval and confrontation—vital to the process of mourning—is incomplete. Despite recent scholarly arguments about the contamination of our collective memory by cynically exploitative, self-serving interests within the American Jewish community,[4] the deeper cultural effort to diminish the felt distance between American Jews and the European past, to reconnect imaginatively, emotionally, to the Jews of Europe and what happened to them is actually in process. American Jewish literature after 1980 testifies to the need and the nature of that process and also empowers readers to move through it. As Jane Tompkins has suggested, these writings clarify issues alive in the culture though obscured by habit, by confusion, by inattentiveness. They also provide "society with a means of thinking about itself." When Brenda Patimkin's plastic surgery begins to call up the blood spilled elsewhere by European Jews, when Eli sees himself in the emaciated, bereaved dark person wearing Eli's green suit, fiction does its cultural work: raising into awareness— if only in the form of questions or angry responses—issues whose power to disturb the order of our lives keeps them closeted behind the cashmere sweaters.

The term "new wave" was first applied to American Jewish writers who undertook this cultural work in the eighties and nineties by novelist Thane Rosenbaum, former literary editor of the magazine *Tikkun*.[5] In his view, their work reverses the flight from ethnic identity so common in earlier American Jewish writing. He believes they participate in a kind of "neurotic millennial return" to commitments rebelled against by immigrant writers and all but abandoned by writers of the fifties, sixties, and seventies.[6] But the shape and the consequences of renewed interest in the Jewish past, I think, vary as writers lift different threads of the fabric of collective Jewish experience that had once seemed so tightly woven, so whole. Sometimes nostalgically warmed, sometimes stifled by the Jewish past, immigrant and postwar writers had tended either to embrace or to discard it. But writers of the new wave may be enraged by the violence that tore it apart, or carefully skeptical about its virtues, or imaginatively inspired by its power, still, to move them.

Some writers of the new wave try (rarely unambivalently) to draw from the fabric of the Jewish past one—or several—of its various threads of the Jewish past: of spirituality, traditional piety, or textual study; of intellectualism, or political or social activism, for example. Or they engage again the conflicts with "tradition" that earlier generations set aside. Some confront the violent erasure of the European past by reinventing it. Longing to experience what was first lived in and then lost during the Holocaust, some writers anxiously, obsessively press imagination to raise the walls of home in a wasteland. And once the homeplaces begin to take shape in their work, they mold and

turn them, holding shadowed portions to the light while surfaces more nostalgically familiar recede into darkness, shedding
sentimental associations as their insides and undersides become
visible. The grotesque and the darkly comic find a home in these
reimagined spaces, often stripped of comfort because they are accompanied by the rage and pain of their violent loss.[7] The tendency in these writings to critique as well as recollect, to see
clearly as well as to honor the past, suggests that "return" may
overstate what appear more like gestures of urgent, but intermittent, reconnection.

I consider first, within this group, writings by children of
people who survived the Holocaust. Because their work confronts directly the legacy of the destruction of European Jews, it
functions also as a kind of lens that brings into focus several salient issues in the literature of the last decades. I believe this is as it
should be. These writers belong to us for they were raised here,
not in Europe. Unlike the survivors, who grew up in a world we
cannot know, the second generation shares our cultural memories and speaks to us in our own language. Yet they also stand
closer to that center of radical destruction—like the crater left
by a bomb—in which our dead, and much of the culture they
created, are lost. Reversing my mother's insistence that the rehabilitation of European survivors and their reentry into the mainstream should be central to the work of American Jews after the
war, these writers set the crater itself, smoldering still, at the
center of their fictional worlds. And the buried pain and rage that
radiate from that place transform language, and narrative structure, and character in the stories of the second generation, fractur-
ing the old world rhythms of talk that distinguished Malamud's
and Bellow's work, disrupting the forward flow of story, shiver-
ing into jagged shards, each one edged and lethal, the carapace of
self within which so many postwar American Jews moved into
the universities and law firms and publishing houses. Thus, gestures of "reconnection" in stories of the second generation often
release the panic that turned the attention of my mother and so
many others in her generation away from the Holocaust

The dangers of inattentiveness come very clear in stories of
the second generation, which uncover what Paul Celan called the
"little secrets" of our collective past. A poet who survived the
Nazis, Celan observed that "the little secrets are still intact, they

still cast shadows." Overwritten now by the violence that would have erased them, significant elements of the collective past survive. Avoidance of their shadows condemns some protagonists in second-generation stories to breakdown: a young lawyer on the corporate fast track is suddenly stalled in an elevator and hauled off to the cattle cars; a young artist crumples at his drawing board, envisioning heaps of corpses piled all around him at the moment of his greatest success. Through the lens offered by these protagonists it may even be possible to perceive consequences in the world outside the stories. If it is true, as John Hollander suggests, that "we have as yet had no great Jewish literary culture in English"[8] perhaps it is because inattention to the "little secrets" has confined American Jews to the surface of their experience, away from the deep sources of energy and imagination that lie beneath the rubble of the past—in which creativity as well as terror abides.

The work of second-generation writers brings light to those dark places by writing large the residue of the Holocaust that stays within the way our collective perplexities have taken shape. Children of survivors are equipped for this task partly by the accident of birth. Like all of us, they live within the emotional geography of their parents; thus their voices remain faithful to that landscape in a way that other writers cannot approximate.[9] Unlike some writers who "witness" the Holocaust, in Norma Rosen's phrase, only "through the imagination," second-generation writers witness the legacy of that trauma through its emotional residue in themselves. Their imagination constructs from that residue fictional worlds they never knew, in which conventionally smooth surfaces break open, allowing the grotesque to surface to the interstices. And as they perform that task, their work reconnects readers—emotionally, imaginatively—with losses that have not yet been mourned. Psychoanalysts and historiographers insist that the past haunts and hobbles us until its losses are mourned. Chapters 2 and 3 of this book argue that memoirists and "fictionists" of the second generation move us toward this end.

Among the "little secrets" that they and other writers of the new wave uncover, still "intact" beneath their "shadows," three have become the subjects of later chapters in this book. First among them, the effort to reconnect the gritty texture—the warts and wrinkles—of reality to the image of the world "before" Auschwitz discloses a contemporary uncertainty about what "home" means. The Jewish world destroyed by the Nazis became what Anne Karpf calls "mythological" in the memory of survivors and refugees. After traveling for the first time to Poland Karpf remembers: "the first shock was that the country really did exist—after all those years as a mental category, an abstraction, its materiality astonished me."[10] In some writings by the second generation and others of the new wave, protagonists undertake journeys that embed mythic places of loss and suffering within the often abrasive experience of lived geography. They complicate the word "home" for American Jews; they reconnect our sense of homeland to a world vastly different now from the one that expelled, imprisoned, and murdered its Jews, from which traces of a Jewish presence have been largely erased. In other writings the effort to imagine homelands the writers never knew is saturated not only with anxiety, grief, and sometimes rage for losses too massive to bear, but also, at times, with clear-eyed appraisal of the sacrifices exacted by traditional culture. Chapter 4 of this study considers the nature of "home" in new wave writings.[11]

Chapters 5 and 6 discuss the ways in which reconnection with the "little secrets" of the collective past highlights a radical transformation in the way we think—both as individuals and as Jews—about identity. Most pointed in second-generation literature is the postmodern, post-Auschwitz, now highly theorized sense of the individual self as fractured, strange, unrecognizable to itself in its ceaseless changes. These chapters develop the issue of identity in new wave writings through the lens of gender. No other subject reveals more fully the startling range and breadth of preoccupations among writers of this group.

Embodied thinking about gender identity takes on radically divergent forms within these stories. Chapter 5 argues that male writers of the second generation concentrate chiefly on the ways in which the Holocaust reshaped the meaning of "manliness" for Jewish men. Emphasized and reinforced by linguistic edginess as well as by unpredictable eruptions of playfulness and grotesquerie, the dilemma of the postmodern self is embodied in second-generation stories partly within the scars, the handicaps, the psychic and physical deformations of their characters. The eyes of one survivor in Melvin Bukiet's *After*, for example, are permanently damaged because the Nazis made him wear glasses that limited his vision, while the jagged, painful remnants of another survivor's teeth testify eloquently to the grotesquely playful sadism of his captors.

Suddenly, brutally, denied the power to choose, to act, to protect, or to sustain either themselves or their dependents, male survivors and their male children are often marked in second-generation writings by the consequences of these violent aggressions against their adult manhood. But other stories by male writers of the new wave, chapter 5 suggests, focus on the postmodern, post-Holocaust complexities of sexual preference. As they follow the lead of Philip Roth, whose phallocentric view of Jewish identity culminated memorably in the apparition of the circumcised penis around which the ghost of Zuckerman gathered itself in *The Counterlife*, these writers develop the issue of identity partly through the power of sexual desire and partly through the scars—ritual, social, and psychic as well as historical—that mark the bodies of Jewish men.

Instead of "reading the scars" left by the Holocaust, in Dominick LaCapra's words, other writers of the new wave look at the effects of both old cultural imperatives and modern capitalist demands upon our sense of what "womanliness" means. Chapter 6 argues that where the embodiment of Jewish women's identity is concerned, Philip Roth is less a forerunner than the women who wrote in Yiddish at the end of the nineteenth and beginning of the twentieth centuries, who began, to borrow a phrase from Adrienne Rich, to "think through the body" about the effect of old cultural assumptions on women's sense of themselves. New wave writings make visible the "little secrets" that lie at the ethnic roots of contemporary women's issues like anorexia and the reproduction of mothering. These stories clarify the dilemma created for Jewish women by rabbinic exclusions and imperatives of service that are "still intact": shadowy remnants of a Jewish past that weighs, still, upon the work of later writers like E. M. Broner and Phyllis Chesler as well as upon writers of the new wave. If Jewish writers have been "thinking through the body," as Rich advised,[12] for decades in both Europe and America, their stories are working through the surviving residue of a cultural tradition—within specific historical and social circumstances—that has helped to shape the ways in which Jewish women continue to see themselves.

Chapter 7 turns from home, gender, and the body to consider the work of collective memory—which depends upon our power to recover and interpret the "little secrets" of our long history. In some respects, that work is complicated by the Holocaust and by the distance between us and our cultural origins. Second-generation writers "re-collect" by reclaiming images that have been contaminated by the Holocaust: images of showers, of crowded trains, of tattoos, hair, glasses, teeth, smoke, and ghosts are everywhere in their writings, serving the uses of the present as they carry into contemporary experience the memory of past suffering. As they reclaim such tainted fragments of the past, they raise doubts about the existence of divine authority—placing redemptive work, instead, into the human hands of writers. Thus Melvin Bukiet judges the too-late liberators of Auschwitz through his cynical young survivors in *After*. And Thane Rosenbaum arrogates to himself as writer the power to command revelation as one character, naked in a stone shower in Poland, discovers the tattoo on his brother's arm. As these works probe the absence (or impotence? or withdrawal?) of a transcendent power who might render meaningful Jewish suffering and loss in the Holocaust, they raise the possibility of disconnection from the spiritual posture of our ancient sources.

Chapter 7 argues, however, that the still vital connection between new wave writers and traditional Jewish texts mixes what T. S. Eliot once called "memory and desire," irony and longing. Passionately ambivalent, the link between contemporary Jews and their writing predecessors pulses with life. Animated by what I want to call the "midrashic impulse," several works manifest a tendency to "look back" toward foundational texts even as they "move forward," sustaining in contemporary literature many of the concerns that motivated the original, rabbinical midrashists. Beginning with personal essays on biblical subjects by feminists of the eighties, chapter 7 describes the reshaping of the essay as a literary form in the hands of writers like Norma Rosen, Cynthia Ozick, and Jonathan Rosen, for whom the midrashic impulse is pronounced and persistent. It considers as well the fictions in which the psychological and philosophical implications raised within our ancient texts remain vital, perplexing—and inspiring to contemporary writers.[13]

On the whole, then, this study argues that, like contemporary literature of any period, writings of the new wave function in one way like lenses that clarify who we are now, what we fear or wish for, what we need, and how we're doing. These stories also nudge us emotionally, imaginatively, through areas of cultural malaise that might otherwise remain opaque—beneath the surface of collective awareness. At the risk of overemphasizing this point: this process is neither descriptive nor prescriptive—it's not sociology but cultural work.

I have wondered for a long time about the malaise that must lie beneath such cultural work, under the effort to reconnect with what remains and to take up the work of mourning so many decades after the fact of loss. In the view of some scholars the reasons rise out of communal self-interest: protectiveness toward Israel, or the desire of Jewish institutions to bind American Jews into a community. In 1980, however, at the very beginning of the period in which the trajectory of American Jewish writing seems to have changed, Alain Finkielkraut's *The Imaginary Jew*[14] proposed a different sort of explanation that touches "self-interest" at a deeper level. Finkielkraut described himself and other French Jews after the Holocaust as "lost and isolated souls . . . individuals who feel Jewish" but who are "people just like everyone else, trying to convince themselves that they're somehow different from the norm. They're the children and grandchildren of immigrants, handed proud difference as a legacy in trust; they can realize it only through the means they possess: the vaguest reminiscences, a moribund, symbolic system and a language that lies in shreds" (96). Stripped of cultural supports that can tell them who they are, Finkielkraut's Jews evoke the memory of Hitler's victims: stripped of hair, names, clothing, and the social markings that had identified them. Culturally shorn and divested, Finkielkraut's Jews recall the Holocaust to remind themselves of what it means to be a Jew.

But remembering may help us not just to identify as Jews with victims of the Holocaust but to recognize that the loss of their culture and their language—which were also murdered—has left us without those distinctive ways of being Jewish in the world. Now, Finkielkraut argues, many Jews try to compensate for those losses by turning to traditional ritual to express what he calls a bond "that links Jews with themselves (and with their dead)" (98). He observes that this turning is not always effective, for we are not victims, and traditional ritual is, for many of us, not only empty of faith, but also inadequate to our cultural need: "The rites that we perpetuate with the timidity of novices and the clumsiness of amateurs are neither the heart nor the whole of Judaism: they are the remains." Finkielkraut fears they may be all we have left: "the last chance for a people whose other cultures have been killed or turned to folklore. The single and fragile chance that has been given us to move beyond dreaming and to not be imaginary Jews" (99).

Finkielkraut's insight may explain the genesis of the creative impulses that are so powerful in writings of the new wave. They show us what it means to reconnect with the past—without hope of reviving it. To listen to the old secrets so that—engaging with them—one can feel their vitality, setting aside residual pieties that feel empty, and discarding falsenesses of nostalgic sentimentality. To "move beyond dreaming." To see clearly, even to feel what has been lost. And to hold very close what remains. Before we move into whatever comes next.

1

Riddling Identity
The Gates of Roth

When the war was over, American Jewish writers enjoyed a dazzling moment of cultural attention. They differed from their ethnic predecessors partly because they were more fully assimilated into American culture, which muted and transformed—though it did not erase—the immigrant struggle with tradition. They did not share the immigrants' optimism. As their work moved into the generous current of the American mainstream, it carried some of the disillusionment that followed terrible losses: of life, of culture, of confidence in the way the world worked. In many of their stories only the energy and modest goodness that could assert itself, fitfully, in individuals seemed capable of sustaining confidence. Although Malamud's little people, like Morris Bober and Seymour Levin, are entirely naked to a brutal reality, they try to do what they can, because they can. Other protagonists of the fifties—Bellow's Herzog and Sammler, for example—also carry the frightening shadow of the recent past into the vernacular of American literature, writing helpless letters of protest or responding, fruitlessly, to increasingly barbaric human propensities no longer restrained by tradition, or community, or law, or courtesy, or compassion. Some characters confront the emptiness of old promises: Olsen's Eva bravely recognizes in her last moments the broken dream of social justice that had animated her entire life, and even Paley's Faith, knowing how often commitments made to her and her children fall short, keeps running nevertheless toward the possibility of honoring her own commitment to humankind. Despite some bitterness at the way the world works, many postwar fictions articulate a kind of wonder at the energy, integrity and determination of individuals.

But Philip Roth's work distinguishes itself in this field by exposing the fault lines along which individual character breaks down. His early stories prefigure in this and several other ways the general direction of the new wave. Despite the howls of Jewish protest that Roth's work first evoked, it turns an important corner in the trajectory of American Jewish writing, marking what one critic called the "passage from a literature of immigration and assimilation to a literature of retrieval"[1]—a turning that appears even more emphatic in work of the eighties and nineties. Like writers of those decades Roth also probes the condition of postwar American Jewish life, summoning into collective awareness both our disconnection from the "little secrets" of the shadowed past and the inadequacies of contemporary culture. Most important, his work opens the gate to a crucial element of the new wave's literary agenda as it trumpets the discontinuities and incoherencies within the postmodern, post-Auschwitz self.[2]

The dilemma of becoming oneself in Roth's work is deeply connected to his awareness of what happened in Europe. What critics have often identified as "self-hatred" in Roth's work may be seen instead, I suspect, as painfully accurate insight into the more general malaise of postwar American Jews. It's a malaise rooted partly in the difficulty of not knowing how to move forward when it's so disturbing to look back. Neil Klugman in "Goodbye, Columbus," discovering his feelings as he speaks them,[3] is already an embryo writer, caught in "numbness" between Newark and Short Hills, between the "throwing off" tendencies of his Aunt Gladys and the "gathering in" disposition of the Patimkins. A veteran of the European war, Neil knows at least three responses to the European past: the death of affect and purposefulness that follow terrible loss; the desire to cast out what cannot be integrated into the forward movement of one's life; the defensive work of getting and spending that attempts to wall out the unbearable, to protect the self from unspeakable threat. In the "small colored boy" (22) who haunts the Newark library and taunts its stone lions the story discovers yet another response to catastrophe: the longing for return to a time of peace and plenty—before catastrophe. It is a longing comically punctured in the heroine's brother, Ron Patimkin, whose dream of the personal past has disconnected from anything he is likely to experience again.

Throughout the story Neil's disconnection from spiritual certainties of the past underlies his inability to make plans for his future. It touches as well his uncertainty about his love for Brenda. While she is securing the diaphragm he has insisted on, he prays in an empty Catholic church to a part of himself he calls "God," asking "What is it I love, Lord? Why have I chosen? . . . Which prize is You?" And then he feels ashamed, reminding himself that the only prize possible, in the world as it is, is the sexual pleasure, the gold dinnerware, the sporting goods trees that will come to him with Brenda Patimkin (71). In choosing her, he is choosing also himself. When he dresses like her to go running he looks like her, only bigger (50). And the part of himself that he calls "God" laughs at him for imagining that there might be an alternative to the future that Brenda will haul him into.

This dilemma of self-invention will become a persistent feature of Roth's work. At least one contemporary critic has seen in this process as it appears in later works, *The Zuckerman Trilogy* and *The Counterlife,* a "peculiarly diasporic playfulness"; she believes that Roth's characters are privileged to "try out any role, any character, without paying the consequences of fixed identity."[4] But writers of the new wave—particularly writers of the second generation—see as less "playful" the uncertainties about the self that Roth's protagonists write large. "Malamud and Bellow," one new wave writer has said, "knew what they could become. They came from Delmore Schwartzland, an immigrant place. And they knew where they were going: to the University of Chicago, with leather patches on their elbows. But we were born out of Auschwitz, so we look in the mirror and we don't know who we are. We get to where Malamud and Bellow wanted to be, and we get stuck in elevators and hauled back to the cattle cars."[5] Seen through the lens of Auschwitz, "a fixed identity" becomes a kind of privilege that Roth doesn't allow his protagonists, and that writers of the new wave will deny their protagonists as well.

To some extent, of course, identity has always been a major theme of American Jewish literature—concerned since its immigrant beginnings with the conundrum of ethnicity in a multicultural society: with "passing," for example, or with faithfulness to one's origins.[6] But the vagaries of the individual self that become apparent in Roth's work and later in the new wave have complicated and intensified this long-standing literary interest, absorbing into story postmodern theoretical speculations on subjectivity and agency. What does it mean to draw theory into the discourse of fiction? In part, it means to seize the feeling of ideas: to see what Wordsworth called the "impassioned expression" upon the face of science.[7] But it also means to follow the logic of ideas to their most likely human ends.

We cannot speculate about the nature of the self without consequence, the novelist insists. What our lives become will carry the traces of our radical skepticism about the possibility of resolving conflicts; of our doubt that we can reconcile ourselves to limits imposed by our choices; of our belief that we contain more possibilities than any single choice can realize; of our disappointment that we are separate from one another however strong our longing for connection. These ideas will shape our experience. We live them out, the novelist shows us, not only in the ways we interact with one another but also in the hidden moments when we try to understand who we are, how we got to be who we are, why we run away from what we desire—or reach for what we know will do us harm.

From the beginning, Roth's stories touch a particularly troubling dimension of postmodern, post-Holocaust thought and experience by allowing protagonists to live out the consequences of our lost confidence in the wholeness, and stability, and agency of the self. After Neil Klugman, Roth focused on the figure of the writer to explore these consequences, probably because the necessary narcissism of writers provided both an ideal medium and a perfect excuse: "His *self* is to many a novelist what his own physiognomy is to a painter of portraits: the closest subject at hand demanding scrutiny, a problem for his art to solve—given the enormous obstacles to truthfulness, *the* artistic problem" (Roth's emphasis).[8]

In *My Life as a Man* (1974) the writer Peter Tarnopol both lives and writes out his preoccupation with this "artistic" problem, demonstrating the human consequences of our lost confidence. Unable, even with the help of a psychiatrist, to unravel the threads out of which the disasters of his life appear to have been woven, Tarnopol marries and divorces, publishes and then falls silent, seeks love and then drives it away without ever being able to understand either the genesis or the logic of his behavior. His turnings and returnings remain baffling; his internalized images of his parents remain matters of intense dispute; and his power to make decisions and to act on them is severely damaged. When a bookstore clerk recognizes him and asks: "whatever happened to you?" Tarnopol can only respond "I don't know. . . . I'm waiting to find out myself." "Waiting"—not "trying" or "wanting": this character's agency has yielded to a passivity that leaves him trapped in endless debate with his psychiatrist over incompatible readings of his own past and motivations. Tarnopol is truly imprisoned within the dilemma of the self. After meeting the bookstore clerk, he walks to his psychiatrist's office through the noisy chaos of Manhattan, hearing only the "bookstore boy's heartfelt question" and his own "bemused reply": "That was all I had heard," he remembers, "through the world-famous midtown din which travelers journey halfway round the globe to behold" (236–37). In this novel, the self becomes a sealed echo chamber from which there is no exit.

The pathos underlying the bravura transformations of later works like *The Ghost Writer* and *The Counterlife* is clear in these earlier stories about the failure of agency, stability, and coherence in the postmodern self. Roth's work also begins to clarify some particularly Jewish wrinkles within this dilemma,[9] for he links it, in part, to losses that followed the trauma of the immigration and, then, the destruction of European Jewry and its culture.[10] One such loss has been the erosion of traditional spiritual and cultural assumptions that once defined and stabilized the self. In the empty church where Roth's earliest protagonist asks, "What is it I love, Lord? Why have I chosen?" the writer imagines the condition of this character—alienated from the collective spiritual wisdoms that might once have guided such choices.

The causal link between the loss of collective assumptions and the radical discontinuities in Roth's image of the self is not hard to see. When collective memory no longer confirms traditional values and beliefs, when texts and teachings—which once carried traditional assumptions through exile, across borders and generations—get forgotten or lost, it grows harder not only to know what one is supposed to want but also to reconcile desires that tear across self-defining boundaries. Thus the stories that lead to *The Counterlife* (and later to *Operation Shylock*)[11] trace the emergence of a primary theme in Roth's work, in which writers/narrators/protagonists and their brothers double and redouble themselves, transformed in some works into body parts and in others into pornographers, zionists, "diasporists," émigrés, surgical victims and survivors, as they process without guidance or traditional restraints the choices that will define their lives.

Traditional moral imperatives, Roth argues, once identified Jewish characters (like Malamud's Morris Bober or Bellow's Artur Sammler, for example) with "conscience" and Gentile characters with "appetite."[12] Consequently, older Jewish men, often the fathers or father figures of Roth's protagonists, usually do the right thing for their wives and offspring, even though they end their working days with "stupendous" headaches (*My Life as a Man* 3). Roth's young protagonists, driven by uncurbed aggressions and desires, will remember—with piercing ambivalence—the circumscribed lives, anchored in spiritual and moral certainties, of their fathers. But, unanchored in such certainties, the younger men will be unable to replicate those lives. Instead, they will constantly remake themselves, demonstrating by each transformation an uncertainty and fluidity of identity no longer restrained by collective spiritual or moral commitment, untutored by traditional teaching.

Roth's legacy to writers of the new wave includes not only this poignant awareness of generational loss but also the stylistic wackiness and unpredictability that follows in its wake. For example, Jonathan Freedman has noticed that at the center of *The Ghost Writer*, a novel that confronts the loss of multiple fathers and father figures, Roth writes a scene in which Zuckerman first masturbates ("he is, after all, a Roth hero," Freedman observes),[13] then rereads a novella by Henry James, a literary father figure, and finally stands on top of the novella, to get close enough to the ceiling to eavesdrop on the supposed ghost of Anne Frank in the attic, where she is trying to seduce another literary father figure, the aging Jewish writer, E. I. Lonoff.[14] Freedman's interest in this scene is to describe Roth's "revisionary, but also recuperative" attitude toward Henry James. But from the perspective of the new wave, the scene raises other issues. It compares the unrestrained but frustrated sexual desire of Zuckerman, the writer/son, with the writer/father Lonoff's disciplined refusal to embrace Anne—and his inability to send her away. A man of an earlier generation, the already married Lonoff is restrained by inhibitions Zuckerman no longer possesses. But even Lonoff is not entirely reconciled to the sacrifices these inhibitions exact.

The scene destabilizes Zuckerman, catching him off balance in several ways. Literally, he is shakily perched on the work of a writer who was both notoriously reticent about human appetites and also unabashed by the voyeuristic tendencies of many of his narrators and artist figures. The James story that elevates Zuckerman close enough to the ceiling to eavesdrop on the attic recapitulates in a different sexual register the moral/sexual conundrum of the scene Zuckerman overhears. Roth catches the multiple ambivalences of both scenes in the physical and moral precariousness of Zuckerman's pose—stretched out, as it were, between them. He realizes the "indecency" of his position yet exploits it nonetheless. And the conversation in the attic deviates wildly from the norms of literary seduction scenes, running madly amuck in the riot of possibilities open to the postmodern imagination. Language here, as often in writings of the new wave, moves into a new register to keep pace with the new rhythms, complexities, and imaginative gaminess of such situations. In *The Ghost Writer,* then, Zuckerman confronts the predicament of the young writer in the world after Auschwitz, dazzled by the vision of old restraints that now seem "mad, heroic,"[15] daring enough to risk eavesdropping on the wild improbabilities of human behavior, yet saddened by the pain they provoke and terrified of the consequences for the writer who would faithfully report them.

The shakiness of Zuckerman's literal position and the ambivalences that threaten his moral balance also suggest the difficulty of stabilizing and unifying his sense of self—a difficulty that will become a crucial problem in Roth's work after *The Ghost Writer.* Each new version of every protagonist will enunciate a different value system and possess its own powerful authenticity. But other characters in Roth's stories who become aware of the power of alternative and incompatible value systems will lose their grip on gender imperatives and bodily self-images. The Zuckerman of *My Life as a Man* (1974) will repeatedly have to ask—and need to be told—what "manliness" consists of. In *The Counterlife* (1987), of course, the circumcised penis that appears to Maria after Zuckerman's death figures one response to such a question.[16] Writers of the eighties and nineties will develop in the scarred bodies and psyches of their male protagonists further insight into the problem of wounded, uncertain manliness and phallic authority after the Holocaust.

Roth's novels also write large, in the transformational slipperiness of their protagonists, the difficulty of understanding oneself in a time when characters have lost awareness of and confidence in the collective wisdoms of their past. As early as 1974 disparate retellings of a single life in *My Life as a Man* suggest the impossibility of getting at anything like a "true" or "real" story of oneself. Even a Freudian analyst's reading of this protagonist/narrator's life becomes only another in a series of endlessly disputable interpretations.[17] What has been lost, then, are not only the collective assumptions that once grounded and stabilized a core of personal values, and not only a way of reconciling inner conflicts by moral discipline, but also a way of interpreting experience: of knowing what it means. Roth never loses sight of the ways in which traditional pieties and understandings narrowed human experience. Especially sexual experience. But in their absence, as *The Counterlife* demonstrates, narrative perspective, upon which we depend for insight into character and event, becomes multiple: psychology, sociology, religion, and history—both collective and personal[18]—flash by like lenses that turn into mirrors as they transform story itself into a kaleidoscope.

The Zuckerman trilogy tropes the loss of old, integrative and interpretive, certainties in the deaths of the Zuckerman parents, the radical destruction of the old neighborhood, the deterioration of the protagonist's body, and the erosion of his confidence in himself as a writer. Reflecting on his condition, Zuckerman thinks: he "had lost his subject. His health, his hair, and his subject. . . . What he'd made his fiction from was gone—his birthplace the burnt-out landscape of a racial war and the people who'd been giants to him dead. . . . Without a father and a mother and a homeland, he was no longer a novelist. No longer a son, no longer a writer" (*The Anatomy Lesson* [1983]).[19] New wave writings about "home" will be permeated by this sense of exile and alienation and by the questions of uncertain identity that it raises.

Folded into the personal losses that fragment and destabilize identity in the Zuckerman trilogy and epilogue are the "little se-crets" that point beyond intimate personal griefs toward historic, collective anguish. The effort to reconnect with this collective di-mension of loss occurs repeatedly in Roth's early work, beginning with "Eli, the Fanatic," who assumes the dress of a Hasidic survi-vor.[20] Less obviously neurotic than Eli, Zuckerman carries in his wallet the word "Holocaust" written by his dying mother who had never spoken the word aloud (*Anatomy Lesson* 465).[21] But Zuckerman's efforts at reconnection are highly problematical. He keeps trying to reach beyond the limits of his own narrative into stories of survivors and the European past. But their stories won't take root in Roth's fictional American world; moving them into another culture diminishes the stories and renders them opaque.

Like the dignified and tragic figure of Kafka who dwindles in America into a shabby, inarticulate, refugee Hebrew school teacher,[22] survivor figures in the Zuckerman trilogy are reduced to pathos as they elude Zuckerman's narrative struggle to draw them in.[23] The putative ghost of the gifted diarist Anne Frank, transplanted to America, can't write anymore. Once she is "free to come and go, free to clown around, free to pursue her every last expectation" in the "presence of the lake, and the tennis courts and Tanglewood," she can't produce the "deft" and "elo-quent" and "witty" sentences of her European ordeal (*The Ghost Writer* 137).[24] Similarly, Zaga, the Polish therapist, cannot tell her own story in New York, and Zuckerman discovers that he cannot tell it for her: "Her story wasn't his stories and his stories were no longer his stories either" (*Anatomy Lesson* 544). Finally, the Yid-dish manuscripts he tries to smuggle out of eastern Europe get stuck there, in the custody of the police. Although Zuckerman dreams they will help him to break out of the "suitcase" of him-self, these stories cannot be "retrieved."[25] They can't help him to escape imprisonment in his own story, trivial and irrelevant though it now seems (*Prague Orgy* 782). He can see the Yiddish stories but neither read nor understand them. And he can't take them home. Thus Roth looks forward to the midrashic writers of the new wave as he tropes both the need and the difficulty of re-storing to American Jewish experience a sense of the collective past that appears, now, beyond reach.[26]

The Counterlife confronts the dilemma of both personal and col-lective identity by writing and rewriting stories of two brothers who, one after the other, attempt to anchor themselves in ethnic connections on one hand and individual relationships with women on the other. As they try to stabilize—perhaps to define—themselves by connecting with something or someone beyond their personal boundaries, they suggest the assimilative and the reconnective options that have always confronted American Jews and that become urgently vivid in writings of the new wave. Roth dramatizes these options in the mutually exclusive attachments (romantic or ethnic) between which Nathan and Henry Zuckerman vacillate. Both alternatives are motivated by desire,[27] either for a beloved woman in her various—usually non-Jewish—incarnations or for reconnection to the collective experience and wisdom of the Jews.

Drawn both to non-Jewish lovers and to Jewish commitments (Israel for one brother; ritual circumcision of offspring for the other) both Zuckermans live out choices that define only fragments of themselves—and cannot secure any lasting connections. The dentist brother, abandoning both his gentile mistress and his Jewish wife and children to live in an Israeli settlement on the West Bank, cannot see the implications of his choice as clearly as his brother Nathan, the writer. But Nathan is no more successful than Henry in anchoring his sense of himself in either a lover or an ethnic commitment. If he alienates his beloved gentile wife by demanding that their baby be circumcised, he knows that without her he will have what he calls "no outer life of any meaning, myself completely otherless and reabsorbed within—all the voices once again only mine ventriloquizing, all the conflicts germinated by the tedious old clashing of contradictions within."[28] He cannot have both the woman he desires and a self-defining commitment to what she sees as a "boring and regressive and crazy" connection to the Jews (*Counterlife* 314). Neither choice by itself, moreover, promises to make coherent or stable the conflictual elements that this character now recognizes as essential parts of himself. Thus this novel captures the postmodern, post-Holocaust condition by denying the possibility of resolution to such conflicts and by insisting, like Finkielkraut, that once we have lost our grounding in a collective, historical identity—the self becomes a series of imaginings, performances.

As the novel tracks protagonists through their successive reimaginings of themselves, it baffles, delights, and frustrates expectations, inviting us, as one recent critic noted, "to embrace and be liberated by the duplicity" of experience.[29] It also shows us, as Roth observed, that our "contradictory but mutually entangling stories . . . constitute our hold on reality and are the closest thing we have to the truth."[30] But as it moves through a whirlwind of endings, beginnings, and transformative experiences, the repeatedly broken, self-contradicting[31] narrative also makes visible its protagonists' frantic attempts to unify and to stabilize themselves. At times they try to hold on to the common pleasures of the good personal life: to lovers, to wives, to mentors, to the sexual and/or verbal interactions that promise to rescue them from the "isolating unnaturalness of self-battling" (*Counterlife* 311). At other times they reach instead toward connection with a collective, ethnic identity: learning to speak Hebrew or participating in ancient ritual. "Circumcision," Zuckerman thinks, "confirms that there is an us, and an us that isn't solely him [the unborn child] and me" (*Counterlife* 324). But as Finkielkraut observed of his "imaginary Jews," these efforts usually fail to anchor the fragmented, post-Auschwitz self that gets driven in many directions at once by powerful currents in Roth's work.

I would not minimize the subtlety and complexity of Roth's oeuvre by suggesting that this brief treatment of one element of his work does critical justice to this writer—or to the extent of his influence on later writers. But for the limited purposes of this study, perhaps these observations will suggest the ways in which Roth's early work frames the problem of identity for American Jewish writers of the eighties and nineties. Roth furnishes them with a set of assumptions about subjectivity and agency that diverge radically from assumptions about the collective past— without entirely banishing either its memory or the rebellious fury it once evoked, and without denying a persistent longing for comforts it once afforded. These—sometimes revolving, sometimes swinging—doors, I believe, form the gateway to stories of the new wave.

2

Writing the Pathos of Belatedness

Second-Generation Memoirs

To the riddle of identity that Roth introduces into American Jewish stories, second-generation writers add another layer of complexity, for they see very clearly another post-Holocaust wrinkle in the worn fabric of general human experience. Born into a world already in process, all of us begin—belated. The sense of belatedness is particularly keen for American children of Jews who survived Hitler. They come "after" the destruction of European Jewry.[1] They enter a place with no visible ruins, invisibly scarred by what happened elsewhere, earlier. But the scars are present to them, for they were born into the emotional landscape of their parents' lives—a landscape haunted by the European past. The literature of the parents' generation bears witness to that past, bringing the wound of its devastation into the moment of reading. But the work of the children, the second generation,[2] makes visible the scars that have become the legacy of that past. They write the pathos of belatedness that belongs, in some measure, to all of us who imagine the residue of trauma without having experienced it, who mourn the loss of what we never knew, and who assume responsibility for what one novelist has called "second hand" memory.[3]

All the writings of the second generation could be said to transform that pathos into praxis. The literature they produce does what Jane Tompkins called "cultural work," for it defines certain aspects of our own reality; it helps us to see ourselves through the lenses and mirrors of its sentences, and it enables us to recognize what we share with these writers.[4] Some critics question the value of this work. To them, as James E. Young has observed, it seems "self-indulgent" to become "more absorbed in . . . vicarious experiences of memory than . . .[in] the survivors' experiences of real events."[5] One wonders about the usefulness of such comparative judgments. One reviewer has even complained that "the whole category of the 'second-generation survivor' is a bit dubious," that "there is something falsely derivative or made up about such a status and that it would be wiser to restrain a reaching after honorary victimization on the part of those who were not 'there.'"[6] One wonders about the usefulness of such comparative judgments. The work of the witnesses, the primacy of their experience, speaks for itself. Incomparably. But the resonance of that experience in our time and place is another subject—a subject that we share in some measure with the second generation. We also come "after"; we also enter an invisibly scarred world; we also need—like them—to understand the work of remembering, to clarify and acknowledge residual damage, and to mourn our losses.[7] These shared issues distinguish—from the ordeal of the catastrophe itself—the experience of "aftermath"[8] and the cultural work that properly belongs to it.

The work of remembering makes it possible to mourn, but memory has become a particular problem in the aftermath of the Holocaust. It has been valued and encouraged for centuries by Jewish writers. But since the Holocaust we know, thanks to Lawrence Langer, that memory can be contaminated by trauma.[9] When we try to recall trauma, as psychologists since Freud have understood, we tend to repeat it.[10] Unable to experience it fully when it happened because it didn't match anything we knew or could imagine or understand, we go over and over it, trying to master by repetition what initially overwhelmed us. All the crucial human experiences—of thwarted love, of loss, of pain—probably follow this path in our mental and emotional lives. Writers have always been able to show us how trauma happens to us; they move us toward mastery of experience that once eluded the mind's grasp by helping us to think what we might otherwise only dumbly suffer. In the aftermath of the Holocaust that work becomes essential because the residue of suffering—still unmastered—continues to haunt our collective lives.[11]

This residue works its way to the surface of awareness in different literary forms. But their burden is the same: to make thinkable, perceptible, the nature of experience in the aftermath. Fictions do this by imagining lives scarred by an unimaginable past; they create "worlds" haunted, like our own, by events that not only shadow but trivialize everything that comes "after." Memoirs address this sense of the present by taking as subject the lives of the writers themselves. Unlike artists' self-portraits in which warts and wrinkles become windows through which one can see the legacy of time in its gifts of spirit and character, the self-portraits drawn by memoirs of the second generation show us simply why—in the wake of trauma—memory needs to happen. And how it happens: how, from the residue of parental suffering, one distills intelligible images and rational data that empower memory without healing or redeeming it. Their work proceeds through several phases: they reshape images of their parents; they recover their parents' stories, clarifying the distortions that obscured them; they trace the legacy of trauma in tangled relationships within the family; and they chronicle the development of their own voices—in which the story of the aftermath can be told and the work of mourning that belongs to it can proceed.

Reconstructing Parents and Their Stories

We know what it means to reshape parental images, for the parents of our childhood are never the parents we know as adults. Children of the second generation need to revise not only childhood illusions but also cultural images of their parents. Neglecting evidence of Jewish resistance to the Nazis,[12] journalists and historians after the war constructed "survivors" chiefly as "victims"—defining them exclusively by what had been done to them. To be sure, the war's immediate aftermath furnished powerful evidence for such images. When liberating armies entered the concentration camps, the visible damage sustained by those who still lived leapt into unforgettable photos of men and women so attenuated, so fragile, that only their mobility and verticality distinguished them from the dead who lay everywhere, unburied. Later, when the allied armies administered other camps for newly liberated but now homeless people, they became "displaced persons." They provided abundant evidence of their vitality: marrying and producing babies at an extraordinary rate; setting immediately to work organizing educational, cultural, and political activities, undaunted by impossible circumstances. But, as Atina Grossman has noted, observers in the camps saw the DP's as "hopeless, depressed," afflicted with "inertia" and an "air of resignation," unsuited to any kind of normal life. Both sympathetic and hostile witnesses regularly and graphically bemoaned the "uncivilized" state of the survivors. They seemed oblivious to "the most elementary rules of hygeine" (297). Grossman recalls a "powerful contemporary consensus . . . that the survivors were 'human debris'" (298).[13]

When inmates finally made their way out of the DP camps these images of their abandonment and despair were further contradicted by the facts of their recuperation. Their readiness to acquire languages and other skills necessary for adaptation to new cultures was only part of the plentiful evidence their lives would offer of resurgent vitality and determination. But the earliest psychological research, undertaken in order to qualify them for reparations, quickly revived awareness of "survivors" as products of what they had suffered: in the public mind they remained primarily objects of Nazi abuse.[14]

For their children these images, incompatible with direct experience of their busy, energetic parents, created confusion that remained uncorrected by any coherent narrative of their parents' lives in either the family mythology or the public domain. Julie Salamon, for example, recalls that her "parents never seemed like victims to me—quite the contrary, they seemed much stronger than most people."[15] Thus one important task of the memoirists has been to reconstruct both "survivors" and their children as subjects of their own stories. Without neglecting either the suffering, or the residual damage, or the powerful vitality of their parents and themselves, the memoirs engage both personal experience and public ignorance and misunderstanding. From that engagement with disparate, often incoherent and painful data, they emerge as neither psychological case studies nor social history. They enter a three-sided conversation in which personal stories of hardship, abuse, and resilience are interwoven with both historical and psychological research. They construct subjects where before there were only objects: victim/parents who had suffered and survived the Nazis, and damaged children who inherited from them a legacy of trauma.

Because we usually become the subjects of our own stories, children's memoirs restore voice—the emblem of subjective status—to their parents by rescuing their stories from silence or incoherence.[16] In part, silence overtakes parental stories because the roots of narrative spread back into a place and time before the writers' birth. But many of these parents were also unwilling or unable to speak of the past.[17] Thus these memoirs note gaps in parental narratives that were sometimes painful, sometimes frustrating, sometimes infuriating. Helen Epstein, for example, remembers her father's occasional silence as "a great big open hole I could fall into if I wasn't careful. My father often got lost this way. He would stop in the middle of a sentence and his eyes would go vague. . . . I was sure he was in that brown-toned world of photographs among all the people who lived in the yellow envelope in his desk" (*Children of the Holocaust* 58–59). Joseph Berger's father also remained "silent, silent to his friends, to his children, even to his wife."[18] Though Berger longed to record his father's early years and his six beloved sisters by reporting faces, names, anecdotes, his father would not speak of them. The memoirist laments that his father's story "will vanish like ashes and smoke." The image he crafts to stand for what must be remembered but can't be spoken dignifies these absent women by linking the silencing of their story to the vanishing of the six million in Nazi crematoria.

Even when parents did speak of the past, their voices were not fully heard by their children. Virtually all children of the second generation whom Epstein interviewed confess that they couldn't remember what they had heard of their parents' stories. In part, memory was baffled by the intermittent, fragmented nature of the narratives.[19] But the greater obstacle lay deeper, in feelings that saturated parental recollections but were not, could not be expressed. For example, Epstein, like many of her informants, was puzzled at first by how little she remembered of the scraps of narrative she heard her mother tell. Ultimately she understood why. She realized that her feelings were blocked when her mother spoke of the past. Her mother's own "numbness" had taught Helen, without words, that this story must not be felt.

Franci "showed no emotion when she talked. The words poured out of her like blood but they no longer seemed connected to anything she had experienced. She did not show pain and I did not either. I imitated her. I took the words in as they came out. It was information. It was what happened, and there was no feeling attached" (152). Years later, when Helen interviewed her mother after months of interviewing other survivors, she learned that "numbness" had become part of her mother's nature in the camps: "she had first noticed the loss of feeling in Auschwitz, after they had given her the blue number. . . . She had stared at her forearm then and the forearm became two arms, one that belonged to her . . . and one that belonged to that other woman, the one that [*sic*] looked exactly like her but had a number on her arm. From that moment on she had become two people: one who acted and one who watched" (78). Foregoing the personal pronoun "who" when Franci recalls herself as a woman with a numbered arm, Epstein signals the fall into objective status that overtook Hitler's victims.[20] It becomes part of the legacy that this mother transmits to her child. Because Franci had split herself to detach from feelings too traumatic to be recalled, her story obscured the emotional resonance that would have held it in her daughter's memory.

Franci's detachment severed her daughter's emotional connection to the maternal past as well. Epstein recalls that every time she heard one particular story of her mother's cleverness in Auschwitz "a flush of pride would rise up inside me, making me want to smile and cry at the same time. I wanted to hug my mother then, touch her, tell her how smart and brave she was. But somehow, at those times, my body would go numb, the lid of my iron box would bulge and then flatten out again. The moment would pass" (161). In the "iron box" that Epstein carries heavily within her until she fears it will explode lie the feelings generated by her mother's stories—which cannot be felt, or acted upon, or expressed. Because feeling, her mother has taught her, is too dangerous, too destructive to be acknowledged. But the powerful, unacknowledged feelings her mother's story both holds and provokes pull the story beneath the surface of the child's memory, into hiding. This confluence of emotion that connects parent and child becomes the central subject of many memoirs, for it obstructs not only awareness of the parental past but also the emergence of a child's consciousness of itself as a separate being, able to hear, to understand, to speak of a past that shapes it in different ways from its parent. The memoir Epstein writes employs all the skills of the writer/researcher/interviewer to illuminate and record the process of bringing to the mind's surface a knot of narrative that must be untangled before the daughter can know herself as separate from her mother.

To some extent, this process characterizes the growth of all children toward what psychologists call "individuation." But these memoirs particularize, on one hand, the ways in which this universal process carries, for the second generation, the legacy of Auschwitz. And on the other hand, the memoirs seem to gesture metaphorically to the larger, cultural process in which American Jews detached themselves from the world of European Jewry. In the view of some recent scholars, the destruction of that world in the nineteen forties has encouraged among American Jews a nostalgia for the European Diaspora, a desire to find in European thought, and practice, and writing the norms that might validate their own culture.[21] Earlier critics believed American Jews cast off the European tradition out of which their own culture had emerged.[22] In either case, whether by clinging to or breaking an attachment that inhibits individuation, cultural growth may parallel, to some extent, the development of human children—often torn between adopting or rebelling against the ways of their parents until they can begin to see and to speak for themselves as separate beings. Indeed, the superficiality of a culture like the one satirized by Philip Roth's "Goodbye, Columbus"—forgetful and emotionally numb to the European past—seems to mirror the condition of this memoirist whose deeper life is inaccessible until memory comes.

Tracing a Half-heard Legacy within the Family Nexus

To speak of and for oneself, these memoirists insist, depends on clarifying the tangle of feelings that kept parental stories unremembered and untold. The memoirs thus concentrate on that work of clarification. Anne Karpf, for example, declares that "family stories are a kind of DNA, encoded messages about how things are and should be, passed from one generation to another."[23] Breaking that code, for her, first meant realizing how thoroughly "bad feelings" had been "hosed away" (40) from the narratives of her family—and from their interactions with one another. These children, symbols to their parents of restoration and hope, were intended not to grieve, but "to tip the family scales towards happiness" (39). Thus Anne absorbed her parents' past (44) complete with its silenced burden of anxiety and pain.[24] Years later, in therapy, she would ask, "'What is a feeling?'" (39). Her own writer's voice developed only when she answered that question, recognizing the "subcutaneous sadness" (4) in her family's life as a product—not of her own mischief or badness—but of her parents' experience of the Holocaust. In tracing the difficulty of "reading" the family story complete with its emotional burden, then, the memoirs record a process of separation and individuation that is common to all children but peculiarly complicated for children who inherit a parental past so haunted by unspoken pain.

The defenses that both parents and children throw up against the pressure of pain and sadness are remarkably similar in these memoirs.[25] Epstein, Karpf, and Berger all remember the terrific "busyness" of their family lives: "what a talky lot we were, how much we busied ourselves with words and feats, how intolerably empty we found silence" (Karpf 108).[26] But beneath that surface, each child caught glimpses of a parent "unreachably sad" (Karpf 108). One mother's "pain was visible. It drained the blood from her skin, making her appear even paler than she normally was, and the blue numbers tattooed on her forearm almost seemed to blaze. . . . I could see the pain creep through her body, trapped, moving from place to place" (Epstein 50). The "bedrock melancholy" (Berger 281) of these parents, masked by endless work and talk during the years of raising their families and struggling to ground themselves in a new country, haunts the memories of their children who cannot even acknowledge— much less describe—it until they learn to see its origin in their parents' past.

Anger too is part of the literally unspeakable, buried residue carried out of Europe into American families after the Holocaust. Epstein and Berger recall their fathers exploding in sudden rages, triggered by inconsequential offenses. Epstein remembers her father "gripped by something that had nothing to do with us at the dinner table in our kitchen in New York," rage erupting from him "lavalike and furious, impossible to restrain" (58). And Berger describes his father, a "quiet, sheepish man" (40), "rising up in fury" against a neighbor who had threatened his child, "unloosing the accumulated rage of so many years" (41). As a child, Berger remembers being aware "of the darker forces seething inside" his father; "they would peek out at moments when his frustration boiled over and he seemed not to know what to do with his rage. . . ." He and his brother are "terrified of this demon inside" their father (40). Their father is terrified too: "His fury, the inextinguishable mass of it, confused and frightened him also. . . . This was anger welling up at an entire civilization that had wronged him irreparably" (87). Here the voices of adult writers rationalize what small children and their parents could only, dumbly, feel.

The silenced rage of innocent people, abused in ways the mind can hardly grasp, while others either watch or look away, rises to the surface of these memoirs not only in recollections of parental behavior but also, perhaps even more poignantly, in careful analyses of its effects on the children. Epstein reports that psychologists believe survivor-parents often encouraged aggressiveness in their children, taking a "secret delight" in it because "during the war . . . they could not allow themselves to express the aggression they felt toward their oppressors. To do so would be to invite death" (209). Epstein herself, however, remembers chiefly the need to curb her own aggressions—particularly toward her mother, who "could not bear any anger directed toward her. . . . Ordinary bickering, the kind almost all siblings indulge in, unnerved both my mother and father. They could not tolerate it" (169). She is not aware of having felt angry at her own troubles because they were always overshadowed by her parents' suffering. The "landscape" of her parents' past "was so vast and empty" that nothing in the children's lives seemed important (168–69). "'Worse things have happened, you know,' they said, and I saw the war rise like a great tidal wave in the air, dwarfing my trouble, making it trivial" (169). But she often fought at school and with her brother—to express the rage she didn't know she felt for her own and her parents' inarticulate pain. She could find no other channel of expression. Her mother was too fragile to witness this rage, and her father wanted only to see her smile

(171). The sense of not mattering in light of the enormous proportions assumed by the European culture that preceded ours—or of the crime that destroyed it—will hardly seem unfamiliar to American Jews whose accomplishments always appear meager by comparison. Need one wonder why Roth's "Eli, the Fanatic" eagerly exchanges his new Brooks Brothers suit for a survivor's shabby black outfit?

As these writers trace the course of buried feelings from parent to child, however, their voices gather resonance and self-respect. Like surgeons uncovering deep sources of old pain, the memoirists seem to look without judgment or complaint at both their own and their parents' malaise. They develop the writer's gift of vision as they try to see beyond old distress into the logic that accounted for it.[27] As writers they attend as closely to the effect of buried rage on family stories as on family relationships. One of Helen Epstein's informants remembers, for example, that there was a puzzling disjunction between the tale itself and the way in which it was told; she never heard her mother "blame anyone for anything" (40); "my mother never said anything bad about anyone and that really confused me. She would tell me about terrible things and she would make them almost into a nice fairy tale with a happy ending"; "I didn't hear about bad Germans. I just heard about wonderful people. I remember her talking about the friends she was with in Auschwitz and how they took care of each other and when they shaved their heads they started laughing, they thought it was so funny. . . . She was so lucky to have come out, and look what she has now in Canada!" (39).[28] Another of her informants can't "remember any outright expressions of outrage directed toward the Germans. Stories of losses were told dispassionately. . . . The rage and pain remained beneath the surface" (325). These distortions account, in part, for the confusing discrepancies between parental narratives of the past inherited from parents, and historic images of parental victimization. Understanding the logic of such distortions in family mythology is, of course, always liberating for children. But equally important for children who are writers is the hard-won insight into the inadequacy of the narrative itself: its failure to construct what Henry James called a "felt truth" in which events would be consonant with the feelings that must have accompanied them when they happened.

This writerly sensitivity to the vagaries of half-told, half-heard parental stories also uncovers a link between narrative and experience as children's lives became texts in which their parents' legacies got inscribed. For example, Helen Epstein not only learned from her mother to detach herself from her feelings, she also adopted her parents' point of view, identifying with it to such a degree that "their values and ambitions became indistinguishable" from her own (310). She assumed, like one of her informants, that "part of the legacy was swallowing pain, feeling pain" (310) but not acknowledging it. Thus, before she could understand the emotional legacy of the Holocaust transmitted by her parents she had moved to Israel, drawn to "the idea of sinking to the bottom of society" because she wanted "to feel connected to the experience my parents had undergone" (294). She believed anger to be "a privilege that my parents had earned and that I had not. One had to have suffered in order to be angry, and I had been told from the time I was small that I . . . had not the slightest idea of what suffering was" (254).[29] Feelings she couldn't acknowledge, and didn't believe she was entitled to feel, detached themselves from her conscious life. The more she busied herself, the less she felt engaged, for she questioned the value of doing anything at all; "I do not remember feeling anger," she says, "I felt numbness, an absence of feeling that seemed to carry over into other parts of my life as well" (254).

For Epstein and several of the grown "children of survivors" whom she interviewed, then, anger, sadness, and pain descended, unvoiced, into places within them that left them partly numb to their own experience, seeking to replicate their parents' suffering in order to earn the right—perhaps locate the power?— to feel. For Karpf, too, the war became a "yardstick to judge all other experiences." By comparison, everything else had to be good. But her negative feelings, denied, turned inward, transformed into intense self hatred (41). "The angrier I felt, the more charming and compliant I appeared," she recalls (46). The "war," she says, "was now within" (54). Buried anger made her feel dangerous (55).

In the trajectory of these individual lives, stories half hidden in the family emerged as symptoms. Some children of survivors discovered that they had lived out unspoken imperatives generated by their parents' half-told, half-heard stories. Fragmented

parental narratives achieved a kind of resonance in their lives
that usually belongs not to narrative but to myth.[30] Karpf remembers that her parents' stories, "through their power, repetition, and the sheer vehemence of the telling," took on the power
of myth and fable: you knew them by heart, able even to prompt
and remind, you internalised them—they became yours. Is it any
wonder," she asks rhetorically, "that some of us longed to appropriate their narratives for our own lives?" (242). In that spirit of
appropriation, Karpf developed "rescue fantasies" (52), transfer-
ring indiscriminately to "hairdressers, milkmen, shop assistants"
the "compulsion to repair" engendered in her by her parents'
mythic suffering. These sobering insights into the distortions not
of narratives but of lives lived in the shadow of half-told stories
suggest the existential dimensions of a legacy that survived the
liberation of the camps.

The legacy sometimes got written not just in the life but on the
body. When Anne Karpf fell in love with a non-Jew and confronted her first significant conflict with her parents, infected
sores—resistant to treatment and medication—appeared on her
hands, "unerring somatic proof that I couldn't in fact handle it";
the "body," she observes wryly, is "an incorrigible punster" (98).
Here, in the absence of words to express anger and negotiate difference, the body became a text on which the untold story of unacknowledged pain could be articulated. Like Freud's hysterics,
whose bodies expressed what could not yet be spoken aloud,
these children first lived out what they could neither fully know
nor say.

Finding Voice for One's Own Story

Eventually, as critical—sometimes even ironic—perspective developed, buried feeling moved into language, transforming
symptoms into symbols that the mind can grasp and work
with.[31] The initial migration inward—into the family, the body,
the psyche—reveals the path of traumatic experience, unmastered when it first occurred. Karpf's work moves toward mastery
of such experience partly by rationalizing the contexts within
which this migratory path took shape. She traces the history of
the Jews in England in order to understand both the cultural

antisemitism that encouraged her to break off her "Jewish bits" (45) as she grew up and the silence that surrounded Jewish refugees. Like Helen Epstein, who remembers the genteel avoidance of Holocaust issues even at the Jewish Sunday school she attended (157), Karpf describes the "disinclination of the citizens of the new country, its Jews included, to hear about, let alone invite discussion of survivors' experience in the camps."[32] She reminds us that in Primo Levi's dream, "'speaking and not being listened to . . . finding liberty and remaining alone' was felt to be a wound almost as grievous as the original camp experiences, a second abandonment by the world after the first which had taken place during the war" (168–69). The reasons for this abandonment, her research demonstrates, lie in the prewar "history and status of Anglo-Jewry, and in dominant Christian beliefs about the Jews," which she covers in three full chapters of this memoir, placing her family's experience in its historical context. Another two chapters cover the postwar period and the "emergence of professional interest in and concern with the psychological effects of the Holocaust on both survivors and their families" (167). Thus, before she can return to her personal story, the putative subject of every memoir, she develops the public contexts in which that story can begin to make sense.[33] Finding one's voice depends for these memoirists, then, partly on assembling a social context in which the traumatic past can be understood, so that they can rescue the family's experience from the dark place to which the habit of avoidance—their own and other people's— had driven it. To conceive the parental silences that drove negative feelings inward, away from their legitimate targets, as responding not just to personal inhibitions but to public refusals is to clarify the origins of family trauma beneath the scars that have obscured it. That process of developing awareness within a rational, analytical context becomes one crucial path in the memoirs toward the emergence of a writerly voice sufficient to the telling of a traumatic past.

The sense of a context may also serve to protect or to insulate the writer from the overwhelming emotional power of a parent's memory of trauma. One memoir, for example, describes the danger of a moment in which a writer comes into fuller possession of both the facts and the felt truths of his mother's traumatic past. Joseph Berger recalls that when he finally interviewed his mother about her memories he had to "keep [his] distance by acting the dispassionate reporter." As "my mother spins her story, I clamp down whatever emotions I am feeling because I have a mission; after fifty-one years, with my mother in her late seventies, I want to know the entire story, not just the sketchy, sanitized version she has doled out over the years. . . . I am afraid that if I let her pain pierce me, I will not be able to go on with the collecting of facts. . . . I am also afraid that if she senses my sympathy, the wall I have built up that has kept her at a distance, that has let me grow into my own person, will come crumbling down. She will invade, take over in her relentless, flailing way. But her story eventually lets me understand why she requires such control" (80). Instead of allowing himself to be invaded by the feelings evoked by his mother's story of her life in Poland during the war, Berger focuses first on his own fears, and then on his intent to construct a framing context in which this story can be disentangled from its hearer.

A sense of place and an awareness of deliberate reflection on a narrative in process become other contextual elements of this telling: Berger locates himself and his mother securely in the present moment as what Langer called "anguished memory" begins to emerge. Rachel Berger thinks back to Warsaw after a Nazi bombing; there she saw a woman wandering through the rubble, seeking her own lost child among the bodies of small children whose little shoes are scattered around them. Berger quickly inserts an image of himself, listening and thinking: "I sit in this comfortable kitchen in the leafy Riverdale section of the Bronx and it is difficult for me to believe that the woman sitting across from me has been through such hell. I ask her about the incoherent mother she saw and she fills in more details. As she does, she begins crying freely, even sobbing" (135). Instead of being swept into the current of his mother's emotion, he analyzes and interprets it: "As she weeps, I wonder why she expends all her tears for children she does not know yet scarcely sheds a tear when she talks explicitly about her own murdered young brother and two sisters. . . . I suspect that the mother she saw in the rubble crying for her dead children was a palpable figure of sorrow. . . . I believe that in some way the woman screaming among the rubble is herself, Rachel, crying for the little brother and two sisters she left behind in Otwock, for all her lost children" (135).[34] The passage moves inexorably backward through several stages (the Riverdale kitchen, the Warsaw ruins) to the biblical losses of one migratory family; all this is held within the single image of Rachel, the mourning mother who bears Berger's own mother's name. Here, within the several contextual "frames" he has assembled, the adult "child" masters the technical skill necessary to receive his parent's story complete: to hear it, to tell it, to allow himself—and us—the return to a past so deeply traumatized that it has taken fifty-one years to be fully experienced. Theorists tell us that these are the processes necessary to "working through" a traumatized past as the narrative delivers into the light of consciousness its burden of memory and old pain.

Other memoirists develop similar strategies to allow that moment of critical, analytical receptivity to happen, in which feeling can engage—without overwhelming—its hearer. Epstein depends on interviews with other survivors to build a context in which she can put her parents' lives "in perspective," and to "measure them against a community" (336). For her, too, the rational, analytical work of the journalist/interviewer—the detached, professional asker of questions and listener to answers—alleviates the mythic burden of parental stories that weighed so heavily on the emotional life of the child. Taping parental interviews so that the writer can alternately listen and think at will also becomes a strategy that allows mastery of potentially overwhelming material: "Through the process of transcribing my parents' tapes I do feel some kind of resolution. I now know and can retain their stories" (313), Anne Karpf reports. Subjected to rational, critical scrutiny, to editorial control, the traumatic past assumes an appropriate place—free of mythic imperatives—in the memory of the adult child of survivors.

The most audacious of the strategies for achieving mastery of previously traumatic material is the journey home, for going "home" again—though literally impossible—becomes in these memoirs a powerful source of insight into the past and an equally powerful strategy for reconstructing memory and developing voice.[35] All memoirs "go home again" in a metaphorical sense. But several memoirists undertake actual journeys back to Europe, partly to provide what Karpf calls "another level of reality" (145) to a story whose emotional power endures even when it no longer traumatizes its listener. Memories of Europe as "home" are deeply mixed for children whose parents were forcibly exiled.[36] Joseph Berger, for example, remembers that his parents' stories "filled the places where they had been with romance, adventure and the sticky glue of family love" (110) that inspired in him a life-long love of maps. But beneath the romantic image are shadows cast by personal and collective grief, pain, estrangement.

Recent critical work on American Jewish nostalgia for the European "homeland" notwithstanding,[37] such shadows subvert nostalgia by writing large and problematizing specific historical and ethnic components of the European "home." Some memoirs refashion "home" as a place darkened by personal and collective grief, pain, estrangement. For example, although she calls her childhood home "paradise," Eva Hoffman opens her recollection with a bald statement of her enforced emigration from it. Ex-pulsion, however, is not the only shadow thrown back, retro-spectively, on this child's earliest memories of "home." Hoffman remembers her mother, in the "middle of a sun-filled day," "sud-denly, while she's kneading some dough or perhaps sewing up a hole in my sweater's elbow," beginning to "weep softly" as she remembers the death of her sister in a Nazi gas chamber. The Holocaust thus darkens Hoffman's "paradise" from the begin-ning. Happy, protected by a strong father who adores her, yet born in Poland just after the war to parents once hunted by the Germans and unprotected by their countrymen, Hoffman knows, sadly, two incompatible things. She has learned the lesson of the secure, beloved child: that "everything is changeless and knowable."[38] But she also knows the lesson of the vulnerable Jew: that "this moment will not last," that its "fullness," once "per-fectly abundant," "will be gone" before she takes another step as she walks home from school (16–17). This perceptual complexity owes much to the historical circumstances of the war and occupa-tion in whose wake her mother's memories, fully shared with a child old enough to "keep every detail," complicate the otherwise romantic, luminous image of the homeplace and Hoffman's own experience in it.

Virtually every element of the European home Hoffman lov-ingly describes comes complete with its shadow of risk and po-tential loss. Her recollection of other people, Poles, for example, is deeply divided between her refusal, on one hand, to believe that her friends look on her "as a dark stranger," and her mother's insistence, on the other, that "there's an anti-Semite in every Pole" (33). Her own ethnic identity is similarly ambivalent: Jewishness is, at first, "filled with my mother's tears and whispers in a half-understood tongue." But this mother also teaches that "it is something to be proud of—something to stand up for with all one's strength" (32).[39]

Hoffman fashions into a metaphor for this blurry, doubled image of "home" a description of a beloved friend's apartment on the eve of his emigration: it "has been transformed from a place in which people have lived cozily and for a long time into a space from which they are fleeing. . . . The familiar rooms, which used to be warm and muffled with their thicknesses of furniture, now echo with emptiness and the wooden crates that line the hallway" (82). Her perception of place is thus doubled and split even before she leaves home. Scarred by an undertone of remembered coziness within a moment of alienation, Hoffman knows both how crucial attachment to home is to one's sense of rootedness in experience (74) and how fragile, provisional, that attachment turns out to be (83). "Poland is home, in a way," she concludes, "but it is also hostile territory" (84). The initial qualification, followed by the radical contradiction, underscores this writer's achievement of a decidedly antinostalgic, critical recollection of the European "home."[40]

Relieved of sentimentalities, the homeplaces themselves ultimately emerge with great clarity and poignance. Mark Schechner once argued that "there is no agreement about what might be called "home" among contemporary American Jewish writers.[41] But the places of origin that these women writers painstakingly uncover through months of patient research reveal surprising similarities to one another. Whether the narratives are set in Hungary, or Czechoslovakia, or Poland, the urban homeplaces bear a family likeness to one another. Disfigured in every case by ethnic hatreds of the past and by the disabling of women, they are marked as well by the sense of possibility and drama present in great cities, by the powerful presence of protective, nurturing forces within the family, and by awareness of an ethnic community whose status becomes precarious but whose existence always opens a wider lens onto troubles that might otherwise have been experienced as purely personal. These homeplaces are often grounded not in space, but historically—in time—as narratives trace the long presence of Jews in those places back to the Middle Ages.

Only by "acquiring some perspective, by achieving critical distance, by interpreting" these homeplaces, theorists remind us, can the process of mourning—in which second-generation memoirists are profoundly engaged—work through the unmastered past.[42] For the most part, that process is unconscious, occurring beneath the level of language. But in some cases language itself can draw up to the surface of the mind—like the wick of a burning candle—the deep grief, and the longing, that accompany the story of a haunted, lost, traumatized past. In the background of the American/English in which they now write, and speak, and think, the ghosts of other languages—either their parents' or their own as children—are always present. The stories they tell in English of their parents' past was lived in those other languages. And, as Ruth Wisse has recently pointed out, experience undergone in one language is radically changed when it gets told in another language.[43] The new language can even create, if the writer is not careful, "an atmosphere of remoteness" that "insulates" us from the past, as though the narrative "were the closed scar over the wound."[44] Thus in the telling of the past, as in the journeys "home," the problem of language falls like a stone into the deep canyon of memory—where echoes of the mother tongue are still resonant.

Disturbed by those echoes, Gerda Lerner, highly literate in English after refusing for many years to speak or read German, suddenly accuses the Nazis of robbing her of her mother tongue. When the songs of her childhood reentered her memory, she discovered that German still held her "deep memories, resonances, sounds of childhood."[45] The most intimate layer of her past had sunk "into a deep hole of oblivion" (48). But when she began to speak German again, she remembered "what was lost and what it cost and what might have been had I been able to be a writer in my own language" (48–49). She became painfully conscious of the split opened by the loss of the mother tongue: between feeling and thought, between the conscious learned faculties and the rich vibrations of the unconscious. Though she has written many books and founded the study of women's history in English, she confesses that she envies "those who live in the power of their own language," "who were not deprived of the immediacy by which creativity finds its form" (49). Despite her brilliant career as a writer of English, Lerner believes the loss of her original language is a wound that "can never heal" (48).

Lerner's insight into the layer of self that remains trapped underneath the mother tongue offers a poignant glimpse into the complexity of a self-image born of exile. Eva Hoffman also describes the change in her persona when she learned to speak English. When she chose to write her diary in English she feared that Polish had become, for her, "a dead language, the language of the untranslatable past" (120). But in Hoffman the mother tongue did not go silent; rather, she learned, it whispered the existence of a persona hidden beneath the "public" self, "my English self" that life in Canada constructed. English began "to invent another me" (121), she explains. The "I" she cannot write in English survives in Polish, a living residue of the self she "would have grown into" had she been able to grow up at home. Susan Suleiman shares this sense of another self that lives only in Hungarian. As she walks the streets of Budapest, thinking what her "life would have been like had we not left," another exile speaks an awareness that Suleiman shares: "'Every time I walk down the street, it's as if my doppelganger were walking behind me,'" this woman tells the memoirist. "Who is my doppelganger?" Suleiman asks.[46] Who is the self, these exiled women wonder, now lost to me, for whom this place, this language, was home?

In Yiddish, the sense of both a lost home and a lost "other" self rises to the surface of both text and personal consciousness. Myriam Anissimov believes that all the many books she has written in French "have their source in the sparks, the phrases, the words of the Yiddish language. . . . They sustain, crossbreed the edifice of French, which is now merely the support, the vehicle of an emotion born in another world, and developed with other materials from an immense imaginary structure: the charred walls of the shtetl houses, the walls of the ghettos, the walls of the synagogues, the greenish walls of the gas chambers, Yiddish. Each word of the Yiddish language . . . lies in me as at the bottom of a grave, where, rifling through the earth, one digs up bone fragments."[47] The sense of self as a grave in which the past lies buried, but is not stilled, appears as well in the work of Anita Norich, who knew in Yiddish both "the sounds of home and also the sounds of the dead. When my dead spoke to me, they always spoke Yiddish."[48] Though she is at home in America, her "imagination continues to live elsewhere" (238). She mourns continually the losses that happen as she translates herself into English. "Sometimes," she confesses, she feels "translation as an act of violence, of betrayal" for it completes "the work of obliteration carried out in Europe" (246). In these writers the pain and poignance of sustaining through language the pulsing life of a vanished culture deepens one's sense of the losses that American readers, born into English, have yet to mourn. Perhaps as we celebrate the brilliance of American Jewish voices that belong to Bellow's Augie March and Roth's Zuckerman we need to keep listening for the sharp ironies and rhythms of Yiddish that once broke the syntax of Malamud's characters—but surface more subtly in the voices of later writers.[49]

In a more personal context, the sense of loss that haunts every corner of second-generation memoirs owes much to childhood experience in families traumatized by abrupt and violent losses.[50] Anne Karpf, for example, remembers that she'd learned to manage her "fear of loss preventively, by not having: you couldn't lose something you'd never had in the first place" (99). All the memoirs record the anguished struggle to separate from parents who watched at the window for adolescent children to come home, so traumatized by early losses that they were unable to believe in the reappearance of a beloved person who had gone out of sight. It isn't surprising, then, that the death of a parent who lost everything but life in Hitler's camps assumes an extraordinary emotional magnitude in their children's memoirs. Karpf and Epstein work with this universally traumatic event to free it from the specific legacy of loss perpetuated in them by their parents' experience in the Holocaust. For Karpf, the death of her father—"who is ninety-three and wants to die" (281)—"is so agonizing" that she "cannot imagine how losing relatives and friends in their prime, and children, was survivable" (281). At one level, then, her father's death yields new insight into the magnitude of her parents' pain and new respect for their power to recover from it. But because her father's death is "the first natural death in old age in her family that [she's] witnessed" (280), it also draws a boundary between itself and the unnatural losses inflicted by the Holocaust—which had traumatized her parents. "My father wasn't singled out or specially selected for death," she realizes. "For the first time I recognise the meaning of the term 'a natural death'; death to me no longer seems necessarily unnatural" (282). In this new awareness, fixed in a phrase that now means something to her, Karpf records a moment in which the pain of loss can be fully experienced, can assume a bearable, memorable, even speakable place in her life.

The death of Epstein's mother yields a different revelation that also marks a significant phase in the development of her voice as a writer. Franci's death helps her daughter to become aware of the bond that has kept her from experiencing herself as a being separate from her mother. As Epstein lies in her mother's now empty bed, looking about at her mother's room, she feels treacherous because she had never before seen her mother's world with her own eyes and reflected on what she saw there. Reflection both clarifies and distances a bond long obscured by its emotional depth and intensity. Her relation to her mother "was the most passionate and complicated of all" her many relationships. "So intense was our bond that I was never sure what belonged to whom, where I ended, and she began. . . . I wore the clothes my mother made for me, read the books she read, valued what she thought good. I shared my life with her, half-understanding that I was her anchor and that, through me, she lived out alternatives to what had been her own life."[51] The journey undertaken in Epstein's second memoir thus begins with an important clarification: until she can see where she ends and her mother began, she can't detach herself from her mother's traumatic past or develop the perspective that would enable her to tell her mother's story.

As the process of mourning her mother begins to clarify what theorists call "the lost object," Epstein also constructs, from memories of their shared past, companion images of her mother and herself as separate beings whose work likens them to one another. Franci was a seamstress, Helen is a writer, but from the recollected image of Franci's workroom Helen shapes a metaphor that both links and differentiates them as storytellers. As she "stood at her cutting table, considering cloth," Franci "would sometimes pin her present onto a scrap of her past and tell me a story" (13). But "at the end of the day, when the 'girls' swept up and threw out threads and scraps of cloth, I collected threads and scraps of stories, hoarding them, mulling them over. . . . Each was distinct. There were no seams, only wide gaps in the fabric. My mother would never have made a dress the way she told these stories. There was something wrong in their proportions and some disturbance in her telling that prevented them from making a whole. My mother was a master at joining parts. She would scrutinize the way a sleeve or skirt joined a bodice and if the juncture was not perfect, it would preoccupy her until she found a resolution. If necessary, she would let her mind work overnight, then rip everything apart and fix it in the morning. But she never fixed the way she told her past. The parts never fit. They remained separate and discrete" (13). This shaping of metaphor from childhood memory marks the emergence of the adult writer's voice and also yields its own insight: fascinated as a child by those "disjunctures," Helen will undertake as an adult writer to repair them.

The work of reparation[52]—implicit in the process of mourning—proceeds through the journey Epstein takes to Czechoslovakia that cultivates both the critical perspective and the voice necessary to the telling of her mother's past. On this journey she corrects her mother's nostalgic images (47); she supplements her mother's memory (62); she notes omissions and inaccuracies in memoirs (62), diaries (90), and journals that she studies. She supplies the cultural context that allows for interpretation of first-hand reports (96). Ultimately she even substitutes an image of the grandmother her own research has revealed for the photo her mother had framed and hung (101). And then she begins to examine "all the [other] photographs that survived the war, the ones my mother did not frame" (101). The death of her mother has provoked her recovery of the mother tongue as well as the culture that once lived in it. Moving about her mother's country in her own and her mother's language, the adult child masters the past that traumatized her mother by telling its story.[53]

Karpf's progress toward mastery of her parents' traumatic past moves through a more complicated process that includes therapy as well as research but it eventuates, like Epstein's, in a trip that returns her to Poland: the scene of her parents' stories. For her the story of the Holocaust was so tangled with her parents that it had turned into biography; the trip "home" severs history from biography (290). It also repairs the split in her mind between two places that were actually the same place: the Poland that traumatized her parents and the Poland that still existed as a geographical place—beyond her family narrative. As she discovers the enormous "contrast between [her] charged fantasy and the pedestrian reality" (296) she learns to value "the richness and vibrancy of the culture which was snuffed out" (297), and she feels fully for the first time the grief that its loss legitimately provokes (298). She weeps, and weeps, and then stops weeping. The journey takes her through the process that belongs to what theorists call the "working through" of traumatic losses. She acquires perspective on a traumatic past, she achieves critical distance from it (200), she learns to interpret it (209), and ultimately she suffers again the anguish of losing it (215). For her, as for Epstein, the journey "home" has become a journey toward the fully achieved self in whom there is both the capacity to hear and the voice sufficient to tell the story of the traumatic past.

On the whole, then, memoirs of the second generation describe, from their own perspective, the burden and the shaping power of the personal and the collective past—and the effort to hear its story and to tell it fully. As they lift into public awareness both the burden and the creative struggle to shoulder it, they offer this complex story to readers who delayed its recognition for many decades. That delay postponed the labor of mourning losses—both personal and collective—that would, I believe, affect both our sense of ourselves as Jews and the culture that we would make here, in the aftermath of the Holocaust. From one point of view, our culture appeared to grow up "in a different country," apart from the ruins of Europe. But from the perspective of these memoirs, the disconnection seems inauthentic. Beyond the legacy of Yiddish, which continues to animate the cultural lives of American Jews, there is something indigenous in these texts that belongs to life in the English language but remains profoundly connected to the trauma of the European past—even as the writers themselves are both separate from and connected to their parents. In the skill required to recover their story, in the power to separate their own pain from the trauma of their parents, in the readiness to "read scars" critically, analytically, interpretively—without sacrificing their full emotional weight—one sees the qualities necessary to the work of mourning that may still await American Jews.

3

Voice and Mourning in the Aftermath

Second Generation Fictions

Even before images of Nazi paraphernalia, death camps, and ghettos made their way into corporate and popular venues, critics feared that artists might exploit or distort memory of atrocity,[1] might impose on its horror the possibility of redemption, might render it meaningful, amusing, or comely.[2] Despite the persistence of such doubts, the imaginations of postwar artists and writers—who weren't there—have brooded on it.[3] Norma Rosen has called these writers "witnesses through the imagination."[4] Some of them are children of people who were there, who survived Nazi attempts to exterminate them. From these parents, novelists of the second generation inherit what Marianne Hirsch has called "postmemory": traces of the past transmitted unconsciously from parent to child.[5] Out of this dark layer of intensely felt parental life, second generation writers draw the materials upon which their imaginations work—developing the possibilities that memory reveals in the "little secrets" it uncovers. In some respects, these writers are like the rest of us because, as one of them explains, unless you were there, all "thinking about the Holocaust is really an act of the imagination."[6] Second-generation fiction works within distinctive boundaries in the general field of Holocaust literature. Unlike the memoirists, on one hand, who concentrate on the remembered data of their own lives, novelists concentrate on the residue of

pain and unmourned loss that haunts experience after Auschwitz. Unlike the survivors,[7] on the other hand, some of these
writers will not imaginatively enter the camps, or write the years
between 1939 and 1945. Their subject is not, strictly speaking, the
Holocaust—but its aftermath.

Novelists of the second generation read the aftermath through
their own and their parents' scars. For some critics these scars,
which disfigure the memories, the self-images, and the expectations of survivors' children, appear simply to be evidence of
"family disfunctionality," a condition as common in contemporary American experience as addiction and divorce. But second-
generation novelists assume that these scars matter to all of us
who come after. They believe that residual damage is a shadow
cast by the "little secrets" that survive the Holocaust—not only
in the families of survivors but in the world. The assumption
makes sense to me, for the massive losses of the war years touch
us all in different degrees, and they create a traumatic collective
past that neither the survivors nor the rest of us were able for
many decades to confront—or to mourn.

That inability, collective and personal, becomes the field for
the cultural work done by second-generation novelists. Theorists
since Freud have insisted that a traumatic past must be mourned.
But the literature of the second generation suggests that people
who survived Hitler's effort to exterminate the Jews could not
mourn while they struggled back into life. Their struggle gave
birth to children who inherited a traumatized past, unmourned,
as a legacy.[8] Fictions of the second-generation confront that legacy, imagining the wounds beneath the scars, undertaking the
work of mourning that their parents were unable to perform. According to several post-Holocaust psychoanalysts and historiographers, such work serves a collective, as well as an individual,
purpose.

In 1966 two German psychoanalysts first called attention to
Germany's inability to mourn its own "unmastered" past. They
meant by "mastering" a "sequence of steps in self-knowledge."[9]
This process would not cleanse, or transform, or redeem the past
but might make possible a wholesome life beyond it. Freud had
called these steps "remembering, repeating, working through."[10]
The last term, "working through," speaks most directly to the
kind of cultural work the second generation is doing. When

memory of trauma is repressed or contaminated,[11] and when the repetitive acting out of old pain that one cannot bear to remember turns sterile, affectless, then working through becomes crucial to mourning. Later theorists explain that "working through" means "acquiring some perspective" on experience of trauma. It calls for an effort to achieve critical distance from it, to modify it by interpretation, to make ever more specific what was lost.[12] It even requires the mourner to reconnect with it, to acknowledge the anguish that was severed by trauma from the original experience.[13] To do this work one must be prepared to "read scars," for whatever is "not confronted critically does not disappear. It tends to return as the repressed."[14] Also crucial to this process is the presence of empathic, responsive listeners who "provide . . . a space in which the work of mourning can unfold."[15] Art, then, becomes for the second generation a medium through which the voice of the mature artist—critical, interpretive, though sometimes enraged—reaches toward empathic listeners, drawing them into the collective, cultural work of mourning.

The emergence of a voice sufficient to this task is, I believe, as profound a subject of second-generation fictions as it is of the memoirs. But fictions neither analyze nor explain this phenomenon; in them it happens on the page. Its emergence can move us into the work of mourning because it belongs—like other voices alive in our culture—to the powerful, collective discourses that surround us and shape the way we think. But it enters those large discourses very small, human, singular—seeding the imagination with images drawn from individual experience, which speak to individual readers, inflecting the ways they see themselves, and their pasts, and one another. To speak of "the emergence of voice" is to emphasize the individual effort to speak—out of what Lionel Trilling once called the collective "hum and buzz" of cultural noise.[16] In this case the term "voice" also emphasizes the personal struggle of each writer to revision a disabling past—despite filial devotion to parents who endured it and, consciously or unconsciously, shaped it and passed it on.

Around the emergence of voice, like fruits that define the central vine by their attachment to it, cluster other issues hardly separable from one another. These issues will persist in writings by other writers of the new wave. First among them is the effort to imagine—from the perspective of the aftermath—a time before Auschwitz. Sometimes as preamble, sometimes as sad or enraged indictment, sometimes as critical revisioning of the ground from which postmemory and the power to give it voice will spring, works by second generation writers often reconstruct the European home before the Nazis came. Judith Kalman's *The County of Birches* gives us two, deeply mixed, images of that time. In them one begins to see the shape of neighboring issues that will persist throughout the literature of the new wave. From her father's myth of origin the narrator of Kalman's novel learns to conceive the prewar home in Hungary as "the lap of familial love," engendering "affection that spilled like change into the grasping hands of all the children." On his family's prosperous farm Gabor felt he had been born "between the cornucopious thighs of Mother Earth, between the Tigris and Euphrates as he loved to say, the very source of life."[17] Though "history stormed around us" Gabor's family "enjoyed a perpetual calm. . . . We felt no matter what went on outside, we were protected and blessed" (40). That prewar "golden era of wealth and community and in-soluble family bonds" (58) implants in the narrator's father a layer of confidence in people that even the war and the murder of his parents, siblings, first wife and children can't erase. "My father anticipated decency in others before he would suspect anything else," the narrator remembers (62).

Some deep things in him do not change, but he is not entirely impervious to the multiple murders and uprootings that scar the trajectory of his life. Kalman represents these scars in the way her narrator embodies this father. A man of "European height," he is diminished when he must leave his homeland; in his daughter's eyes he becomes "small only by North American proportions" (68). Even before he reaches America, on the day he leaves Hungary after the revolution in 1957, his young daughter recalls a moment of visible change in him: he closes the front door and by the time he joins his wife and children at the end of the path "his shoulders had rounded, his chest sunk into his belly. He turned into the father of my childhood, the one I really knew. The man who never again trudged through fields of corn or patted the flanks of horses, who from that moment was always close by our sides" (68). It broke him, she believes, "to see his children re-pelled so virulently by the living earth, and severed from the generations who had cultivated this land, loved it and nourished

it and built from it a dynasty" (68). Out of her beloved father's
memories, which encourage his daughter to search for and to
speak the meaning she finds in the past, she fashions poignant
images of the European home as a place of both plenty and deprivation and of the man whose body articulates without words
the effects of his losses.

Embodiment and gender become persistent issues in second-
generation writing—and in other writings of the new wave. From
the story of the life of Sari, her mother, before the war, more emotionally complex images of home and family—also persistent elements of this literature—emerge. Even the great elm tree in which
Sari and her younger sister climb and hide as children is marked
in Sari's memory as a place not only of play but also of danger,
pain, and family conflict. Because Sari's father fears in the tree
the evil forces that he senses in the world around them, he punishes Sari—unjustly—for her small sister's escapade in its thick,
high branches. The novelist will link with Sari's remembered
pain and her anger at this guilty but unpunished small sister a
later scene in Auschwitz. There, while the now adolescent little
sister is brutally beaten by a guard for no reason, Sari feels "cap-
tive to the love that forced her to witness. Helpless, mute, numbness instantly filling the cavity as it was torn open inside her,"
she watches as her innocent sister's skull is split open and her
nose smashed (24). Despite immense differences, the two scenes
are linked in several ways. In both, there is the terrifying injustice
of unmerited physical punishment. In both, a similar cluster of
feelings—of fear, and love, and helplessness before danger—link
Sari to her father. Most important, Sari's childhood rage at her
younger sibling now appears an impossible luxury within the
larger context of their suffering in Auschwitz and the murder of
their parents. By pairing these scenes Kalman twists and deepens
the meanings of "sibling," "family," and "home" as this narrator
mourns the loss of her own innocence by recovering not just the
generosity of her father's past but also the emotional complexity
of her mother's deeply traumatized memories.

Images of the past, then, emerge from second-generation work
on the time "before" as sites of divergent, sometimes conflicted
feeling and memory. They come through the imaginative process
richly layered. In them, specific, detailed moments both connect
with and contradict one another, deepened and complicated

by mature insight, saturated by feelings that once clung to those moments and now reappear in their images. Trauma neither blocks nor erases them. In this way, the novelist not only reconstructs what her parents have lost but mourns it, restoring the anguish that eludes memory as people struggle to survive such losses.

Gender and the body also emerge as important elements in these images of "before." Never as fully embodied as the narrator's father, the mother in Kalman's novel suggests both the power of her youthful sexuality, and its excision from her later life. In the narrator's reconstruction of her mother's past, Sari's passionate desire for her first husband drove her through barbed wire onto his pallet every night for three weeks in the labor camp (48). She will meet and marry her second husband, Gabor, very soon after the camp is liberated. But she will demonstrate in this second marriage, after Auschwitz, no residue of desire or sexual generosity. Rational, deliberate, always fearful, haunted by horrors she can never entirely ignore, this mother transmits to her daughter not only troubling messages about gendered helplessness and loss but also an image of home as "a terrain blasted by uncertainty, loss and terror." Unlike Gabor's "golden" image of a past that sustains his trust and hopefulness. Sari feeds the war to her infant daughter as she spoons food into the child's mouth: "The war came to me with all that is good. It dawned on me like my own sweet flesh and buds of toes" as the child learns both the "pale hand that held the spoon to my mouth" and "the impatient withdrawal of that hand" (47–48). Both the child's and the mother's feeling are alive in these early interactions with the mother's body. "Home," here, becomes deeply ambiguous, a site of both sustenance and sudden loss. The invisibly scarred female body, still a source of nourishment, becomes a source of contamination as well, because of the knowledge it transmits and because of the loss of agency and desire it exemplifies.[18]

Without making direct reference to what came after, Melvin Jules Bukiet's *Stories of an Imaginary Childhood* lace the imaginative reconstruction of "before" with foreshadows of the imminent catastrophe.[19] The stories also explicitly center that reconstruction in the emergence—from the pieties and simplicities of the European past—of a singular artistic voice. Bukiet's "imaginary" Prozowice is alive with both the grotesque and the conventional elements that we have come to associate with shetl life. There are the loving parents, bewildered by their deviant offspring; there are the village whore and the gravedigger. All of them are even larger, warmer and more fecund, in their different ways, than life. But Bukiet's portraits of people and events gleam ominously with suggestions that call up the murderous future. Like the elm tree, disfigured by the father's fears in Kalman's *County of Birches*, allusions to torture and fire to come, to skeletal bodies and skulls with silvered hair ("Virtuoso" 3, 5, 6),[20] darken Bukiet's tale of a young boy's futile romance with the violin. When the young narrator's veins stand "out like tattoos on my skinny arms" in a subsequent story about antisemitism and adolescent appetite ("The Apprentice" 33), it becomes clear that there is no way back to before that doesn't begin with Auschwitz.[21] Unlike historians, who try to clear the image of the past from the shadows of retrospect, second-generation writers do not try to recover the shtetl as it may have been but to reconstruct it in the light of what happened to it. For Bukiet and other second-generation writers, the Holocaust now grinds the lens through which all images of home can be seen.

Self-hatred, ambition, transgressive desire all belong to the young narrator of Bukiet's *Stories*—as if to highlight qualities hidden in more sentimental images of both the shtetl and the artist as a young boy. In part, these characteristics mark the child of conventionally pious, loving parents who accept, even though they cannot understand, his defiance of the limits that govern their lives. This narrator trades his quilt—handmade by the women of his village, a symbol of his "entire past"—for a gypsy boy's bicycle that allows him to feel different, superior. On the bike the narrator zips "past the greybeards weighed down by their Bibles. Unbent by circumstance, I was taller, quicker than the villagers. I was of a new, frictionless generation to whom the old laws did not apply" ("The Quilt and the Bicycle" 55). While the other villagers bend their heads during prayers to the Kohanim, he looks directly up at them ("Levitation" 19); when his neighbors emerge from the water into which they have ritually cast their sins, he swims further out, praying to be lifted up above both them and the law of gravity ("Levitation" 24–27).

Entitled by artistic power, he aspires "to the estate of wings and wheels" ("Nurseries" 169) because his voice, his vision, has created the world in which they exist. There was "something about having shaped another person's world," he discovers, "that gave one legitimate power over him" ("The Blue-Eyed Jew" 125). Still virgin, he does not impregnate the town whore with the child he helps her to deliver. But the experience of bringing a new life into the world marks the "ecstatic" loss of his own virginity: he knows "this was sex," and his "earthly passion" is consummated as the baby he delivers initiates him "into the mysteries of life" (164). This figurative displacement of sexual consummation onto an act of midwifery accords to the artist, who brings the world of "before" into being, both power and privilege. It is a new, imagined life, not a recuperation of the old, that he brings to light.[22]

In this narrator Bukiet develops the trope of the embryonic artist who inherits a past he cannot recuperate but must imagine. And tell. The drama of emergent artistic voice is nearly palpable in these stories.[23] When the narrator recovers his quilt from the gypsies he takes on the warmth and complexity of the past. Its burden becomes his "story," the story of a "hero" who aspires to a land that offers him both beauty and jeopardy; it "was the prize I had sought, and found" ("The Quilt and the Bicycle" 59). He sees himself in this land not as an innocent child of the shtetl, beguiled by its beauty, dependent on its warmth, subject to its authority. Instead he is like the serpent in this soon-to-be-lost garden, already wise to its vulnerabilities, already scarred by knowledge of its imminent suffering. He uses his verbal cunning to win the love of women, to "manipulate and distort" ("Sincerely Yours" 74); his stories attempt not to honor the created world but—more critically—to "comprehend" it ("The Woman with a Dog" 95); he finds his voice as he learns, through a ventriloquist's dummy, to see his own flaws, to acknowledge his caustic, provocative, and controlling nature ("The Ventriloquist" 103–13); he even steals from a celebrated, aging poet an opportunity to substitute during a public reading "his own for the poet's words" ("New Words for Old" 139–46). Here and in two other stories Bukiet introduces the image of a snake to insist that the power of the artist is not innocent. Unlike one character whose devotion to the shtetl goes with him when he emigrates (129), this boy brings "exile" wherever he goes.[24] As he looks at the European home through the lens of Auschwitz, he sees in every lighted candle the flames of the death camps, in every act of love the shadow of loss.

Like parables that refuse to sever home from exile, past from present, Auschwitz from Prozowice, these *Stories of an Imaginary Childhood* refashion earlier, immigrant visions of the old country and the emergent artist's voice by seeing them as they are now: wounds under scars made by the Holocaust. Bukiet's later work refashions the figure of the survivor in a similar way, creating in the matrix (patrix?) of second-generation memory parental figures morally and spiritually as well as physically and emotionally scarred by experience of the camps. Bukiet's *After* begins with the liberation of the camps. Here he imagines the brave new world that reshaped those who survived. Dominated, like the world of the *lager,* by commerce and cynicism, the postwar world takes up—where Hitler left off—the refashioning of European Jews. Some things have changed: liberated prisoners, once objects of malice, are now objects of sympathy.[25] But they are still objects: bureaucrats still group them in masses, erase them as individuals, list, regulate, even exploit them as a "refugee industry" develops among politicians and journalists (17). As Fischl, a former yeshiva boy, journeys "home" to search for the young bride taken from him by the Nazis, Bukiet contrasts the world of "now" with the one "before." The web of train tracks across Europe still exists, but "now" there are seats and windows where "before" there were only cattle cars; the conductor smiles instead of turning him in to the Gestapo when he identifies himself as a Jew; no guns and dogs meet him when he climbs down into the station that is—surprisingly—still intact; he even locates the shul—now a variety store. But as he turns to the cemetery in search of his wife, Polish children—disappointed that he digs up no buried treasures there—pursue and stone him: "The good children of Jewless Ostrowiec had no recourse but to open their hearts to the treasure within, to search their souls and discover the purity of the hatred they bore like a vein of gold in the fertile Polish earth" (56–66). Ironically reminiscent of all the graveless dead, buried treasure is a dominant metaphor in this work, but what really persists beneath the changing surfaces of both before and after remains deadly hostile to the Jew.

A current of sometimes cynical, sometimes murderous, hostility is the shaping power that transforms both the world and the former yeshiva boys who emerge into it from the *lager.* Information is still useful to them, but their learning is very different from the lessons of the yeshiva. Neither morality nor spirituality has survived. One former yeshiva boy asks, "'Tell me about a God who gives the world to the German murderers and to us, who bow and pray, he gives less than nothing, he gives . . . ,'" to which Isaac replies "Dreck and claptrap. . . . He gives dreck and I've never heard such self-indulgent claptrap in all my life. . . . If this is what freedom brings, then put me back into the *lager* where I can understand what people are saying. At least you knew where you stood, and what you needed. The last thing I needed then and the last thing I need now is theology'" (121). Belief, alive in Proszowice, is "no more" Isaac knows; in the new world Isaac wonders: "'Did Jews survive? I don't know what a Jew is anymore. I don't think that I bear any resemblance to my father or my grandfather or some ancestor with camels. Things are different now'" (156–57). The task of this novel is to assess that difference so that losses may be clearly seen, adequately mourned. The loss of belief introduced here, like the changes Judith Kalman records in images of home, family, and gendered bodies, will become a persistent issue in Post-holocaust writings of the new wave.[26]

Among the losses after Auschwitz Bukiet numbers not only traditional belief but also traditional forms of love: among men "who could not yet grow a beard" and "women whose heads had been shaved," "delicate courtship rituals established across the synagogue barriers that kept the opposite sex at a remove for centuries went up in smoke. . . . They paired like rabbits in a cage as they couldn't when penned in separate cages for the first half of the decade" (187).

The bodies of these men when they leave the *lager* are significantly marked by more than tattoos: Isaac's teeth have been shattered by a sadistic guard who made him drink steaming coffee after exposing him to severe cold "that penetrated so deeply it congealed the marrow in his bones" (5). Morgenstern's "genetic nearsightedness had been deliberately magnified by those who compelled him to work as a counterfeiter, to wear too strong a pair of spectacles to accomplish the fine work they now required"; now he can "see no farther than his knuckles" (38). The damage done by the *lager* will persist not only in embodiments of its survivors in second-generation writing, but also in images of Jewish men throughout the writings of the new wave.

Perhaps equally grievous, Bukiet concocts in a factory that turns books back into pulp, a Swiftian metaphor for the devaluation of all previous knowledge: "It was a library, with a dozen aisles of shelves filled with thousands of brown and purple volumes, and it felt like a library except for a branch of the *papiergescheft*'s conveyor belt that rolled incongruously down the center aisle, carrying a stack of books"; among them one scholarly survivor sees "multiple copies of Sholem Aleichem and Mendele Mocher Seforim, and . . . Ladino poetry in volumes that dated from the sixteenth century" (208). Thousands of books "moved along the conveyor belt . . . and . . . dropped off the edge" like "the workers at Mauthausen. They joined heaps of Hebrew books in a large steel vat while a rusty pipe extending over the edge dripped a clear liquid down the wall. 'Hydrochloric sixteen,'" the overseer says. Fischl, a former yeshiva boy, watches "as the acid hit the covers and turned them to a mash the consistency of oatmeal. . . . He could almost feel the release of the words within. 'Shma Yisroel' rising from the pulp to the heavens as the same words had risen from the owners of those books as they were placed into a different processing center" (210). This metaphor of loss will echo in works by other writers of the new wave who will assess the nature of Jewish experience in a world from which traditional learning, like the Jews who studied and lived within it, has been violently removed.

This novel bitterly, insistently, connects the radical devaluation of books to the fate of people who wrote and read them. Once, the narrator remembers, "Jews had passed through the Regensburg valley on their journey from Spain across Mitteleuropa to Poland, but that was centuries earlier. The return of eighty thousand Polish émigrés would have meant a golden age of culture and learning to the rabbis. The manner of their return now, however, was a boon only to suppliers of bulldozers and lime" (145–46). Learning and human beings become commodities as Bukiet mourns the losses of "before." Like values, customs, and beliefs, they become "part of some universal go round, like the water cycle, rain from clouds into seas, evaporating to form rain for clouds" (210). From such a cycle, meaning disappears.

In such a world, family bonds are simultaneously intensified and attenuated. Isaac's brother, half-blinded by antisemitic brutality even before the Nazis, becomes in *After* a kind of deus ex machina who appears and disappears unpredictably, while all that is left to Isaac of the rest of his family emerges at the end in a vision of their deportation. He sees "every Jew in Eastern Europe on that same train. . . . Isaac could hear the Jews' murmurs from within. . . . *They* were wondering were they were going, when *he* knew damn well and wanted to shout out a useless warning. There were tiny gaps between some of the warped slats of the cattle car. Isaac could see his parents' fingers emerge from between the slats. They were waving 'Good-bye,' their fingers scratching the air. After the train had left, all that remained were the scratches of those fingers on the air, tiny rents in the fabric of being" (362; Bukiet's emphasis). Reduced to scratches of ghostly fingers on the air, the family is disembodied altogether in the world after Auschwitz. As Bukiet imagines Isaac recovering this long suppressed memory of radical loss, the novel acknowledges its part in the work of mourning

The rage inspired by such losses helps to explain not only the bitter cynicism that speaks through many of Bukiet's metaphors but also the failure of his survivor / writer, Benya, who will never be able to write the story of the aftermath. Gentle Benya, called *der schreiber* or "writer," can tell the long story of the Jewish past, beginning with Adam and Eve and "passing from Babylonia to Rome, to Spain, to Mitteleuropa" until "history split wide open. It was 1939." He can even tell the tale of one shtetl boy imprisoned in the *lager*. But then he falls silent, "unable to enter the last chapter of his own saga" (269). Through the rest of his life he would carry "the *lager* with him wherever he went." But his voice will be insufficient to the story of the aftermath. Bukiet suggests that the story of "after" will not be told by those who were there; their energies will need to be spent either on remembering—like *der schreiber*—or on returning to life, like Fischl's wife giving birth to a child, or like Isaac—anticipating America (322). Only their children, fueled partly by the rage that would have diverted their parents' energy and will from the task of reentering the world, will be able to pick up the tale abandoned for the sake of memory and of life by those who came out when the camps were liberated.

In Art Spiegelman's work, images of "before" and "after" are as thoroughly interlaced as Bukiet's; parental images are scarred; and family is profoundly damaged as anger finds a target more intimate than the Nazis or the postwar world. The map on the

back cover of *Maus: A Survivor's Tale* makes visible the interpene-
tration of what was with what was yet to be. On this map Poland
contains not only names of the towns in which Art's parents
lived, courted, and married but also names of the camps that
later swallowed them and all the Jews of Europe. In the fore-
ground, superimposed on this dark country of both "before" and
"during," is a small, bright map of the world of aftermath: "Rego
Park, N.Y." where the son struggles to grow up, to grow into, to
represent and to mourn the story of his parents' and his own
losses. Like Bukiet's work, Spiegelman's narrative does not recover but rather reconstructs a personal, idiosyncratic image of
the European home. It is filtered through the lens of the survivor-
father's selective, often self-serving memories, overlaid—like
Rego Park on Poland—with the equally idiosyncratic and self-
serving responses of his artist/writer son.

The mixed-media form of Spiegelman's two books clarifies
an essential difference in intention between fictions of the second generation and the work of historians, archivists, and witnesses.[27] Spiegelman's works do not seek objective knowledge of
the Holocaust for the sake of recovering or memorializing it. Instead he makes parables that imaginatively represent, that explicitly reshape what survives of the past by turning Jews, Nazis,
and Poles into mice, cats, and pigs. His works seek to imaginatively reconstruct a traumatic past—together with its aftermath—
for the sake of interpreting and mourning it. This labor eschews
objectivity because it needs to be, simultaneously, expressive,
critical, self-reflexive, and saturated with affect.[28]

Like other writers of the second generation, Spiegelman links
the Nazi atrocities to the damage they left behind. In *Maus* there
are the father's story of the war years, on one hand, and the postwar suicide of his wife, Anja, Artie's mother, on the other. But in
this work as in others of the second generation, these subjects—
which re-present the European home, what happened to it, and
its aftermath—reveal a narrative process that underlies them
and gives them form. The narrative process upon which they depend is the emergence of the protagonist's voiceand the work of
mourning that it performs. Spiegelman suggests the centrality of
this process to the narrative as a whole by literally centering in
Maus the four-page story of Anja's suicide and its aftermath, by
allowing these pages to break the chronological scheme of

Vladek's and Artie's joint story, by disrupting in them, with human images, the dominant animal metaphor that controls figuration elsewhere in the work, and by accomplishing here and in the text that follows the radical disembodiment of the survivor-mother. Even her voice disappears. *Maus* makes explicit its roots in this particular traumatic loss and Artie's effort both to survive and to mourn it.[29]

This work of mourning is so painful, so many layered, so long delayed that even his father's account of imprisonment and abuse in his prewar European home appears almost tangential to it. To be sure, one cannot look away from witness testimony; there are no subjects more compelling of entire attention. *Maus* does not look away, but it embeds Vladek's testimony within its deliberate scrutiny of Vladek himself. Beneath the specific horrors of his experience, his tale reveals his dedication to survival, his inability to mourn. When he speaks of himself as a young man he emphasizes the strength, resourcefulness, and good looks he possessed during the terror of the prewar years, qualities that will become crucial to his survival in the camps. He struggles to sustain this self-image in the aftermath. But he is scarred in many ways by Auschwitz and its legacy. His glass eye and fragile heart, his obsessions and compulsions, his medications and Exercycle workouts mark him both physically and psychologically as damaged. His fragility becomes manifest when his wife dies; his grief then is so overwhelming that he must shut it down in order to live beyond it. He has learned in avoidance and repression the fundamental lessons of survival. Never consoled for Anja's loss,[30] he will marry again; he will even destroy Anja's journals to prevent them from depressing him.[31] He makes clear the difference between surviving and mourning that differentiates the task of the parent from that of the child.

In Spiegelman's work Vladek's voice and image are persistent. But they are everywhere companioned by the voice and hand of his son—who must both survive and mourn. Artie filters and subverts his father's narrative even as he reaches past it to connect the experience of traumatic loss to feelings that Vladek cannot allow himself to recognize. Artie will carry through this story of the aftermath—as he tries to reconstruct his mother's past from Vladek's fragmentary and often self-serving memories, as he searches for her papers and rages against his father for having destroyed them—the work of mourning Anja's death that Vladek cannot perform. She is, as many critics have noted, entirely absent from this text—except insofar as her survivors reconstruct her. Not Anja, but her loss is the subject that grounds Artie's work.

Like a frame for the resentments and misunderstandings her loss inspires, and for the multiple efforts to dismiss and the attempts to comprehend it, Artie's relation to his father becomes the context within which Anja is mourned and from which the mature artist emerges. Inadequately recognized by Vladek, who never acknowledges Artie's feelings and who calls him—at the end of *Maus*—by the name of an earlier, lost child, Artie turns his rage against his father. But Spiegelman, the artist/writer, sees through Artie's anger to both the vulnerability of the father and the need of the son. The persona of the artist/writer develops through the drawing and telling of Artie's and Vladek's story. Wearing the striped uniform of Auschwitz in the central pages that tell of Anja's suicide and Artie's breakdown, the artist/writer testifies to the power of the *lager* to reach beyond itself, into the death of Anja and her survivor-son's sense of himself. But Artie, unlike Vladek, is not permanently overwhelmed by this loss. Initially stricken by it, Artie first breaks down; but then he develops the power to produce this work. He reconstructs this family past; he edits his father's words, revealing what the father would hide; he organizes the sequence that structures Vladek's narrative; and he embeds his father's story of the past within the story of their failed and painful but ongoing connection with one another.

All of Vladek's story can be heard only through the filter of his relationship to Artie. Artie's voice plays over, under, and all around the father's fragmented memories, complaints, criticisms, and pleas. Artie's reactions to his father's eccentricities shade a reader's response to them but also allow one to see their sources in Vladek's earlier suffering. One must see always double in this text: the damaged, unloving but needy father prodded by his resentful, unloving but needy son to furnish the material out of which this work of memory and mourning can be fashioned.

The process shaped by the text responds directly to the requirements set out by theorists for the work of mourning: what trauma has obscured is clarified in this work. The emotional effect of a painful past is represented in specific, graphic—even critical—detail as Artie draws himself dwindling into the child receiving his father's excessively but understandably grim lecture on starvation as the test of friendship.[32] The mature artist can see and interpret what the child could only feel, can critique the cruel inappropriateness of Vladek's lecture to his small child and also understand its appropriateness to Vladek's own experience of Auschwitz. Specificity becomes crucial as Artie encourages Vladek to describe a crematorium so that, as writer/artist, he can diagram it exactly (*Maus II:70*). The past is critically examined and interpreted—as Vladek reveals and the artist draws the mixture of grief, fear, and self-concern within his avoidance of the place where four Jews, friends, have been hanged by the Nazis for dealing on the black market (*Maus:83*). As Artie recalls that his own grief and guilt were overwhelmed by Vladek's needs after Anja's death, the artist/writer reveals the emotional ground from which the son's grievance grows against his father. Always the story and drawings reconnect events with their affects: once Vladek has described the Gestapo roundup of all the Jews of their village, the artist/writer draws him slumped, despairing, over his exercise bike. Artie's rage and bewilderment at his father's highhandedness (*Maus:68–69*) in another scene are as clear as his contempt for Vladek's stinginess—whose roots in Auschwitz the tale makes very clear to us without softening Artie's annoyance at them.

One gift of this work is its power to elicit feeling for both the parents and the child: for Anja, desperately needing to be reassured that her son loves her, and for Artie, equally desperate to disengage from the overwhelming needs of his war-damaged mother (*Maus:103*); for Vladek, offering what love Auschwitz has left him to offer, and for Artie, rejecting it because it is insufficient. As in Kalman's work, the figures of both parents and the emotional sustenance they offer are scarred by the damage they sustained in Auschwitz. Emerging from the guilt Anja's suicide inspires, from rage against a father insulated by his own, old suffering from the needs of his son, the hand-drawn signature that closes *Maus II* affirms the identity of the artist/writer, born and evolved out of grief and mourning, beside dates that mark the beginning and end of this process in the origin and completion of this work.

Spiegelman's *Maus*, then, tells the emergence of an artistic voice sufficient to the task of mourning a complex, destructive past. His works trace in the interplay of survivor and second-generation experience the scars left in both generations by Auschwitz and also the difficult, patient, brilliant work of reading and writing them. That they are not healed in the process testifies here, as in all second-generation work, to a residue of pain and loss that will not be erased. Thane Rosenbaum's trilogy of fictions begin and end with that recognition. Like other writings by the second generation, they read within the families of his protagonists, on their bodies and in their emotional and spiritual lives, the scars of a traumatic past. But they develop the story of emergent artistic voice not in the interplay of survivor/parent and child but by differentiating memory from the entangling web of postmemory.

The artist is not yet visible in the first, widely anthologized and often discussed story of *Elijah Visible,* which features what Freud would have recognized as the "return of the repressed." In the sudden arrest of a young lawyer's late night descent by elevator from the upper stories of his office, the unmastered parental past overtakes a child of the second generation. The sealed space in which he is stalled fills with the sights, sounds, and smells of the cattle car that took his parents to Auschwitz, and the trajectory of his own life shifts to make possible the work of mourning left incomplete in his parents' lives. This protagonist, Adam Posner, is broken into different personae in each chapter—like light passing through a prism. Time is also broken in this work; its chapters move in a zigzag path, generally backward. Here, development of both character and plot means moving to the place where the scarring began.

Rosenbaum's "before" is located not in Europe but in America, not in the Nazi past but in the personal past of his protagonist where memory needs to be extricated from postmemory. Whether Adam tries to evade or to court the past, whether he distracts himself from this work by pursuing non-Jewish women, or summons into his troubled life the surviving European relatives who know the family history, he is drawn back little by little into the world of his own childhood. Only when his scars can be seen separate from those of his parents will Rosenbaum's protagonist develop the critical, interpretive, empathic perspective that even his narrator doesn't possess until the end of this first work.

The trilogy as a whole will close the perceptual gap between Rosenbaum's protagonists and his narrators, like the gap between Artie and the artist/writer in Spiegelman's *Maus*. In the first work, however, Adam Posner cannot see what needs to be seen. As a young lawyer, he cannot separate his parents' trauma from his own: drowning in his parents' memories, he experiences a stalled elevator as though it were a sealed cattle car. As an academic, he lives and works within the web of Holocaust literature and history, taking on the burden of a past he never lived, always late for appointments because the Nazis were always on time, feeling inauthentic because he was not there ("An Act of Defiance").[33] As an artist, he attaches himself serially to unsuitable women, allowing one of them to disrupt his first ritual gesture of mourning for a mother whose power subverts his work as well as his life ("Romancing the Yahrtzeit Light"). Though Adam cannot mourn because he can neither connect nor disentangle his own malaise from his parents' past, the novel itself reconstructs, in both specific and increasingly critical ways, the damage done by Auschwitz to Adam's parents and their effects on this child of the second generation. One chapter ("The Pants in the Family") traces the inability of small Adam's father to hold on to his child or to cope with the illness and death of his wife. This father's body has radically deteriorated within the child's memory. Adam recalls wrestling on the carpet with the once strong man later confined by multiple heart attacks to a wheelchair, remembers a childhood of "tiptoeing around the house, being warned daily of his impending death" (43). "I came to you with a heart filled with loss," his father tells him (51). From this "afflicted creature," the refugee "with the haunted past" who survived "months of hiding in the forest," "years in the concentration camp," and the "slaughter of his family," the child assumes too early the crushing burdens of adult responsibility (43) that the father cannot bear. But the narrator sees clearly the loss not only of the vital father but also of the abbreviated childhood that Adam will need to mourn.

Adam's mother's scars ("Bingo by the Bungalow") will be even more difficult for this child to "appreciate" (108). Outwardly she is marked not only by the numbers on her arm but also by "an unforgetting purple scar molded on her forehead" (110). Inwardly, she is damaged in ways we cannot see. But the story reveals the wounds that Adam bears because of her un-specified, earlier suffering. When her husband dies, "her sanity began to leave her. She was losing her memory, her sense of place, her essential bearings, her grip on reality" (119). When she violently punishes Adam for revealing secrets he doesn't know, about hidden bullets and hidden bread, the narrator sees that "the child was too young to understand; the parent too mortified to concede the injury—to both of them" (120). But Adam cannot yet command this insight.

This mother figure will return in Rosenbaum's second work, *Second Hand Smoke*, as his protagonist moves closer to a narrative perspective that can see—through the harm she does—to the wounds under her own scars. Only "authorized persons" (who have become authors?)—the sign on their abandoned summer bungalow points out—can see into this painful past, can read the mother's as well as the child's scars.[34] Rosenbaum's later protag-onists will move through rage and blame toward acceptance of her—like Artie who becomes, as artist/writer of *Maus*, capable of both criticizing and empathizing with damaged parents and the family they made. As these writers become more fully aware of their own wounds, they read more insightfully the scars of their parents.

Relationships figure one important benchmark of the trans-formation these protagonists must undergo. The Adam of *Elijah Visible*'s next-to-last chapter begins to see what the narrator sees: that the pattern of Adam's adult relationships has been shaped by early losses that damaged both his parents and himself. In this chapter Adam reconnects with a childhood friend whose father died when the boys were very young. After they recall the effects on the friend's family of this strong, playful father's sudden death, and the effects on Adam of that family's sudden depar-ture, they realize the devastation created by these losses. "'Way too much for a ten year old. We then realized,' Adam says, 'that my mother was right: we would never be safe, or feel safe'" (182). Adam's mother learned in Auschwitz what she taught Adam in Miami Beach. But, like Vladek's lecture on starvation as the test of friendship, the lesson wounds instead of protecting the child. After the old friends weep together, after they share the sense that their lives have been futile quests for what is unalter-ably lost, they play catch in the airport until one friend's plane departs. In the interrupted game—whose very form depends on keeping a ball in the air, on repeatedly breaking and reestablishing connection with it and with one another—the narrative offers an image of the kinds of relationships Adam has known throughout this work and will know, with some important changes, throughout the trilogy. In the broken marriages of Rosenbaum's later protagonists, in the interrupted frisbee game that the writer/protagonist of Rosenbaum's last novel plays with the ghost of his errant wife, one sees the shadow of this paradigmatic game of catch interrupted by the sudden departure of one player.

To see this shadow, and to conceive the relational pattern it suggests, is to move beyond suffering, beyond repetitive memory, to another place. *Elijah Visible* works toward that movement by returning, in chapter after chapter, to moments of Adam's past. The goal of these efforts to reconstruct the personal past is to differentiate the child's experience and memories from those of his parents. In the first chapter the adult child crumbled under the weight of his parents' memories. In subsequent chapters Adam moves into moments of his own adolescence and young manhood that reveal, incrementally, not only the damaged parents, but also his own formative years, traumatized by the legacy of their past. The change in perspective achieved by the work as a whole can be measured by comparison of the first and final chapters. When the elevator doors open in the first chapter, the elevator has become a cattle car; Adam has become a survivor: "The stench of amassed filth was evident. . . . Adam was sitting on the floor, dressed in soiled rags. Silvery flecks of stubble dappled his bearded face" (11). There is no narrative distance here to clarify the difference between second-generation postmemory and survivor experience, between Adam's hallucinatory experience of a past he never lived and the actual experience he is living in the present, between stalled elevator and cattle car.

But in the final chapter the narrator can make the necessary distinction. In "The Little Blue Snowman of Washington Heights," the smallest Adam, rendered by his parents' residual paranoia "incurably anxious" in kindergarten and suspicious of both solicitous school counselors and uniformed policemen, escapes his protective teacher and trudges home from school alone in a blizzard, insulated in boots and parka appropriate to a winter in Siberia, unwilling to ride the bus with the other students because it "wasn't part of the plan, not the scheduled escape route" (203). Here the narrator sees the child's malaise in painfully specific ways: the dreadful appeal of the "little red light house," no longer dominated by the great bridge that looms above it, sufficient on its own to rescue others (196); the parents' stories of real terror and no rescue that the child must keep secret (192); the anxiety attacks that alert teachers to Adam's malaise (200); the child's numbing readiness for the loss of his parents— "they had long ago warned him of the precariousness of life, and the possibilities—no, the certainties—of their imminent deaths" (202). The narrator's most vital insight into the child's dilemma comes when he arrives home and enters to find both parents, naked, "shuddering in the darkness. Two pairs of terrorized eyes—the withering remains of the master race" (205). In this visionary moment the narrator sees and understands what Adam cannot yet grasp. Even more important, as the chapter differentiates the child's from the parents' terror, the existential and psychological connections between them remain strong but finally become clear. Here the narrator can see both the imprisonment of the parents in their own past—and the child, bound by their as yet unread scars to his own ordeal, still too young to understand or to take up the work of mourning.

Reconstruction of the personal past for a second-generation writer is neither a symptom of self-absorption nor a bid for sympathy but—like the effort of other second-generation writers to reconstruct the Europe of "before"—an essential condition for the emergence of artistic voice and the beginning of mourning. Drawn back little by little into the world of his childhood, Adam's returnings are not the futile repetitions that distinguish traumatic memory. They recover the past in a way that allows it to be fully felt—but also known, worked with in the mind. The image Rosenbaum offers of this process, which becomes an emblem of the work of imagination on a traumatic past, appears in a chapter called "Romancing the Yahrtzeit Light"—a chapter that tells the story of Adam as an artist who betrays the memory of his mother by liaisons with gentile women. He even interrupts the ritual of mourning that has energized his work by allowing his mother's memorial (*yahrtzeit*) candle flame to be put out by a woman who makes love to him on the table beside it. Afterward, his work declines as his love life improves. He forgets his loss. His mother's "aborted yahrtzeit candle" becomes an "indistinct memory."

But imagination will not let it go. The artist removes the unburnt wax from its glass, pulverizes the glass "into crystal shards," and slaps them "upon a canvas that he intended to paint entirely in black" (31). In the darkness of that painting's virtual "world," the bits of broken glass call up both the personal past—the dead mother—and the collective past that holds the memory of *Krystallnacht*—the night of broken glass. These bright, dangerous fragments illuminate the darkness of his painting—suggesting the way in which imagination recovers what the rational, analytic mind doesn't, yet, allow itself to know. Multiple illuminations that recover past losses recur at the end of the story, when Adam's current girlfriend stands on tiptoe to light the star on her Christmas tree. Her pose repeats the Shabbat candle-lighting pose of Adam's mother at the beginning. Adam falls asleep under her tree, "curled up like an unwrapped present, a lifeless ornament, the keeper of the flame" (33). The now-extinct fires of Auschwitz, once witnessed by his forgotten mother, live in the background of that final image, which refers ironically as well to the *yahrtzeit* candle that Adam failed to keep alight. Adam cannot see here what the writer and narrator of this story see: that remembering—however painful—can restore vitality not only to his art but also to his life.

The process of coming to see what imagination already grasps works itself out through this first novel as Adam moves through different phases of his earlier life. In every phase he confronts the damage sustained by his parents in the Holocaust—and the emotional legacy they passed on to him. Both the unmanned father—his physical fragility an embodiment of his damaged sense of self—and the powerful, destructive, deeply traumatized mother suggest that these potentially lethal data of the post-Auschwitz family must be reconstructed, set like the shards of the pulverized *yahrtzeit* glass within the darkness of Adam's initial descent into memory. The sharp bits of shining glass that once held a survivor/mother's memorial candle are the memories that belong to Adam; the cattle cars belong to the world of his parents. The novel differentiates but links them, allowing one to see through the child's suffering—to the damage done to his parents.

To some readers, this double vision is objectionable; it seems to equate the suffering endured by survivors of Auschwitz with the ordinary pain of family experience. But there is no such equation suggested here. The writer uses the child's pain as a lens to focus first the parents' failures of love and patience and tenderness, and then the old suffering that lies behind them. Both the child and his parents bear scars that must be read. Memory and imagination become the readers. And we become the empathic listeners, who learn not only to recognize the legacy of the Holocaust in the dysfunctions within second-generation families but also in the hardening of our own responses to vulnerability and dependence in the aftermath of atrocity and collective loss.

The rage that follows such recognitions becomes another issue for the artist. In Bukiet's *After,* it energizes the bitter humor, the cynical wit of the artist. In Spiegelman's *Maus,* after destabilizing the artist to the point of breakdown, it fuels the engagement between himself and his father out of which the work— and the mature artist—emerge. In Rosenbaum's second novel, *Second Hand Smoke,* rage makes of memory a kind of nightmare from which the protagonist cannot awaken. "It's like you're possessed," his estranged wife tells him, "Your eyes are burning with rage. It's the look of the Six Million in one fragile, but very frightening, face."[35] In Duncan, anger at what the Nazis did to his parents and at what they did to him spills into the streets of New York and the souvenir shops of Warsaw. He can see the difference between their suffering and his own, but as he gathers in the shards of both his own and his abusive mother's traumatic pasts, enraged memory breaks the continuity of the narrative, destroys his marriage and career, and finds expression within the narrative voice and the images that distinguish Rosenbaum's work.

Duncan Katz exemplifies Freud's warning that unless we mourn we are doomed to repeat the past. As the narrative cuts and crosscuts between Duncan's mother's and his own violent experiences, the novel shows us "flashbacks" as the "ultimate prisons" in which Duncan's life is trapped (18). Groomed by his mother, Mila, to become a warrior, he fights. Denied by her, from the beginning, the nurturing that teaches confidence and trust, he is hard—yet fragile. Refused by her even the sop of wine offered to every Jewish male infant at his circumcision, abandoned as a child in neighborhoods that victimize children, forced to compete at football and wrestling, Duncan hates this mother—and those who rendered her unable to love. Even the narrator attends to the damage she has done. He sees beyond Duncan's distress to a scene in which Mila—before abandoning in Poland her first son, Isaac—burns into his arm her own numbers from the *lager*. The narrator knows that as she nurses this baby to still his screams after the burning, he will take in with his "mother's milk" the "fateful kiss of second hand smoke" from the chimneys of Auschwitz. In this novel the mother's body becomes the medium through which the poison of the camps is transmitted. And the bodies of her male children are scarred by her legacy.

This narrator also sees that Mila has survived extermination. And has been deformed by it. He will insist on the complexity of her maternal legacy. Duncan's tenderness toward his daughter unconsciously mimics his mother's carefully concealed gestures of devotion to him; she has saved even the curls shorn by his first haircut as he saves a curl of his own child's hair. Even in Mila herself, some residue of generosity and compassion survive. Having won at poker large sums of money from other patients in a hospital where she is dying of cancer, Mila returns the wager of a young boy who has lost his arm in an accident. She shows him her own arm, tattooed in Auschwitz. When the boy says, bitterly, he "would rather have your arm than the one I am missing," Mila replies: "I know. It would be better. You are young; this should not have happened to you." Her response neither masks her pain nor minimizes his. Removing from Mila the heavy burden of maternal responsibility to teach what she has learned, Rosenbaum reveals a woman rendered empathic by guilt and her own suffering. In this way—like Spiegelman's artist/writer who can see the sources of both Artie's and Vladek's suffering— Rosenbaum's narrator refocuses the rage of Mila's children on those who abused her without losing sight of the ways in which that abuse scarred her sons.[36]

Second Hand Smoke not only creates a narrative voice sufficient—partly by virtue of the pain and rage it expresses—to the work of mourning but also plays with iconic images of the Holocaust in such a way as to decontaminate memory for the one who remembers. The repetitions in which outraged memory imprisons Duncan Katz are different from the ways in which art recalls and reclaims, like Adam Posner and the bits of *yahrtzeit* glass, the shards of a terrible past. This novel differentiates the unmediated, literal work of remembering from a process that asserts ownership—if not mastery—of a past so painful that it

would otherwise overwhelm the rememberer. Rosenbaum introduces the most dangerous bits of Holocaust memory into the ongoing lives of his characters—as if to inoculate them against the
deadly effect.[37] Sometimes he recontextualizes these dangerous
fragments of the past, shifting their tragic valence toward comic
ends. The fake showers in Auschwitz that poisoned millions of
Jews become, in *Second Hand Smoke,* real showers in modern
Warsaw, where two brothers separated by the Holocaust will discover one another. In the third novel, *The Golems of Gotham,* the
ghosts of eight survivors will be discovered by the son of survivors in his shower. Sometimes the change in context simply
familiarizes an image of the contaminated past, diminishing its
power to overwhelm by rendering it ordinary. The cattle cars
that carried so many Jews to their deaths, and stopped Adam
Posner nearly dead in his tracks, reappear casually in *Second
Hand Smoke* as New York subways, "where lights flickered on
and off like a strobe, drawing attention to all those faces in spasm
with misery" (87).[38] Instead of universalizing the cattle car by
calling attention to the forced migrations of other peoples, instead of exploiting this image to suggest a connection between
industrial commodification in our own time and the transport
of Jews to the crematoria,[39] Rosenbaum's images simply suggest
that the world we know is haunted, still, by the painful, unpro-
cessed residue of the crime against the Jews.

Sometimes a change in the context of a Holocaust image renders it revelatory: the tattooed number inflicted on Duncan's
mother in Auschwitz and later scalded by her into the arm of her
Polish infant becomes an agent of identification when he is reunited with his brother, Duncan. The new, specific power Rosenbaum adds to this image does not change its original deadliness.
The pain and humiliation of this marking remain vivid in the
novel. But beside the continuing power of this image to brand, to
punish, to dehumanize both the one who bears it and the one who
inflicts it, the novelist gives it another, less destructive power: to
inform, to connect, to make recognition possible. "It's all in the
numbers," a character in Rosenbaum's later novel, *The Golems of
Gotham,* will say, when a child of the third generation uses her
grandparents' numbers to recall their spirits after their deaths.[40]
Arrogating to the artist, rather than to God, the power to transform the residue of atrocity in this way, Rosenbaum suggests that

to own the past is to play with it, to reclaim it, to turn it seamed-side out so that the terror still alive in it can be felt—but survived.

Like the artist, Adam Posner, who pulverizes an empty *yahrt-zeit* glass and sets its fragments into the midst of his painting's darkness, Rosenbaum resets and reframes these potentially killing bits of the past so that one can remember without succumbing to them. He suggests that one treats the past in this way simply in order to live with otherwise unbearable postmemories. Like the paintings of Anselm Kiefer, made partly of ashes, partly of burned and twisted metal, partly of fragments left behind after the immense devastation of the Holocaust, the fictional worlds of Rosenbaum's novels are built out of and upon ruins, constructed of debris that litters the European past. Significant elements of that debris: broken glass, railway cars, tattoos, stripes, gas, showers, smoke, hair, reappear again and again in his works—as though there were no other materials with which to build a life.

Rosenbaum's third novel, *The Golems of Gotham* concentrates on the ordeal of the writer in such a world of ruins. In it the novelist, Oliver, suffering from writer's block, imagines back into life as golems the spirits of six writers who committed suicide after their liberation and the loving, worried ghosts of his survivor parents—also suicides. They return to rescue the world—and also the writer/protagonist—from forgetfulness. But the world is unredeemable. Though the golems close down the tattoo business, end the shaving of heads, eliminate stripes on zebras and showers in bathtubs; though smoking stops, chimneys disappear, and subway cars will not run when people are packed too tightly into them (129–35); though even Con Edison switches from gas to electricity (137), forgetfulness persists. In Holocaust denials, in the waning of public interest in Holocaust memorials, museums, and college courses, in "indifference and amnesia" (385–90) the weight of the murderous past sinks again below the level of collective attention. Thus this novel accepts as a given—like the two before it—the task of living with a past that cannot either be forgotten or adequately remembered or redeemed.

There is no divine agency in this work to draw meaning from historic outrage. From the parental suicides during a sabbath service at the beginning, through the seder at the end that features a Haggadah amended to highlight the still unanswerable questions about human suffering and the failure of divine intervention, this novel—like the suicidal Rabbi who turns up in Elijah's place—refuses the consolation of redemption. But the novel places within the power of its writer/protagonist's imaginative memory the possibility of owning the past without becoming another of its victims. The suicides of the golems raise for Oliver the threat of perishing under the burden of memory and postmemory that Rosenbaum's entire oeuvre confronts. In part, this novel tracks the deterioration of its writer/protagonist as he faces this threat. His hair turns white; he dreams incessantly. He writes to relieve his pain. He nearly commits suicide. But he survives. He reconstructs the images of survivor/parents to reveal, beneath the fact of their abandonment, their continuing concern for him; he reimagines the motives of his estranged wife to suggest, beneath the fact of her abandonment, her continuing love for both him and their daughter.

Beyond the plot that traces Oliver's developing power to read the scars of those who have hurt him, the novel offers two other, complex, representations of a strategy that could make mourning possible in a ruined and forgetful world, still haunted by the half-buried memory of atrocity. In Oliver's daughter, Ariel, one such image becomes visible. She has "hair . . . the color of late afternoon sand and her eyes, large and round, were the kind of ambivalent blue that turns gray in the backlit sun. She had an immobilizing smile. . . . Her nose was slender and her lips thin. She was tall for her age with long arms, sloping shoulders, and the awkwardness of body that came from growth spurts that couldn't quite keep pace with the rest of her development" (12). In her, the writer conceives the possibility of a future unmarked by trauma. But the instrument she plays, a weathered, battered Klezmer violin rescued from prewar Europe, links even her future with the outrage of the past. "This violin looked more like a bastard piece of wood that had been sent out to sea and had returned water-logged. The horsehair strings resembled copper wire, and the fingerboard was no straighter or sturdier than a rotting gang plank. . . . in addition to its misshape, its color was coarsely rough-hued—a weird, bruised blue—as if it had been dragged behind for miles. A mongrel violin of folk origins that looked as though it had been rescued from a band of musical gypsies" (14). Like that instrument, the writer's imagination rescues from its worn and bruising path what must be carried forward. Oliver knows that "the artist has no other choice. Repression is not an option. Neither is forgetting, nor denial" (38–39). What imagination reconstructs from the ruins of the terrible past is all there is, now, to make music with.

The sound of that music, roughened and bruised by shards of the personal and collective past, is in the narrative voice that shapes, dominates, saturates Rosenbaum's novels. Sometimes that voice rages or passionately preaches; sometimes it mocks or satirizes; sometimes it doubles over, laughing; and sometimes it deepens with longing or despair. One critic has heard in this voice a "self deriding humor that is part armor, part X ray, a source of protection and of revelation."[41] It is not always easy or pleasant to hear. But it is compelling, because it calls readers explicitly to attend critically, interpretively, empathically, imaginatively to the past. It comes as close as one can imagine to the voice of mourning. Like the voices that emerge from the works of other writers of the second generation, it describes that process in its own terms: gathering the shining, lethal shards of what is left after atrocity. And with them, very carefully and fully conscious of what has been brutally taken away, making the world again.

4

Recalling "Home" from Exile

Revisiting the Past

Writings of the new wave move energetically, innovatively, into the stream of Jewish writings about home. One of the most intimate of the "little secrets"—obscured, now, by the shadow of the Holocaust and rendered especially precious by the recurrent history of exile—the image of home stirs both personal and collective memory. It focuses longing, and loss, and the memory of early security—in some cases claustrophobia—on a place that is always somewhere else. As Sidra DeKoven Ezrahi has observed, Jews have built these feelings not only into political movements and family myths but also into stories: the biblical narrative of Rachel's departure from her childhood home demonstrates that "the safest and most enduring hiding places" for the "household gods" of "deserted homes were the stories that contained and superseded them."[1] Among writers of the new wave those stories take the forms of fiction, essay, and memoir. They have in common the motif of a journey that can move in several directions simultaneously, toward several goals. A home-bound journey can carry a writer toward a sometimes vexed and provisional reconnection with both an ethnic and a personal past. It can move toward insight into the trajectory of an individual self and its often damaged bond with the family that shares its exile. It can lead to clearer realization of places to which the roots of self still, atavistically, cling. And it can achieve either acceptance of loss or imaginative recreation of the sites of origin—drained, now, of sentimentality, seen in ways too complex, even too dark, to be compatible with nostalgia.

When Women Writers Go Home Again

Perhaps because the domestic and family roles of men and women have differed for such a long time, home often appears to resonate in different ways for them. For women writers of the new wave, recollections of home are inflected principally by gender and by new ways of imagining "the self." The sense of self as a constant, indwelling presence used to be everywhere in Western literature. But presently, as Patricia Waugh, Teresa De-Lauretis, and many others have noted, more complicated and disturbing insights into the—by now, highly theorized—issues of subjectivity and agency are familiar elements of contemporary critical discourse. These issues, I have suggested, enter American Jewish literature in Philip Roth's Zuckerman stories, which challenge, as Eugene Goodheart observed years ago, "the realist assumption of 'a natural being, an irreducible self.'"[2] In *The Counterlife* in particular, Roth demonstrates that the "unified self is sheer illusion" (441).[3] As Roth's narrative knits and unravels the stories of two brothers, it enacts—and fixes in American Jewish literature—the postmodern sense of the self as essentially unstable and discontinuous.

In much recent work by American Jewish women writers of the new wave, this postmodern awareness of the complexity of "selving"[4] is coupled with a persistent interest in the constructive power of the search for origins. Deviating in this respect from earlier works by writers like Edna Ferber and Fanny Hurst, who realized themselves by leaving home and family,[5] American Jewish women's memoirs and novels of the last two decades revisit the places of the authors' or their parents' childhoods. Responding to felt discontinuities within their own experience, writers highlight the continuities that their searches bring to light as they reconstruct places of origin that disappeared in the Holocaust.[6] They also play out dramas of reconnection with the European home-in-exile in which memory is the prime mover.[7] In their work, the effort to recall home can take the shape of a literal journey back to

Europe during which the writer reengages with—but doesn't necessarily accept—Jewish ways of being in the world. Or, this effort can become research, which seeks out fragments of a collective or parental past.[8] Or it can appear as the imaginative, unsentimental recreation of a place where Jewish life once flourished. Immigrant memoirs and fictions tended to thrive on implicit contrasts between then and now, there and here. But women's writings of the new wave—almost always marked by awareness of the Holocaust as a divisive, fragmenting, destabilizing force in contemporary experience—seek continuities, often imaged as reconciliation with people long estranged from the writer. They reveal an important secret: that the journey home can still shape— for better or for worse—the writer's own sense of herself.[9]

Perhaps the most striking feature of the memoirs is their insistence that the journey home begins with estrangement—a separation not freely chosen but rather forced upon protagonists. [10] An initial sense of alienation from home is often represented as a rupture in personal, filial relationships: like the relationship of the writer to her mother or sister. Kim Chernin's *In My Mother's House: A Daughter's Story*—in some ways a precursor of new wave women's memoirs—establishes this pattern as it sets the writer's intense, prolonged estrangement from her mother at the very beginning of her journey home. Chernin's memoir insists that the image of home she seeks to recall is deeply shadowed by her sense of estrangement from it. But when Chernin decides to return to her mother's house the narrative invokes her memory of long alienation from that place and from the mother she now reencounters. "Since I was a small girl," she remembers, "I have been fighting with my mother."[11] Their efforts to clarify and to honor their differences, and also to reconnect with one another, form the dramatic center of the memoir. In Jewish women's recollections of home, the difficulty of connecting with other women— friends as well as relatives—often measures the distance between writers and the places they seek to recall.

The subtext of Chernin's memoir is the struggle of mother and daughter to summon into being, through remembering and retelling, the homeplaces that shaped them. For Rose Chernin, Kim's mother, home is a Russian shtetl. Kim cannot recollect her own, American home—and her mother's painful, frequent absences from it—without reaching behind it to the place of her mother's girlhood. What Rose has become, her daughter knows, "grows up out of her past in a becoming, natural way" (15). But the trajectory of Rose's growth is marked from the beginning by gendered and ethnic complexities that are characteristic of the European home and that will reappear in later memoirs, by deprivations, oppressions, and the struggle against them. As many historians have noted, and as I have observed elsewhere, Jewish tradition excluded women from authority in communal and religious life and denied them the education enjoyed by their brothers, fathers, and husbands.[12] Ironically, Rose's family was descended from the Vilna Gaon, "a famous rabbinical scholar of the eighteenth century" (9).[13] But Rose was born into a "village where most women did not know how to read" (15). Thus scholarship—and the spiritual life and social status that Jewish tradition links with it—were closed to her, as to her mother and sisters. Her mother especially, "that poor, broken woman" (15), haunts Rose Chernin and sets in motion the struggle that will dominate her developing sense of self. Easy going and gentle, unable to "stand up for herself," Rose's mother was displaced first by her own father's second wife and later by her emigration to America. Unable to adjust to the new world, "she lived through most of her days in that sorrow of mute protest which in her generation was known as melancholia" (15). When she became suicidal, her abusive husband committed her to an asylum—from which her daughter, Rose, ultimately rescued her.

Even before this rescue, however, Rose had conceived herself as a fighter: "I would lie awake at night and remember [his] fists beating at her, breaking her down. Destroying her. And I knew it would not be me. I would not be my mother and no child of mine would be my mother" (39). Kim, Rose's daughter, will ultimately uncover the "helplessness and sorrow . . . the sense of unbearable despair that lives, forbidden, beneath" her mother's adult persona, which foregrounds her "will to fight" (82). That will—formed partly by witnessing her mother's suffering and partly by experiencing her own deprivations as the immigrant daughter of a broken woman—drives Rose into political activity as a leader of the American Communist party and explains the commitments that often diverted her attention from home and daughter. Rose recalls that once she identified the cries of Jews attacked by Cossacks with the voices of American workers attacked by police on horseback, she knew the shape of her adult self: "I had fought for my mother and now I was ready to start fighting for the people" (92). Thus, memory of both the personal and the collective European past, saturated in retrospect by the residue of both ethnic and gender discrimination, grounds and intensifies adult political commitment in a very different culture. Seeing herself as champion of those whose spirits are broken, who cannot fight for themselves, Rose's political activity in America "renews once again [the] ancient battle against the limiting of women" (107) that broke her mother's spirit in the Jewish shtetl.

Recognition and acceptance of difference becomes in this memoir the most salient ingredient in the reconstruction of their relationship. Unlike Rose, her daughter, Kim, will define herself not as a political activist, but as a poet—reacting, in part, against the preoccupations and absences of her warrior mother. Again unlike her mother, Kim will feel a "futile nostalgia . . . a sense of loss" (32) for the vanished spirituality of shtetl life. She tries to explain to her mother that "What we—my generation—long for, grew up in the shtetl": "a sacred dimension to daily life, which held its own alongside the terror and the violence" (106). The juxtaposition here, of spirituality and suffering, embraces a disjunction that often scarred the experience of European Jews. It also overlooks the particular problems of women's handicaps in the European shtetl. Kim believes, for example, that her aunt's gifts as writer might have been nourished by the spiritual life of the shtetl. But her mother is contemptuous of this belief, knowing firsthand, as Kim does not, the forces alive in that culture that silenced women. For Rose, politics takes the place of religion. But for Kim, precursor of the "new wave" women writers who will take up again—some to reclaim, others to transform— the thread of spiritual and cultural practices that alienated their parents, later writings will chart the course of her search for a woman-friendly religious life. Unlike Rose Chernin, but like later women writers of the new wave, Kim will engage—instead of abandoning—the spiritual conflicts that alienated her mother, conflicts engendered in Jewish women by a tradition that excluded them from learning. The image of the lost home-in-exile that their joint narrative constructs will be rescued from sentimentality by Rose's anger—and also augmented by Kim's longing.

As this mother and daughter listen to one another's stories, the differences between them will become mutually acceptable. The dialogue will even disclose resemblances beneath the differences. Most important, perhaps, the "storying"[14] of these women clarifies for both of them an underlying connection that binds them to one another—no longer secret beneath the similarities and differences that have obscured it: "I seem to grow out of my mother" (184), Kim says. And Rose gives into her daughter's hand the power to write both her own and her mother's story: "who I am, what sort of person I am in the world, we must hear later from you" (184) she says as she passes the narrative of women's "selving" to her daughter like "a gift of fire, transported from a world far off and far away, but never extinguished" (16). Beginning in a daughter's return to her mother's house, moving through memory first to the shtetl, then to the America of immigrant Jews, and finally to the world of the sixties, this memoir recalls home in every venue as the site of women's struggle: against poverty, ignorance, abusive authority on one hand, and between genders, ethnicities, and generations on the other. It is the site as well of the ethnic sources of spirituality and inherited wisdom that will animate the daughter's future work. Darkened at the outset by estrangement, suffering and loss, this narrative journey of return reveals, nevertheless, the formative power of both the places it recalls and the process of recollection—which offers the memoirist a path that leads forward, into her own future, as well as backward, into her mother's past.

In later women's memoirs of the new wave, the fact of initial estrangement occupies an even more decisively historical and ethnic as well as a filial context. Unlike Chernin whose parents were immigrants, Helen Epstein, Susan Rubin Suleiman, and Eva Hoffman are children of survivors or refugees from the Nazis. Gerda Lerner and Marianne Hirsch are themselves refugees. Thus the Holocaust explicitly darkens recollections of home among these writers of the new wave. Their journeys of return fashion in the mind places that, as Marianne Hirsch observed, have really been "irreparably changed or destroyed by the sudden violence of the Holocaust."[15] Exiled "from a world that has ceased to exist, that has been violently erased," these writers "remember" home by recounting the story of their return (419–20). Expulsion—rather than immigration—marks the outset of all these later narratives of home as the writers struggle not only to reconnect with but also to see clearly, beneath the shadow of their forced departures, the place that cast them out.

The effect of this dark memory—like awareness of women's struggle with tradition—on the antinostalgic resonance of home cannot be overestimated. Gaston Bachelard, a philosopher of science who turned his attention to art when he began to understand that "the poetic image is a sudden salience on the surface of the psyche,"[16] explains: "Asking a child to draw his house is asking him to reveal the deepest dream shelter he has found for his happiness. If he is happy, he will succeed in drawing a snug, protected house which is well built on deeply-rooted foundations" (72). But if a child is unhappy, the house he draws will reveal his distress. Bachelard remembers drawings by Polish and Jewish children who had lived under the German occupation during the war. They drew "motionless houses, houses that become motionless in their rigidity. This rigidity and motionlessness are present in the smoke as well as in the window curtains. The surrounding trees are quite straight and give the impression of standing guard over the house" (72). Thus terror drains the vitality of home from children's images. One suspects that new wave memoirs by American Jewish women attempt in part to undo that rigidity, to recapture the energy for life that was also part of the places of their parents' or their own ordeals, whose images have gone still and static under the darkened memory of antisemitism, patriarchal repression, and expulsion.

That attempt is deeply inflected in new wave women's memoirs, as it is in Chernin's work, by the desire for both clarification and reconnection. Gratifying this desire is not simple, for as narratives of return problematize places of origin, they also fracture chronology and disregard contextual boundaries, moving in several directions at once: backward through memory, and forward into new relationships to the past; outward into collective history and politics, and inward into the deep reaches of personal experience. Anger and bitterness provoked by both personal and collective experience figure significantly in the process of clarification. For historian Gerda Lerner, for example, the journey home begins with the recognition that collective Jewish experience in Germany largely determined the shape and scope of her choices in America. Her compulsion to do history, she believes, rises from her early malaise as a German Jewish woman; she works to clarify the link between herself and her consciousness of "other members of the Jewish community."[17] For much the same reason that Rose Chernin became a communist, Gerda Lerner became a historian—because of the connection she felt between her own suffering and the historic experience of the Jews.

Like Chernin, Lerner adds to ethnicity the complicating element of gender, denying nostalgia and rejecting Europe—on both personal and collective grounds—as a source of norms for a Jewish woman's life in exile. Being Jewish in Germany before World War II, Lerner remembers, "set one apart. Jews were not 'normal,' we were not right, we were different." But because she was not only a Jew, but also a girl, "the life-line of Jewish learning was out of my reach. All I got was indoctrination in gender restrictions and a thorough exposure to the great silences—the denial of the past, the suppressed voices, the absence of heroines. . . . Thus I became a Jew and a Jewish woman and double difference became imprinted on me—not pride, but embarrassment; not collectivity, but exclusion" (7–8). Reacting against her remembered exclusion from "the life-line of Jewish learning," Lerner refuses to set foot in a synagogue, a boycott she maintains for over fifty years (8), which extends as a woman the exile imposed upon her as a Jew by the Nazis. Like Russian-born Rose Chernin, Lerner abandons Judaism and turns instead toward feminism, substituting political activism—itself, ironically, a feature of European Jewish women's experience—for religion.

Laura Levitt's *Jews and Feminism* incarnates most recently this refusal to sentimentalize traditional Judaism as a spiritual home for Jewish women. Levitt, like Rose Chernin, will define herself politically: as a liberal American feminist. But unlike Rose Chernin, who remained estranged from traditional Judaism, Levitt, whose father's acculturation resulted in the surrendering of their Jewish tradition, returns as an American feminist "to study Jewish texts . . . to come to terms with this complicated legacy."[18] Thus, in some new wave writers the journey home provokes desire to retrieve what has been lost or denied. The trajectory of "selving," for them, is bent by desire: to take back what they believe has been withheld. For others, the European home remains a place in which gender, coupled with ethnicity, meant deprivation, alienation, and exile. Their self-realization is shaped by the effort not to remedy or compensate for past losses but simply to see them clear, to feel and to mourn them, and to hold them in remembrance. "After you remember and record," the memoirist Susan Rubin Suleiman tells herself, "it's time to move again—not toward new forgetfulness, but toward new experience."[19] This mode of engagement, which refuses to abandon or forget even as it refuses to dwell nostalgically on the past, is characteristic of women writers of the new wave.

Sadness and the seductiveness of remembered mysteries also play a part in these recollections as these post-Holocaust memoirists work to reconnect early childhood uncertainties with muted echoes of collective tragedies. Marcie Hershman traces the thread of her own ethnic identity to a collective past that was largely silenced. When Hershman remembers her grandparents' stories of their past, she hears "in the silence and afterbeat" when the story is done, "a hint of the wider, sadder history that was also our heritage."[20] Haunted by "the pauses within my grandmother's stories, the shadow slipping inside the light suburban joy, and endlessly the cries I both feared to hear and did not hear," Hershman finally turns her attention " down to the very base of where I lived," to listen to "messages I hadn't wanted to take in and claim as part of my own life" (154). To hear those secret messages she travels to Germany with her brother, returning to an earlier family home, "the land that had filled the nights and our hearts with emptiness in our spacious, safe childhood home" (154) in America. Breaking through the silence in her grandmother's stories, Hershman recovers a sense of home that remains connected, still, to the place in America where she lives.

The sense of penetrating silences to discover a connection whose vitality enriches one's own life is particularly strong in memoirs like Suleiman's or Helen Epstein's, which describe the journey home partly as a search for the lost, beloved, mother. In some cases she is the mother in her own European girlhood, young and playful before the difficult years of adolescence, exile, and marital disappointments. Or she is the mother of the writer's childhood: happy and strong before the disturbances of the Holocaust. "How I had loved her, my beautiful mother who knew how to play," Suleiman recalls after her mother's death; "I had to take my children to the place where I had known her as a young woman" (11). Like the pilgrimage to that place, the writing itself performs its own part of the work of mourning.[21] As it moves between America and Europe, between now and then, the fluid narrative movement itself begins to reanimate the image of home and the estranged mother that had gone rigid in memory with pain and loss.

The effort to clarify and reconnect—twin desiderata of all these memoirs—anneals estrangement and also constructs the memoirist by revealing the formative power of circumstances over the never fully understood little secrets that estranged mothers from their daughters. Suleiman's memoir of return will uncover at last an explanatory seed of bitterness that estranged her for many years from her mother, healing through the work of the journey itself this filial conflict that can finally be understood within the wider context of the mother's life. As Suleiman remembers her mother "mourning her first love" (138) and suffering her husband's repeated infidelities (190), her research also brings to the narrative surface the historic sexism and antisemitism of the culture that formed and finally expelled her mother. These personal and historical clarifications free the memoirist to recognize "traces" of her mother in herself, a residue that reforms a connection shadowed—as human connections often are—by unspoken pain. As she unfolds the documents that her search for origins has uncovered, as she places them "one on top of the other," they not only "tell a story"; they also confirm that "the continuity of generations has prevailed over war and destruction, and I am the beneficiary of that victory" (219). Confronting, at the end, her anger at her mother and the deliberate forgetting that followed, Suleiman—like Epstein at the end of her memoir—is liberated by this journey of remembrance. Her trip to Budapest is a return in two ways: she has made herself at home there, relearning the language, making friends, learning to move freely around the city. She has also reconstructed her mother's life there, clarifying and repairing the filial connection between them. Both accomplishments reshape her sense of options and agency: in short, her sense of self. Helen Epstein too will uncover the cultural and historical matrix of the Holocaust that destroyed her mother's expectations for herself and silenced her memories of the camps. She will refashion the bond between them, reshaping the maternal image that her memory will keep, so that her own life can continue separately, after the beloved mother is gone.[22]

These memoirs usually open with the large historical fact of collective expulsion and exile and narrow, in the end, to the most intimate personal and family estrangements. They suggest that culture, history, family, self are inextricably layered, like Suleiman's documents, or folded into one another. Lerner opens her volume of essays *Why History Matters* by addressing the collective, cultural issues that shaped her sense of herself as a woman, a Jew, a German: gender, ethnicity, and nationality tucked inside one another like nested Russian dolls. But later in the collection Lerner also attributes the long estrangement from her beloved sister, and their reconnection, to the most intimate loss and recovery of "deep memories," of the "sound, the rhythm, the forms of [her own] unconscious." She believes that Nazism stole these from her when it stole her native language—"as it had stolen all my worldly possessions" (33, 48). Personal losses are thus folded into the collective loss of home, culture, language. Epstein and Suleiman also interweave the collective with the personal, the form of their memoirs lacing together the most intimate pain of personal loss and betrayal with the public, political, social facts of antisemitism and the suppression of women.

Perhaps, as Gerda Lerner and others (discussed in chapter 2) observed, the loss of one's language of origin is one of the most profound and damaging of the consequences these writings describe. But women writers of the new wave agree that language is also the one certain way to get home again. The strongest thread through the labyrinth of exile and forgetfulness is language. "Language equals home," Alice Yaeger Kaplan insists; "language is a home as surely as a roof over one's head is a home."[23] It is the place where our bodies and minds collide, where our groundedness in place and time and our capacity for fantasy and invention must come to terms (64). Its loss is chief among the losses mourned by exiles.

Susan Suleiman sets it in the first line of her memoir when she recalls that everyone on the bus that took her family away from home, to safety in exile, "spoke a language different from our own" (4). "American speech," she says, became her home; "although I never forgot my native tongue, my knowledge of it was frozen in time" (8). She refreshed that shred of memory when she returned to Hungary to "unforget" what she had once known. The process is difficult, but revelatory. First she tests herself by asking a new friend whether she can "'pass' for a native Hungarian or whether he could tell I didn't live here the moment I opened my mouth." But then she asks herself why it should matter to her whether or not she passes as a Hungarian? She has transformed language into a sort of trial or test of her "at homeness" in her native place. Realizing this, she begins to see more clearly the part of herself that still worries about not fitting in anywhere, even in her native city. As her vocabulary and her accent improve, and as she learns her way around Budapest again, she realizes also that one assumption she had conceived as fundamental to her life in exile is not correct. One home, one language, does not displace another, as she had always believed it did. Budapest doesn't displace other cities where she feels at home—any more than English displaces Hungarian or French. Instead each place, each language, is added to the others; "when I leave here," she knows, "the door will not slam shut behind me" (171). Thus both her sense of her self as multiple rather than single, and her complex engagement with many "homes" in the world, have been profoundly affected by her return to Europe and her reclaiming of the mother tongue.

Two recent novels by women writers of the new wave draw this sense of multiple homes and selves into the full light of conscious attention. For American Jews, these writings suggest, the European world that vanished with so many of its people in the Holocaust remains a haunting presence. Perhaps because, as Ezrahi and others suggest, it has been "incompletely mourned." And perhaps, as I have argued elsewhere (in "Traumatic Memory and American Jewish Writers"), fiction participates as fully as memoir and autobiography in the work of mourning, by reimagining in all its concrete specificity what cannot be remembered because it was never directly experienced. Even as they participate in the process of mourning, moreover, fictions also embody and dramatize issues that can remain deeply embedded in other modes of discourse. In this way, recent novels by Rebecca Goldstein and Lilian Nattel perform what Jane Tompkins describes as "cultural work"(see introduction above); they augment the work of autobiographers and memoirists whose journeys home recall through travel and research what novelists reconstruct imaginatively. The distinction is truly problematical, because the boundaries between literary genres—and between the mental processes they enact—are permeable. Memories are always already partly imagined. And even research—which demands that we select, that we withhold or emphasize certain things at the expense of others, that we spin narrative out of random data—calls deeply on imagination. Indeed, one might want to argue that once any kind of data makes its way into language, it becomes a kind of fiction. Perhaps the way a reader encounters a text will be different, and perhaps the degree of imaginative freedom a writer allows herself will differ according to genre. But modern readers do well to season with a healthy measure of skepticism their willing suspension of disbelief in all texts.

In the shtetls imaginatively reconstructed by Rebecca Goldstein and Lilian Nattel, as in the one remembered by Rose Chernin, the "ancient limiting of women" is a salient, persistent feature. The struggle against it subverts nostalgia as it shapes the pattern of strong women's selving. In Shluftchev by the Puddle, a Polish town remembered by Goldstein's *Mazel*, "girls were all supposed to be pressed out from the same cookie cutter, anything extra trimmed away."[24] Thus Leiba, mother of many children, teller of true stories, can sing only in the dead of night because Jewish men are forbidden to hear a woman's voice (51). One daughter's struggle against such limits ends in suicide; another's in rebellion. Fraydel, a profoundly creative, "pious woman" never "taught to read the Hebrew prayers" is "in love only with what was marvelous and strange, with things too bright or too dark to live anywhere but in her mind" (89, 128). If "she had been a boy, they would have called her an *illui*, a prodigy" (127). But because she is a girl, they call her crazy. She dances with the gypsies and longs to run away with them. She reads and makes stories— hungrier for words than for food (68). As she grows up she falls silent, angry not "at a 'this' or a 'that,' at a something that could be altered or erased, emended or ended." She feels anger "with the world itself." And just before her arranged marriage to a man she doesn't love, she drowns herself.

Fraydel's death is mourned untiringly by her small sister, Sorel. For this child, "the whole look of the world" had "shifted when Fraydel came near. An excitement swept after her, like the long swirling train of a noblewoman's dress, and it rearranged the world" (71). Unable to rescue her from despair, unable to foresee or forestall her suicide, Sorel at first clings to the memory of her lost sister. But she wakes one morning "with her sense of the world reinstated" (165), hungry for life in a world that was changing, opening herself to the political and intellectual excitements of Warsaw after the family leaves the shtetl. She defies limitation by gender, taking a name, Sasha, that is "a man's and a woman's, too" (199). And she becomes an actress in the Yiddish theater, telling Fraydel's story at her first audition and speaking in the "quivering Galician voice" (240) that had once been her sister's: "a voice . . . like a reflection on unstill water" (19), a voice "that wouldn't let you go, that held you fast" (240), a "voice like no other come from out of the lonely wind" (243). Sophisticated now, made "theatrical by its mastery of . . . a Yiddish so highly Germanized that really it was hardly even Yiddish anymore" (209), Sorel/Sasha's voice tells of loss and estrangement, liberating into public life the night songs of her mother as well as the now silenced storying of her dead sister. Retelling Fraydel's tale of the beautiful girl who—like Fraydel herself—deserts her crooked betrothed to dance instead with death, Sasha not only restores the voices of her beloved sister and mother, but also carries into postmodern, urban consciousness the pathos and tragic loss of women's gifts in the shtetl.

Like Rose Chernin, made into a fighter by despair at her helplessness before the suffering of women broken by shtetl life, Sasha rebels against the home of her childhood; its "atmosphere made unbreathable by piety and ritual . . . she had taken no small pleasure in breaking the tiresome taboos with as much noise and commotion as she could muster. . . . And her spirit of rebellion hasn't given an inch over the years" (19). Unlike her mother who accommodated herself to the limits of the shtetl, and unlike her sister who was broken by them, Sasha strides into a world first opened by the enlightenment and then destroyed by the Holocaust.

Gender, culture, history thus cooperate in the "selving" of this character whose own daughter and granddaughter carry forward into America the gifts of women that could not flourish at home in the shtetl. These two American women of different generations bracket the novel's interest in both the past and future: the daughter is a student of myth and classics; the granddaughter is a scientist. They also bracket evolving attitudes among feminists toward men and marriage: one arranges to use an attractive man whom she will never see again to father her child; the other settles into conventional domesticity. The novel is deeply concerned with the shape of time, circling back and forth narratively to suggest the interlacing of widely divergent moments in each character's life. The present becomes a kind of frame for the past here, as Goldstein reconstructs both the shtetl and the urban world of the *Haskalah,* engaging like other new wave writers, with those segments of European culture. She uncovers in the process alternative possibilities that were open to gifted women within those homeplaces: accommodation, rebellion, self-destruction. In three shtetl women, a mother and two daughters, she allows readers to envision the "doppelgänger" self that haunts the imagination of the memoirists.[25]

Formed partly by restrictions like those that shape Goldstein's shtetl women, characters in Lilian Nattel's *The River Midnight* develop a collective power that makes possible the imagining of more generous options for female selving. In Nattel's Polish village of Blaszka girls learn early that "a woman doesn't do what she wants, only what she has to."[26] One woman, for example, gives thanks when her rebellious niece is temporarily transformed by remorse into a meek and "proper girl at last, as obedient as anyone could ask for" (167). Learned men, powerful authority figures in the shtetl, tolerate "only black and white, kosher and *trayf,* pure and impure"; they have condemned this woman to "the no-man's land of the *agunah,*" the abandoned woman whose husband has disappeared without divorcing her and who is forever forbidden to love or to marry again without his consent (154). This woman—and others like her in this novel—see clearly the limits that shtetl life imposes on them, but manage to transgress them in ways that preserve the continuity of shtetl life without entirely foreclosing the satisfaction of individual needs. Nattel's portrayal of the shtetl as home thus imaginatively enlarges women's options, problematizing without rejecting the culture of the European home.

In Nattel's women, ethnicity fosters a sense of gendered identity that is—though restrictive—both benign and powerful. Concentrating on not one but four female protagonists, the novel develops from the beginning a strong sense of what "selving" might have meant to European Jewish women. Each protagonist will be restrained by the "ancient limiting of women" in traditional Judaism. But each one, supported by the others, will move through those ancient limits toward fuller self-realization. The *agunah*, one of four girls who called themselves "*vilde haya*," or wild creatures, will ultimately transgress the traditional injunctions, quietly taking a lover while her community looks the other way. Another of these girls, deprived—by the domestic and maternal cares of a large, beloved family—of the intellectual life her father prepared her for (35–36), will initially mourn her inability to study in Warsaw. But after a disillusioning visit to that city, whose intellectual ferment seems detached from the living truths of her life in the shtetl, she begins to write and to publish stories in Yiddish—the shtetl language she had once despised. She has learned that what she knows about life "can only be said in the *mama-loshen*," the mother tongue of shtetl Jews (100)—rather than in Polish, German, or Russian, the languages of the intelligentsia (75). A third woman, longing for erotic satisfactions withheld by her loving but impotent husband,[27] will discover pleasure in innocent pursuits that moderate her need, quiet her demands, and ultimately restore her husband's sexual prowess. And a fourth, the fearless healer-midwife, Misha, unmarried but heavily pregnant, teaches the women that "even a woman trapped in the ordinary way, worn out from her pregnancy, with her feet swollen, isn't completely helpless" (102). Later, alone in labor as the community gathers for Yom Kippur, Misha's moans will summon to her aid all the women of the shtetl.

The spirituality of these shtetl women deviates markedly from traditional expectations. But they neither abandon nor rebel against tradition. Rather, they adapt it to their own needs. During the highest holy days, for example, they gather at the grave of Misha's grandmother—herself a healer and midwife—and pray "that their mothers and grandmothers and great-grandmothers would intercede for them with the Holy Court. . . . At this time of year, as at other times of life and death, dread and relief, danger and birth, the women stood together arms linked, a net that gathered up their compassion, and let their grudges fall through" (177). One of the "*vilde haya*," in despair, prays to her mother, sister, grandmother for help: "to all of the women with their dangerous gifts" (176). And on the night of Misha's labor, the women of the shtetl leave their section of the synagogue to help her: "the *mekhitzah* can't contain them, they are like the river in spring flooding the banks with wild excitement, carrying its rich mud to Misha's garden. The women flow from the gallery, all of them, so many women pouring down the stairs and across the square as if all the women that ever lived in Blaszka were flowing down to Misha" (180). The powerful fluidity of the image articulates the collective strength of an ethnic and gendered community brought together by a single purpose. It suggests as well what the plot as a whole demonstrates: that the gendered limits imposed on these women are as little likely to contain their energies as the banks of a river in spring.

Here, the image of home as shtetl and the possibility of female solidarity and satisfaction within it are imagined in ways that deviate significantly from the recollections of women who actually lived there. The difference between what we imagine and what we remember does not always come so clear. It points, one suspects, to a recognition and a desire articulated also by Goldstein's novel and Chernin's memoir: a recognition that women of the shtetl possessed enormous creative power. In Nattel's work, such recognition is accompanied by the wish that this power might have found expression, that mothers, sisters, friends might have, collectively, circumvented the restraints that worked to silence and suffocate them as individuals. One wonders whether such a wish also finds expression in the memoirists' efforts to reconnect with mothers and sisters from whom they have become estranged.[28] In *Mazel*, Goldstein imagines the rebellious sister, Sasha, carrying into an American future, through her daughter and granddaughter, the gifts of her mother and sister. Goldstein writes a final scene set in the American diaspora that gathers three generations of loving women into a communal ritual. Traditionally observant in many respects, yet hospitable to its women's gifts, the culture that supports this ritual remembers Fraydel and the bitter cynicism her loss and all the other losses still engender—without missing a step in the collective joy of a wedding dance. These fictions that recall home-as-shtetl from a woman's point of view restore to its image the erotic, imaginative, and fully embodied givens of women's lives there, as well as the pathos of women's struggle against traditional restraints. In the memoirs, the site of this struggle and renewal is only the family, not the community. But in the fictions, sisters, friends, neighbors, as well as mothers, daughters, and granddaughters carry forward gifts that individuals cannot always carry alone.

In these works by American Jewish women writers of the new wave, then, novelists reconstruct the gendered repressions of the shtetl and imagine the female bonding that might overcome them, while memoirists engage with the urban European past, probing the silences of their exiled mothers and sisters to clarify and to reconnect with the homes and the languages that shaped them. "Each one of us," Bachelard believed, "should speak of his [*sic*] roads, his crossroads, his roadside benches: each one of us should make a surveyor's map of his lost fields and meadows" (11). In such maps these women writers are tracing not only the homeplaces of the past but also the shape of the self—the family, even the community—that might spring from them.

When Male Writers Go "Home" Again

Male memoirists and fiction writers, unlike their female counterparts, augment the discourse of home by deepening one's sense of the ambivalence that clings to both the place itself and the journey that recollects it. Gender issues recede in these works. For the most part the drive toward renewed continuity with the past, when it appears at all, is deeply—abidingly—conflicted. Instead of seeking reconnection, most of these writings emphasize the historic, the moral, the psychic and cultural complexities that weave into the memory of the place of origin a durable residue of estrangement. They reshape the image of home by asserting a darkly skeptical awareness not only of the ambiguities that permeate imaginative memory but also of the resistances that rise like snapping dogs against recollections of the Jewish past.

Ironically, the least shadowed of these works is a memoir in which the Holocaust itself functions as a kind of home, becoming the medium through which a recently divorced young father forges a more centered sense of himself and new connections to his small sons. In Daniel Asa Rose's *Hiding Places*, "Daniel" takes his children to Europe to discover the places that allowed his family to hide from, and thus escape, the Nazis. The memoir also moves, in alternating chapters, backward: into Daniel's childhood and the multiple betrayals of both his own Jewish identity and his surviving relatives. In hiding for many years—not only from the Jewish part of himself but also from his grieving

mother's stories of the Holocaust—Daniel knows that as a boy
he "couldn't do the one truly brave thing that is asked of any
human being, and that is to be who he is."[29] Blaming his "Con-
necticut family" for "beating back our blood history, brutally
crushing our own traditions" (48), he tries to drive his own
"roots deep" into the collective and the family past by retracing
the path of his relatives' flight. Finding their hiding places, deci-
phering the clues to their suffering and resourcefulness, become
for him and his children a symbolic process of reconnection with
the past, and with one another.

This memoir suggests that closer contact with the historic ordeal of a family and a people may provide a "center" (375) from
which feelings can reach out—not only to the delicate, subtle,
surviving remnants of the writer's own family but also to other
Jews—like the "Hasid" he and his boys encounter on the trip
home: "if we aren't family, who is?" Daniel wonders. As his boys
call out from the balcony of their hotel in Brussels, former head-
quarters of the Gestapo, that they're "Jews from America" (377)
the memoir affirms their connection with a collective identity
that has emerged from the journey they have undertaken together. The constructive element of this journey is this renewal of
connection.

But in the process, Europe is definitively distanced. It becomes
the place one sifts for evidence of a terrifying past. Though it furnishes reminders of the resourcefulness, bravery, and luck of
those who survived it, this land rouses no memories of life or culture before catastrophe. In his surviving relatives Rose distinguishes traces of a culture eloquent in its restraint, powerful in its
delicacy, subtlety, and gentle humor. But withered now, and fragile. Europe furnishes no living sense of a "homeplace" to him
and his children; its nightmares knit them more closely to one
another and to other Jews, but they carry nothing else of it home
to America.

In much the same way, a memoir by David W. Weiss (*Reluctant
Return: A Survivor's Journey to an Austrian Town*), son of the former chief rabbi of Wiener Neustadt in Austria, subverts the possibility that Europe may be seen as home by tracing carefully the
psychic and historical legacy of damage and loss still linked for
the memoirist with the town from which he and his family escaped. Though he returns at the behest of Christians who seek

reconciliation with the survivors, his account of that experience is most intense when it records the ambivalences that preceded it and the enduring abrasions this place has etched in his sense of himself. "The people among whom I grew up declared one day in 1938," he writes, "that Jews were not really of the human species; to have thought that they were had been a grave mistake. In the light of that discovery, I stood bare, no longer *Mensch*, debased in all my aspects down to my blood and genes. Perhaps the threat to identity is especially damaging in the years a boy passes through to manhood: If I am a non person, what then am I, how can I move on?"[30] Radical denial of his humanity in adolescence has left him, he acknowledges, deeply scarred. He has become "the proud Jew who cannot keep his tail from wagging when admitted to the club" (18); he has known "only too well the overwhelming need to be accepted, a need that was not fulfilled in the time and place of my youth" (33). Now the father of a sturdy, loving family, an Israeli scientist whose work is respected throughout the world, Weiss never loses sight of the fragilities masked by his reputation and status, fragilities that testify still to the trauma of his family's expulsion from their home. Despite his pride in the family he has fathered, despite his persistent awareness that Austria is a "land soaked with Jewish blood," he longs still "for the normalcy of everyday relationships" there, in the "place that once had been home" (13). He dreamed for years of "walking its streets just one more time, of seeing its houses and the trees in the . . . park where we used to roam." He knows "the draw is atavistic, despite all the bitterness that went with the ejection from childhood and the knowledge of the alternative that had awaited those who couldn't escape. I do not really comprehend the urge but neither can I resist it" (23). Thoroughly at home in Israel, in his work, in his life, he resists at first the invitation to return to Austria because he is still afraid that "to be handed the forbidden apple of belonging at the source of its archetypic withholding might be more of a temptation than I can overcome" (34).

In Weiss's reading of his own scars, as in his careful tracing of the—unopposed—Nazi extermination of Austrian Jews and the story of his family's escape, the subtext of this memoir subverts its own explicit intention. He wanted to describe the overcoming of initial resistance, to portray the healing effects of the weeklong

ceremony of return arranged for a group of Israeli survivors by a
group of Austrian Christians. He describes briefly, but more effectively, however, another kind of "return" in his recollection of
his first journey to Israel: "a stunningly personal recovery of the
past . . . the plain, overwhelming knowledge of being home" (92).
The return to Austria yields no such recovery. Though he ultimately responds with warmth and generosity to the Austrians
who arrange the ceremony of return, though he believes the experience teaches him to see more clearly the once-hated Austrian
"other" in all his ambiguities, "for us who once called this land
home, it is also very empty" (139). It remains a "wasteland" (16,
189) to the very end of the memoir.

In these two memoirs the Holocaust is the primary shaper of
the image of home. By expelling or murdering its Jews, Europe is
drained in these recollections of whatever vitality sustained Jewish life there for centuries. Despite Egypt's expulsion of its Jews,
André Aciman's *Out of Egypt* recalls not only a home in a different continent but also a place still saturated by the exiled writer's
longing. Aciman writes of Alexandria and its environs, the place
in which his family lived from 1905 until 1964 when his father's
business was nationalized and they were expelled, taking pleasure still in its remembered scents, sounds, and appearances.
One hears "the stirring of long spoons in tall lemonade glasses"
and "the persistent whispers of . . . two women" woven into the
afternoon rest of the small boy in his grandmother's apartment.[31]
The "drone of the old Bedouin bagpipe player . . . the call of the
bread-and-biscuit vendor, and the ice cream vendor after him,
and then noises made by neighborhood boys" (247) mark his
days of summer at the beach. One sees the child and his gover-
ness rising in the morning, opening "the door to the veranda,"
seeing "past the sand dunes and the aged palm trees . . . basking
in Sunday silence—the pale-blue sea, glaring in the morning
light" (284). Sunlight, here, is a nearly palpable presence. One encounters it in the feel of wool on the skin, in the look of uphol-
stery near a window or of freshly washed linen carried up dark
stairs to a terrace "where a sudden, blinding spell of heat and sunlight dazzled our senses" (107). One even learns, with Aciman,
to mark its gentler manifestations: when the sun begins in the
morning to "pound the flagstones . . . a cool breeze swept
through the streets, and something like a distilled, airy light

spread over the city, bright but without glare, light you could stare into" (324).

Beneath this sense of a world laid open to light, fragrant and humming with vitality, however, the memoir constructs a well of darkness. The sounds of neighborhood boys in summer recall their deadly kite fights with razors and sharpened bamboo. The gentle light of early morning, "without glare," opens a day in which the boy must secure the passports that will take him and his family away from Alexandria, into exile. His father, "facing the night" before his arrest, looks out the window and says: "It's a small city, but I hate to lose her"; "Where else can you see stars like this?" And the boy thinks: "They might torture him, and I may never see him again" (322). Dark stairways and dazzling sun; stars upon a night sky; love of home and terror of loss—ambivalence becomes the soul and shaping genius of this memoir.

Embedded not only in a place but also in an extended family, the ambivalent image of home is constructed partly by portrayals of the boy's relatives. Aciman describes one gentle, bewildered grandmother "who was always eager to come to anyone's defense, partly because she was kind and didn't like to encourage slander, but also because her little rebukes always seemed to force people to intensify their original indictments of others" (60–61). He recalls the family's intimate care for beloved servants—whose odor they find offensive (105). He even recalls the profound ambivalence evoked in him by his deaf mother whose unnatural voice, "louder and higher than most" when she "shouted goodbye in the morning" made him pretend he hasn't heard her, made him "put some distance" between them, made him envy "other boys their mothers, their sweet, hearing mothers."

He also remembers, however, that she understood and forgave him for his embarrassment, letting "out words of love" to him that "weren't even words, just sounds reaching far back into her childhood to a time when she couldn't even speak—half-words which she sometimes yelled out in the water when we swam together, her voice muffled by the sound of waves, thinned of its coarseness, kind as a seagull's" (98–99). In the tenderness of these recollections, the intimate connection between this mother and this child comes clear: "My thoughts were her thoughts, just as her thoughts were my thoughts," he recalls (101). But one strand of this tender connection is formed by his concern for her, his anguish at realizing that "she would always be deaf, never hear music, never hear laughter, never hear my voice. Only then did I realize what it meant to be alone in the world, and I would run to find her in this large house that became so quiet, so empty, and so very dark at night, because nighttime in our part of Alexandria was always somber and murky, especially with my father out so late every evening" (101). The natural darkness intensified by the infidelities of his handsome, generous father, the recollected parents testify, like every other element of the Alexandrian home, to the shaping power of ambivalence.[32]

Beneath Aciman's feeling for his large family as a whole, the memoir recognizes the darkness of their collective insecurity as Jews in Egypt. They refer frequently to the precariousness of their situation. They criticize the behavior of other Jews: "'It's because of Jews like them that they hate Jews like us'" (25). They mock themselves as *"parvenus juifs"* (33). Accosted on the street by hostile boys, one uncle denies he is a Jew (184). They argue— in several languages—about whether they belong to Turkey, to Italy, or to France (172). The boy's father, who has briefly considered converting, recalls as they look at their apartment, emptied on the eve of their exile, "witnessing his parents' emptied home" many years earlier, "on the day they had left Constantinople. As had his father seen his own father's home. And our ancestors before that as well. And so would I, too, one day, though he didn't wish it on me" (300). Loss of home—not home itself—thus becomes the Jew's legacy to his child.

Against this loss the presence of family forms a kind of temporary defense. During times of war, they gather in the matriarch's apartment, from "Cairo and Port Said, and some from as far as Khartoum" (24), spending their days tending to business but gathering in late afternoon and evening to eat and sleep—some on mattresses on the floor, to hear Schubert played by one aunt on the piano and to listen to the radio in rooms darkened for fear of air raids. Remembering these times the memoirist knows that "even if I disliked almost everyone in this room, it was good to be with them" (186), to relish the "strangely comforting certainty of coming back to a stuffy room full of stuffy people bound together by the need to huddle in the dark" (187). When the "all clear" is sounded, he thinks: "I would miss these nights . . . not the war itself but the blackout, not my uncles or my aunts but the velvety hush of their voices when we turned off the lights and drew closer to the radio, almost whispering our thoughts in the dark, as though the enemy were listening in on us as well" (207). Always in this memoir, darkness—both literal and figurative, personal and collective—is the matrix out of which grows the comfort and security associated with home.

Ambivalence continues to structure Aciman's later work, for the process of imaginative memory has become his central subject. Both the memoir and his later essays dwell on this elusive process: moving toward it from different angles, shining different lights into its obscure working place. He understands the way memory both invents and reconstructs from fragments held in the mind. On the night his father met his mother, she gets into her car, "one foot resting on the pavement as she fumbled with the keys." After she is gone, "all that remained of her . . . was the memory of that white satin shoe resting on the pavement, tilting sideways as she struggled to unlock the other doors" (69). Later, when his father "felt the memory of her features starting to fade from his grasp, like an anthropologist reconstructing an entire body from a mere bone fragment he would think of that shoe, and from the shoe work his way around her foot, and from her foot, up her legs, her knees, her gleaming white dress, until he had reached her lips and then, for a fleeting instant, would coax a smile on a face he had been seeing for years across the street but had always failed to notice" (69). Here the very process of imaginative remembering is laid bare; as the boy's father builds on a residual grain of perceived experience a whole human figure suddenly become significant—and responsive to him.

From the work of imaginative memory, Aciman seems to draw his most powerful emotional experiences. Long after his grandfather died, the boy recalled by the memoirist discovers that what lingered in his garden "was not his presence, not even his memory, but that vague sense of well-being that would fill his sunlit garden when I came looking for him, hoping to hear his cane or his billiard cue, so that we might pluck guavas" (127). For years the boy, passing this garden, would think: "What if he happened to be there right now?" On an evening just before the family has to leave Egypt, as the boy walks with friends "to visit a woman called La Leila," he passes this garden again: "I was thinking of other things then and had drunk too much wine, but the thought had come so naturally, and with such persistent urgency, that from the man I was about to become that evening, I would gladly have borrowed five minutes to go ring his doorbell and check one last time" (127). In *Out of Egypt* this powerful desire to "check one last time" will blossom into longing that begins even before he has left home: "suddenly I knew, as I touched the damp, grainy surface of the seawall, that I would always remember this night, that in years to come I would remember sitting here, swept with confused longing as I listened to the water lapping the giant boulders beneath the promenade. . . . I wanted to come back tomorrow night, and the night after . . . sensing that what made leaving so fiercely painful was the knowledge that there would never be another night like this, that I would never eat soggy cakes along the coast road in the evening . . . nor feel the baffling, sudden beauty of that moment when, if only for an instant, I had caught myself longing for a city I never knew I loved" (339). Even before memory comes, longing endows home with a depth and pathos that will nourish later experience. In later essays Aciman will look more closely, more analytically, at the work of memory and the longing for home. Years after he has been sent into exile he muses on the persistence of his longing for home, wondering "why . . . unlike the body, which sheds everything, the soul cannot let go of anything but compiles and accumulates, growing annual rings around the things it wants and dreams of and remembers."[33] He recognizes that beneath his awareness of all the other cities he has loved, Alexandria remains. In the end even Paris and Rome, whose memory he retrieves in New York, "are really the shadow of the shadow of Alexandria, versions of Alexandria, the remanence of Alexandria . . . reminding me of something that is not just elsewhere but that is perhaps more in me than it ever was out there" (*False Papers* 49).[34] The phenomenon he calls "remanence," the shadowy presence of the past beneath experience of the present—like the barely perceptible ghost of water trapped in an underground place (*False Papers* 44)—helps him to understand the power that Alexandria retains over his imagination.

He imagines memory, like a dowser seeking the ghost of water, moving back and forth over dry rocky soil, seeking the ghost of home. The image returns when he revisits Alexandria, years after having been expelled from the city and long after he has made New York his home. On this trip he discovers at the grave of his grandfather the power of ritual to both evoke and relieve the anguish of longing for ghosts whose remanence persists. Unmoved by his visit to the city and to the cemetery, distracted by the presence of his guide and the warden's family, he is suddenly drawn into an ancient ritual practice when the warden pours fresh water over the marble slab covering his grandfather's grave, "flooding the whole area, wetting my clothes . . . allowing the stone to glisten for the first time in who knows how many decades. With eager palms, we all go about the motions of wiping the slab clean. I like the ritual. . . . I want it to be my job. I don't want it to end. I am even pleased that my clothes are wet and dirty. . . . 'Are you happy now?' I want to ask my grandfather, rubbing the stone some more, remembering a tradition practiced among Muslims of tapping one's finger ever so gently on a tombstone to tell the dead that their loved ones are present, that they miss them and think of them. I want to speak to him, to say something, if only in a whisper. But I am too embarrassed. Perhaps this is why people say prayers instead. But I don't know any prayers" (*False Papers* 18–19). He has come to Alexandria to "bury the whole thing, to get it out of [his] system, to forget, to hate even, the way we learn to hate those who wouldn't have us" (*False Papers* 5). His experience of the city has been dryly analytical—until the moment when he enters this ritual. Immediately afterward, he encounters his doppelgänger—"the person I might have been had I stayed here thirty years ago" (*False Papers* 19)—and realizes that although this city is "no longer home," his mind will always turn back to it, for "one never washes anything away." Within the self, as within the cities one lives in, the ghostly shadow of the past—with all its unlived possibilities intact—remains.

Like dowsing, the ritualized gesture of washing the old stone in fresh water becomes for this writer a figure that "captures the confused, back-and-forth, up-and-around, congested nature of ambivalence, of love, and of nostalgia" (*Out of Egypt* 139). Elsewhere he calls this repetitive, ritual motion by other names, seeking a word to describe the reversals that characterize his experience of exile, his longing for a place that is no longer home, that nurtured him and cast him out, that is full of sun and darkness, that he both loves and hates, whose remanence abides in every other place that takes him in. And whose ghostly presence in himself his longing continually reinvokes. In the end, he believes, the "ultimate homecoming" becomes "the act of recording the loss" of home (*False Papers* 144). He has learned to "re-create Alexandria the way the rabbis, in exile, were forced to reinvent their homeland on paper, only to find, perhaps, that they worshiped the paper more than the homeland" (*False Papers* 157).[35] The labor of recollection and the anguish of loss have become two poles that create the momentum of life in exile. Between them, memory weaves and reweaves the web of feeling with words that refresh the past—like water on an old stone—without washing it away.

In the stories of Steve Stern imaginative memory performs a similar function, making explicit the work of fabrication that accounts for the image of home his work recalls.[36] Neither Europe nor Egypt, the American immigrant past becomes the site that Stern's imagination recollects. The process of recollection itself becomes one of his most important thematic preoccupations. Like a strand of bright, thick yarn deliberately unwound from a spool, the immigrant past in an early story ("The Book of Mordecai" in *Lazar Malkin Enters Heaven*) weaves its way through the memoirs of a dying man. Installed in a dark corner screened off from the family living room, uncle Mordecai falls—like his nephew's canary that toppled from its perch days earlier—"beak first into the past," taking up the labor of recollection that will terminate in the writing of his birth and the nearly simultaneous moment of his death. Driven, the narrator believes, by fear, Mordecai writes continuously: "composing his memoirs back to front, subtracting year after year."[37] After years of pleasant interactions with the narrator's small family, Mordecai withdraws into the work of memory.

This labor involves no literal journey across oceans, no research—only remembering. Behind the screen decorated with flowers he looks "like a scribe in a cloud of roses" (174). But his work transforms both him and the place in which he writes. The deterioration within and all around him alienates the entire family except for the young nephew who narrates the story and supplies his uncle with food and notebooks to write in. "His filthy waistcoat was emptied of its paunch; his several chins collapsed into a wattle. Stubble frosted the hollows beneath his cheekbones, and his hair boils over" as the corner in which he sits becomes a "slum. Peach pits, zwieback crumbs, fishbones, half-empty cups of Ovaltine, and blowflies littered the floor" (173). In the Yeatsian "foul rag and bone shop of my uncle's corner" (178), the thread of the American immigrant past is slowly, deliberately "reeled in" (179). This curious mode of recollection dignifies the disheveled memoirist who accomplishes it: as the uncle weeps over his "hemorrhaging memories," his nephew realizes that "the emptying of Uncle Mordecai" is "so much more important than his filling up" (180). Like Aciman's rabbis who begin to worship—more than the place itself—the paper on which the homeland has been reinvented, Mordecai's memoir— "a dubious sort of book that begins at the end and vice versa"— becomes for the nephew a "holy book"; it is his Uncle Mordecai's "gift, and I live in constant fear of losing it" (181).

As Stern constructs this metaphor for the artist who imaginatively recollects the Jewish past, the literal family home is carefully differentiated from the past-as-homeland that Uncle Mordecai struggles to write. The befouled "living room" in which he worked can be purged after Mordecai's death—"restored . . . to its original serenity" (181). But Mordecai's story has revealed the dark, untidy joys and desperations in which the sanitized, orderly present is embedded and from which, while it lives, it draws its vitality.[38]

To accomplish this revelation becomes for Stern the work of the writer, dependent on a muse who knows the Jewish past. Whether the muse is a beautiful young immigrant woman who died before she could finish her own work ("The Ghost and Saul Bozoff" in *Lazar Malkin*) or a gnarled old hermit living in a sewer on whose walls he has crayoned "mementoes of the Old Country" ("Bruno's Metamorphosis" in *The Wedding Jester*), whether the writer falls in love with his muse or simply leaves her a glass of fresh milk, his work begins to "remember the world" ("The Ghost" 188) only when it recovers the past. The writer Saul Bozoff sees the immigrant past as a "birthright he'd been denied," in which "the supernatural mingled . . . casually with the mundane. Peddlers, spinsters, and piecework tailors had frequent commerce with fallen angels; bakers and seamstresses braided and embroidered their handwork with arcane spells" ("The Ghost" 192). Through the "rent in the fabric of reality" ("The Ghost" 208) that enables Bozoff to imaginatively encounter such a world, he glimpses the "communion of archaic and slaptstick sensibilities, [the] illicit marriages of Old Testament and pagan themes" ("The Ghost" 192) that once appeared in his muse's stories and will now revitalize his own writing. In these stories, imaginative recollection is a gift passed to the writer from another world, a world he never knew but one that becomes home to his imagination because it preceded the less vital Jewish world in which he lives.[39]

The creative joy and dignity of Bozoff's work, however, are not unmixed. In one story the writer first needs to accept his dependence on a muse he cannot control; then he must acknowledge that the times they recollect together were not, as he had believed, "innocent" ("The Ghost" 234). "'From the fruit of the tree of the knowledge of good and evil,'" his muse tells him flatly, "'we had our lifelong stomachaches'" ("The Ghost" 234). In a later story, the writer must not only accept his dependence, make "peace with his emptiness," but also learn to feel "that the grimacing stones, the waist-high ferns, that deserted quarry, that broken chimney, that oak, had at least as much significance as himself." [40] Meaning begins to come from the place where his muse lives, instead of from his own world, or from within himself.

The writer's dependence on and attachment to the world of the past is at first, for Stern's writer persona Saul Bozoff, a source of heady exaltation. In love with the young immigrant woman who opens the immigrant past to him, he first learns the pleasure of making stories "whose typewritten pages . . . winked at him and shimmered, words like electric minnows, like a veil of northern lights" ("The Ghost" 221). Even after his muse's ghost leaves, the inspiration she has given him remains. Bozoff's protagonist, Felix, blocked like Bozoff by a picture of the past that features only "ashes and umbrellas of flame," climbs out of his cellar to discover what will become Stern's own subject: "a neighborhood on top of a river bluff mercifully spared by the Lord, full of cunning old world Jews" ("The Ghost" 248). No longer impeded by images of destruction—shadows of the Holocaust that darken the little secrets of the past in many of Stern's otherwise antic stories—Felix tries to shut down but is overwhelmed by "hordes of wild Jewish daughters and horny cheder boys" who stream— irrepressible—into his work ("The Ghost" 249)

In a later story in *The Wedding Jester,* this attachment to the world of the past—like Uncle Mordecai's withdrawal from the pleasures of family life into a corner where he empties himself of memory—divides the writer's spirit from humankind. Drawn out of himself as he exorcises a demon from a young bride's body, his spirit becomes "a vagabond . . . content to let the winds of fancy blow me . . . forward or backward in time" while he seeks another embodied persona who "can manage, with grace, to live in two worlds at once" ("The Wedding Jester" 213). This sense of eternal dividedness edges darkly an otherwise comic story with an otherwise characteristically antic ending. The concluding tale in this collection ("A String around the Moon: A Children's Story") offers to "children" a more upbeat fable about the creative work of a sorcerer who restores to life a moribund Jewish neighborhood by tying a string from his finger to the moon. The image of creative power drawn from somewhere else to this needy, exhausted place remains an image of two worlds unalterably divided, linked tentatively by a tenuous, uncertain connection through which vitality streams. Imagination's home, as always, is somewhere else. Transformative energy comes from there to the writer, only by way of the creative imagination. And the one who imagines is either tied to it or divided within himself by attachments too profound to uproot. The ambivalence that Aciman characteristically negotiates through the oscillating movements of memory and the agency of language becomes in Stern's stories a tragic condition of separation and brokenness that his writer-characters struggle—either to overcome or to sustain. Stern's work suggests that the distance between ourselves and the collective home from which we came may be as important a source of brokenness within contemporary Jews as the Holocaust and its destruction of European Jewry.

Stories that recall home as the world of the immigrant past— as Stern imaginatively reconstructs it—suggest that this essentially tragic condition belongs to all of us, not just to writers.[41] In the imaginatively recollected past, innocence and spirituality set in motion forces that victimize both those who possess such virtues and those who would persecute them. In the early "Moishe the Just" (from *Lazar Malkin*), a desperately poor and aged junk collector attracts the attention of neighborhood boys who have been convinced by their ringleader that Moishe is one of the thirty-six "lamed vovniks": "one of those for whose sake God neglected to destroy the world" ("Moishe" 6). The boys are peculiarly susceptible to this belief because the "world" they live in, like the one we know, is shadowed by terrible "news from abroad" ("Moishe" 7). They need the old man to prove himself by performing a miracle, so they contrive an accident that will surely kill him. But in the last moment the murderous ringleader saves Moishe by sacrificing his own life. In him the story makes very clear the ambivalent reactions—then and now—to innocence in a fallen world. As Stern recalls it, the world of the immigrant past is as torn as our own by villainies and saintlinesses that sometimes exist within the same confused person.

The severity of this profound confusion deepens in a later story, "The Tail of a Kite" (from *The Wedding Jester*), where hostility to a saintly rebbe whose prayers enable him to levitate alienates a child from his father. If the European past as women writers recollect it is darkened by hostility toward Jews and the repression of women, Stern's image of the immigrant past is tainted by its antagonism toward what one assimilating immigrant patriarch calls "the blind superstition of our ancestors preserved in amber." How "did it manage to follow us over an ocean to such a far-flung outpost as Tennessee?" he wonders. "Let the goyim see a room like this, with a ram's horn in place of a clock on the wall . . . and right away the rumors start. The yids are poisoning the water, pishing on communion wafers, murdering Christian children for their blood. . . . A room like this, give or take one flying rebbe, can upset the delicate balance of the entire American enterprise" (10–11). The stubborn, assimilationist materialism of this father moves him, hedge shears in hand, to the room where a saintly rebbe, reverently watched by the father's own child, rises into the air, held to earth only by a cord around his waist. The boy's father is momentarily moved by the "wonder" of the rebbe's ascent. But he cuts the cord that links the rebbe to the earth. The rebbe floats free and the child leaps after him, holding fast and rising with the rebbe into the heavens. The father imagines for a moment that he is rising with them, into a "sunset . . . more radiant than a red flare over a herring barrel, dripping sparks—all the brighter as it's soon to be extinguished by dark clouds swollen with history rolling in from the east" (20).

Stern gives voice here to the ambivalent urge toward—and rejection of—holiness that appears in his other stories. In his work neither need nor longing can overlook the residue of darkness—at home in the world of the past—that subverts nostalgia and sustains ambivalence toward "home."[42]

Unlike Stern's several fictions that locate home in the richly imagined American immigrant neighborhood he calls "The Pinch," Jonathan Safran Foer's *Everything Is Illuminated* recalls "home" in the image of a European shtetl. He calls the place "Trachimbrod" and invents its mythic past, tracing its life up to the moment of its entire annihilation by the Nazis. "'There is nothing,'" the town's only resident survivor tells the American grandson of a Jewish man who escaped the massacre; "'there is no Trachimbrod anymore. It ended fifty years ago. . . . There is nothing to see. It is only a field. I could exhibit you any field and it would be the same as exhibiting you Trachimbrod.'"[43] She remembers that in this shtetl, "'everyone had his own family, but it was something like we were all one big family. People would fight, yes, but it was nothing'" (155). But as the novelist re-creates this place, it becomes clear that its animosities and brutalities are not "nothing"; they trouble the grandson's Russian translator who pleads with the novelist to lighten the darkness of his shtetl characters' lives. Though generously laced with comic and tender moments, though framed by brilliantly comic interactions between the grandson/novelist and his Russian translator, the darkness in which Trachimbrod is embedded is so deep that neither silence, nor laughter, nor even the broken play of language that allows one to see through what Stern would have called "the rents in reality" can mitigate or ameliorate the pain of its terrible passing. And the guilt that outlives this shtetl passes, like the pain, from generation to generation, severing bonds that have developed between the American Jewish writer and his Ukrainian translator and also between the translator and his own family. "They must cut all the strings" (275) that bind them to the past, to one another. When memory comes, in this novel, its effect is deadly—not life-giving. And imagination here stirs into vivid, engaging life only what one must—but cannot bear—to lose.

In Aryeh Lev Stollman's *The Far Euphrates* the certainty that home is lost provokes not just pain but also radical insights into the ways in which such loss shapes—may even make possible—individual growth. In this novel home is the place where journeys begin, for the work looks deeply, through its pro-tagonist/narrator, into the reasons why people leave home. The novel frames as well the enduring tension of desire for this place that we leave but also keep: a place so deeply inscribed in the most intimate parts of our brains and feelings that we can neither see it clearly—nor ever look away from it.

Alexander tells his own story in this novel. He acknowledges at the outset that he will not be able to see things as they really are or were: "we can never look back . . . or even directly at the present, and see . . . the everywhere and everything and every-one that is not us."[44] But he tries, nevertheless, to recall and to describe the tangled events and significant personae of his childhood. Drawn—against his rational judgment—back to these formative sources of his being, he appears to seek a way of under-standing why he had to leave them. Through him, the novel fo-cuses on distance and separation, representing them as essential elements of what we imagine home to be. Through him, the novel lifts into visibility a hard secret: that, from the womb onward, home may be the site of our most desperate struggles—a struggle first to receive nurture and care, then to achieve independence, and finally to assume responsibility.

The only living child of a woman whose other pregnancies end in miscarriage, Alexander learns from his mother's best friend, Berenice, about his own prenatal struggle for nurture. When he is ten Berenice explains that he must have been very "clever to hold the door" to his mother's womb "shut" until he "was ready to come out" (70); unlike him, his baby brothers and sisters have all left that safe space and perished before their time. Years later he will dream of being "locked in a dark space, hold-ing the door shut with all my strength while vicious dogs or monsters wait outside to get me" (70). But in the dream, the once-secure space itself becomes threatening as his oxygen begins to run out. In his life, as well, the family space becomes threatening to him and he must use his cleverness to get out, rather than holding the door closed so as to stay in.

"Getting out" means, first, learning to withdraw from a mother whose fears threaten to undermine his confidence and self-esteem. He learns very early the strategy of withdrawal that will liberate him from her. In part, she teaches him the value of this strategy. She has withdrawn from him because her anxiety that he will carry the genetic taint of her brother's mental illness has alienated her from her own child. He recalls that "in her own obsessive worry she became almost afraid of me—to touch me too much, or to caress me" (7). He has seen her employ this strategy in other relationships as well. She leaves home to avoid her visiting mother-in-law, and she turns away in anger, refusing ever to speak again with an old friend who loves her: "That had always been her way," Alexander explains, "to withdraw from what frightened her, from the unbearable, to retreat quietly, as she had long ago retreated from me, to hide deep within herself, beyond the intrusive glare of a rational sun, never to return" (198). His father, too, models withdrawal: closeting himself in his study, creating a rift between himself and his wife. His grandparents have also withdrawn: from a son whose rabbinical career disappointed them and from a daughter-in-law whose genes, they fear, may carry the taint of mental illness. They leave America to return to Germany, refusing visits from Alexander's parents, more comfortable with the home culture that cast them out than with the uncertainties of life and offspring on a new continent.

Though Alexander excelled before his birth at remaining within the space that nurtured him, he learns very young, from all these family models, the dubious virtue but certain efficacy of withdrawal. The novel allows it to happen as we watch. Stollman writes a scene in which the five-year-old Alexander, riding in a car with his mother and two other women, first sees— reflected in his mother's sunglasses—"the broad greenish arc of river" below the bridge on which they are driving. He tries to "snuggle against her" and she draws away. He closes his eyes and imagines himself "a seagull, gliding on air, letting the river breeze lift my wings ever higher. . . . Then I transformed myself and became invisible. . . . From a great and wondrous height, alone, isolated from the earthly world, I peered down at an open basket of sky-blue papyrus holding three tiny women and drifting in the breadth of the Nile" (16–17). When his mother's voice comes to him, as if from a great distance, we understand that he has effectively withdrawn from her. He can see the world now through his own lenses. When another woman's critical observations about his mother have distanced him even further from her, he begins to see "her anew, from afar, as other people might have seen her. Perhaps, I like to think, this even saved me, for I did not get caught up in her unexplained worries and fears" (22–23). The space he has put between them will carry its own burden of guilt and sorrow. But although he will not be able to celebrate his severance from his mother, although he will even assume responsibility for her after his father's death, "leaving home" psychologically becomes for him the guarantee of his freedom to become himself.

In adolescence he withdraws even more severely from the home that seems to obstruct his growth. He covers his windows to bar the intrusive sunlight that seems to order his time, closes his bedroom door against his family, and refuses to leave his room except after dark—when everyone sleeps. He spends a year in that room, reading at night the books his father provides, studying ancient languages, physics, and anatomy. During this time he reorganizes his sense of himself: "It was a process of withdrawal and internal realignment, a painful but necessary rearrangement of the hierarchy that exists in every breathing soul, the structure that mirrors the mystical shape of the living God Himself" (9). This inward journey of withdrawal becomes the analogue of less productive journeys undertaken by his father and grandfather who withdrew from their families in order to go home again—to visit the site of the origin of their people. Preoccupied nearly to the point of obsession with the ancient homeland, the boy's father and grandfather study its history and geography, map its rivers, try to locate its academies. Ironically, they leave home to go home. One of them will return to a family permanently embittered by its abandonment. The other will die prematurely in Baghdad, close to the site of the Garden of Eden—a place that was once watered, as the novel's title, and cover, and initial map suggest, by the river Euphrates. Thus the protagonist's personal journey of withdrawal from his home to his room, from his family to the inner sources of his isolated self, mirrors—like the Hebrew and English letters that mirror one another on the book's cover—the journeys of his father and grandfather who have withdrawn intellectually, spiritually, physically from their family homes to return to the collective homeplace in Eden.

Alexander's father, a scholarly rabbi, explains the powerful attraction of this ancient home: "Our forefathers, strangely enough—and this I believe is the real root of mankind's problem—originally came not from Kana'an, not from an earthly Jerusalem, but from the far Euphrates with its source in Eden, from an impossibly remote and primordial home. We cannot forget it, or ever find it again. I believe this fact has afflicted us to the present day" (163). The novel is replete with afflictions that can be connected with the long exile from home in Eden. In the world of this novel, fetuses miscarry; children die young from incurable diseases or are killed, at play, by cars that invade their backyard; one survivor of the Holocaust, a family friend, is rendered sterile and his twin brother assumes the disguise of a Christian woman because of Nazi surgical experiments; even palm trees, lovingly tended in Canada by the gentle survivor who cannot father a child, are destroyed by a tornado that topples the pots that contain their roots. The world of exile, of rootlessness, and homes that can neither nurture nor protect, is alive with afflictions. In it, characters find themselves "not-at-home" in what Alexander's father calls "places which still somehow frighten us" (162). Their malaise evokes an infant's passage from the relatively quiet and secure darkness of the womb into a clamorous, dangerous world. It suggests as well an adolescent's emergence into the confusions of puberty after the confining— yet predictable—clarities of childhood. And it leads the mind back to the long, perilous exile from Eden that forms the deepest layer of our collective memory of home.

This novel's gift is to develop the link among these sites of struggle, pain, and longing. The link among them is language. Subjected to the estrangements and withdrawals that mar his parents' marriage and damage their relationships with their own parents and their care of him, Alexander saves himself by psychically leaving home. Yet he knows from his father's love of ancient texts, and from his correspondence with scholars abroad who share his passion for recollection of the original home, that language is the umbilicus that is never severed, that can always connect him with that "impossibly remote and primordial home" beyond the far Euphrates. From the sugar cookies shaped like letters that his mother bakes for him; from the Hebrew letters of Genesis that his father reads with him—"where the dotted vowels clustered like bees around the honeyed consonants" (2–3); to the letters on the headstone of his friend—that burn in his imagination like those in the words pronounced by God before

Creation; to the letters of his own name, spoken by God before Alexander's birth, letters and the words they shape connect Alexander to a home that remains accessible to him—however far he may travel from it.

The culminating scene of the novel draws together the promise that has always been implicit in the letters of the ancient language and the problematic influences of family and friends at home. As Alexander, now a young man, prays at the grave of his father, he sees that the ancient Hebrew letters of his prayer belong both to the place of collective origin—"to that place which remains outside time and this earth"—and also to "this world, which is our home" (206). They speak to him now of both Eden and the home in exile. And as he watches, the letters link even more directly the human presences within and around the family home and the divine presence that presided over creation and the collective past of Eden and exile. The letters of his prayer hover before him, gathering themselves into the likenesses of his family and boyhood friends—the damaged, the loving, the fearful, the living and the dead. These human images suddenly appear to him like the guides furnished by God to the Israelites on their journey through the wilderness. He sees that they have been given to him "like so many pillars of cloud and pillars of fire, to lead me through my days and to lead me through my nights" (206). Their images connect him not only to the ancient home, "where we might always go to reconcile ourselves" (206) but also to both the biblical world of exile and the contemporary wilderness of inexplicable pain and sudden loss. After the death of his own and his father's friend, Alexander chooses to "come back to the world . . . even though it might include . . . the part that was death" (190). After his father's death he affirms as well the familiar, beloved personae of that world. Though they have hurt and disappointed and abandoned as well as loved him, they appear now to be "bound up" with the "Mercy" and "Loving-kindness" of God. In this perception the rifts this novel has portrayed—between personal and collective memory, between historic and individual losses, between yesterday's promises and this moment's pain—is healed.

This moment of healing neither forgets nor cancels the darknesses the novel has uncovered within its image of "home." Awareness of those darknesses persists into Stollman's second novel, *The Illuminated Soul*. But this later novel constructs an image of the present in which memory itself becomes home. The novel introduces a Canadian family, a widow and two sons, who live in a small provincial town. A beautiful woman enters their home and their lives, enriching, healing, teaching and bearing with her precious old manuscripts made by European Jews, contained in an antique lacquerware box from the Far East. She is the daughter of a Czechoslovakian scholar who taught her Torah; she has been the wife of a Japanese scientist who saved her from the Holocaust. She is, has been, and remains homeless. But she makes herself beautifully—if temporarily—at home within the family and its house. Her name is Eva Laquedem Higashi. Beneath her story, Stollman has embedded a significant ancient narrative of Jewish journeying and homelessness. The narrative rises partly out of the biblical texts that tell of the Israelites' preparations for setting off from Egypt.

The story that underlies this novel is told partly in the Book of Numbers, in a passage that the widow's older son, the narrator Joseph, is preparing to read aloud in the synagogue on Shabbat. He is working on this passage when Eva comes to the door, looking for a room. When the doorbell rings, Joseph is reading God's instructions to make "two trumpets of silver" for the "calling of assemblies and for the journeying of the camps in the wilderness."[45] As the door opens, Joseph looks at the sunlight that fills their front hall and sees "a soft and spreading light that divided into two broad bands" (66); they seem to him like the "silvery trumpets" he has been reading about. Eva's glorious red hair and the shimmering silk clothes she always wears—sometimes purple, sometimes "blue-green with glints of gold" (67)—recall, for a reader familiar with Israel's preparations for the wilderness, the shining curtains and veils of blue, purple, and crimson that hung within the portable Tabernacle. According to God's instructions, this Tabernacle would shelter the Ark of the Covenant as it travels with the Jews through the wilderness.

From the beginning, the figure of Eva is interwoven in Joseph's mind with the living memory of this long journey, undertaken according to divine command and accompanied, as midrash would have it, by the *shekhina*—God's presence.[46] In their preparations for the journey, in the richness of silken hangings and brilliantly colored fabrics that will go with the wanderers and serve as a sheltering background for the performance of their rituals, one sees a people making friends, as it were, with the fact of impermanence, with the givens of change and loss that accompany movement in time, with homelessness in a dangerous world.

As Eva settles temporarily into the home of the widow and her sons, she transforms the room in which she lives and works, covering her bed with rich brocade, hanging ancient and beautiful images from China and Japan on the walls. Like the ark that accompanied the biblical wanderers, Eva's room becomes the setting for a series of significant rituals. In one memorable scene Eva appears to the family in a long, violet dressing gown, then drapes herself in an even more brilliantly embroidered fabric, and performs for them an ancient Eastern tale of a magic giraffe. In an earlier performance she demonstrates for them the way in which silkworms spin by removing from her abundant red hair two silver pins—elaborate as Torah ornaments—allowing the hair to fall around her face and shoulders. Like the Israelites once awed by the splendor and richness of rituals performed within the undulating folds of their Tabernacle, this family is spellbound by Eva's beauty and performances. She seems to them like a visitor from another world, the beauty of her performances like the beauty of rituals performed in a bright silken tent for a dusty people, weary of traveling the wilderness and longing for home.

She also bears treasures of beauty and understanding into their small world. She carries a precious, ancient miscellany, a receptacle of ancient wisdom. She is herself such a receptacle, for she knows the literature of the Jews, the culture of Europe and Asia. "In these dark times," she remembers her father saying, "everyone must carry as much knowledge within themselves as she can. That is the only way we have to save the past" (82).

In human memory, then, the novel locates a power resistant to the inevitable changes and losses that accompany journeying in the wilderness of time and space. What stays with us, Eva insists, are the intimate changes made in our brains by everything that has touched us. The consoling power of this idea comes very clear in the frequency with which this novel's reviewers have quoted it: "Anything you have ever seen or heard or held in your hands changes you," Eva teaches: "It becomes a part of you. It's a scientific fact. Your brain changes. Why, when we look at each other right now, we are being changed forever. We are becoming part of each other" (111). In a post-Holocaust, postmodern world of multiple discontinuities, whose most precious gifts are constantly passing away from us, she insists on the power of the mind itself to hold whatever has touched and changed it.

This power of mind to absorb change and to redeem what has been lost becomes a kind of promise—held up against the long experience of homelessness. That experience, the novel suggests, belongs to all human beings. Eva has learned, and teaches Joseph, what Asian culture also knows: that no one "in this world has more than a temporary shelter." (72).[47] To the writer of *The Tale of Genji*, "a hut, a jeweled pavilion, they are all the same" (118) because they are of the moment. But for the Jewish family of the novel, beyond the "temporary shelter" of specific texts and particular places, the work locates home within the minds that have been opened to Eva and to the treasures she carries, and have been changed by them. Memory, for this writer, not only recalls but becomes home. This most durable of Jewish wisdoms—that what we have known and felt has not been, cannot be taken from us—reappears in the last decades of this most generous and hospitable of exiles. It reappears no longer as a defense against aggression or expulsion. Now it offers reassurance—perhaps even consolation—for losses too vast and too grievous to be otherwise embraced by the image of home.

5

Portnoy's Successors

*Gendered Ethnicity and the Embodying
of Jewish Men*

It isn't impossible to imagine ways in which the Holocaust
could have shaped the self-images of Jews who survived and
came "after" it. Perhaps no experience is more formative than
abuse. But the sense of self, especially the embodied self, is over-
determined, rooted in many places. Among them—according to
writers of the new wave—are less obvious, more "secret" places,
fashioned well before the Holocaust, and persisting in its
shadow. Alexander Portnoy and his father spring directly from
the imagination of their creator, Philip Roth. But they also bear
the imprint of long collective experience. Like a well-traveled
crossroads, the Jewish male body in post-Holocaust writing by
American Jews is, at least in part,[1] a site of multiple intersections.

The forces that meet in passing at this site originate both
within Jews, and between them and the non-Jewish world. Vagaries of psychological differentiation common to all humans
crisscross here with long-standing Jewish imperatives that allo-
cate prerogatives and power on the basis of gender. The collective past may leave its mark most clearly in the creases made by
the Holocaust in Europe. But the Jewish male body is also deeply
imprinted by a historic residue of ethnic difference. During centuries of life among non-Jews, images of Jewish bodies absorbed
the suspicions and fears of host cultures as well as the anxieties
and priorities of Jews themselves. This complex convergence of

both private and public, individual and collective experience of gender and ethnicity has come to mark the ways contemporary American Jews imagine themselves as embodied creatures.

However original the figures he creates, a contemporary novelist who attempts to embody the Jewish male engages an ancient dilemma in which choices are always already shaped by others as well as oneself. What psychoanalysts describe as a process through which individuals become gendered may contribute to this dilemma in a particular way for Jewish men. From Freud to the feminists, these writers affirm that awareness of gender begins for a man when he identifies with his father and "repudiates" his mother, who lacks a penis and thus differs from him. In a world that empowers men more generously than women, feminists add, what Freud called "the repudiation of femininity"[2] leads not only to the "triumphant contempt" for women that Freud predicted but also, as feminist theorists believe, to a man's denial within himself of qualities he recognizes as "feminine": "feelings of dependence, relational needs, emotions generally."[3] Traditional imperatives, which reserve for Jewish men the privilege of studying Torah and the power that rests in such study to regulate the lives of women, may reinforce this pattern of psychic differentiation.[4] The power of this prerogative began to erode in Europe after the enlightenment; erosion continued in America when Jewish feminists began in the seventies to demand for women educational access to traditional texts. But in collective memory, traditional privilege still supports assumptions of male primacy that continue to mark the construction of American Jewish male bodies in literature.

Cultural and social historians add an ironic layer to this dilemma of gender for Jewish men by suggesting that the wider society and culture—at least from the medieval period on—constructed the male Jew as a feminized "countertype" to its own ideal of manliness. Needing an image against which gentile masculinity could define itself, European culture constructed an image of the Jewish man that reversed gentile norms. While the ideal European male was imagined as physically beautiful, courageous, honorable, powerful but emotionally restrained, the Jew was conceived as neurotically passionate, deformed, dirty, untrustworthy and feeble.[5] Sharing some characteristics with stereotypes of homosexuals and women,[6] "the poisoned image of the Jewish male . . . assumed its modern form and special virulence only toward the end of the nineteenth century. . . . By the end of the century, caricaturists had recorded every nuance of the Jew's ignominious failures to achieve equal status with the gentile male."[7] Long denied entry into the world of agriculture, excluded as well from acceptance into the military officer corps, and ineligible to respond "honorably" to insult by dueling, a Jewish man in premodern Europe was unable to prove himself: he couldn't be quietly heroic, like a peasant facing the elements of nature; he couldn't be "courageous" like a soldier; and he couldn't be "a boon companion, a passionate lover" like the chivalric ideal that persisted into the modern model of European masculinity.[8]

Eastern Europe provided other models of the Jewish male. According to one historian, the "gentle, timid, and studious" model served as a rebuttal and alternative to the aggressive, dominant manliness of the gentile ideal.[9] Another researcher argues that the Bible itself valorizes this nonaggressive model by repeatedly rejecting the "older, stronger, more masculine son" and choosing his younger, "physically smaller, less hirsute, more delicate, more domestic" brother to inherit leadership of the people.[10] Biblical literature had provided images of refined male strength—in Jacob, for example, who can move great stones and wrestle with angels but who resorts to trickery in order to satisfy his aggressive impulses. The persecution of European Jews before World War II, however, gave rise to a Zionist model of maleness that looked back instead to the Bible's proud, self-righteous warriors.[11] And after the Holocaust, American literature produced images of "tough Jews" who "ruptured the nearly two-millennia-old Jewish cultural heritage" that had been based at least partly on gentile hegemonic anxieties, exclusions, and persecutions and partly on Jewish "principles of gentleness."[12]

Both the aggressiveness of Alexander Portnoy and the passivity of his father respond in part, then, to a confluence of assumptions and prejudices about men in general and Jewish men in particular. Roth understood the cultural, and even some of the psychic, forces that had constructed the Jewish male body. He knew also that *Portnoy's Complaint* slashed a new path through the tangle of earlier constructions. He believed that earlier American Jewish novelists, Saul Bellow and Bernard Malamud, had identified the post-Holocaust Jew in American fiction "with righteousness and restraint, with the just and measured response rather than with those libidinous and aggressive activities that border on the socially acceptable and may even constitute criminal transgression."[13] He understood that American culture of the fifties—thought of as "silent" but actually "straitjacketed"—strangely reinforced this virtuous construction of Jewish maleness ("On *The Breast*," *Reading Myself and Others* 88). In 1975 he traced the psychic roots of this construction to the Jewish boy's struggle with his Jewish mother, "the Cleopatra of the kitchen" who was always watching, controlling him ("On *The Breast*" 6). Later, in *The Counterlife*, Roth connected the excessive goodness of the Jewish boy to the too-good Jewish father, whose kitchen table lectures on the "historical struggle between the goy and the Jew" bound his sons to the same nonaggression pact that had constrained him.[14] But when Roth considered the alternative—the "new Jewish stereotypes" of tough, fighting Jews created by Leon Uris in *Exodus* to the great delight of American Jewish readers—he objected to "swapping one simplification for the other" ("Some New Jewish Stereotypes," *Reading Myself and Others* 138). Sexuality, not aggressiveness, his works suggest, was the appropriate path out of the thicket of inherited constructions of passive, repressed Jewish masculinity.

Thus, Portnoy. Roth didn't introduce sexuality into the male protagonists of American Jewish writing; Bellow's and Malamud's male figures perform their share of sexual feats. But Roth's emphasis on sexual appetite becomes obsessive, sometimes even grotesque, and it appears even before *Portnoy's Complaint*. "If we meet you at all," one of Roth's earliest protagonists tells God, "it's that we're carnal and acquisitive and thereby partake of You. I am carnal, and I know You approve."[15] Roth's male characters earn that approval in striking ways. From Alexander Portnoy's autoeroticism to Mickey Sabbath's bizarre pleasures, the male organ dominates a reader's sense of Roth's male characters as embodied creatures. Even after one character in *The Counterlife* has died, his penis reappears to his lover. Talking. The emphasis on insatiable sexuality that drives Roth's male characters through barriers of "personal inhibition, ethical conviction and plain, old monumental fear beyond which lies the moral and psychological unknown" also drives them beyond the confines of earlier constructions of Jewish masculinity ("On *The Breast*" 85).

Male writers of the new wave, whose images of male protagonists reshape the discourse on manliness that they enter, redefine
for readers what it means now to be a Jewish man. The randy adolescent boys of Thomas Friedmann's 1984 novel, *Damaged Goods,*
promise at first to develop further Roth's sense of the male Jewish body as a sexual instrument. Because they are Orthodox boys
who "prick [themselves] sore on the thorns and thistles of Torah,"
their sexual escapades—like Portnoy's—are beset by guilt.[16]
They perform them nonetheless, pocketing their *kippot* as they
leave their neighborhoods in pursuit of girls—transgressing, as
they leave, the boundaries set by traditional prohibitions against
premarital sex. In many ways their antics describe the same
comic arc that Roth's novels embody. But the play of sexual adventure gives way in this novel to the possibility of love, and the
parents' roles in the drama of a Jewish boy's self-realization are
radically altered.

The parents of this novel's protagonist, Jason, reverse the
images of the aggressive, controlling mother and recessive father who belonged to Alexander Portnoy. Jason's father is silent,
critical, rigidly authoritative, controlling. His mother is gentle,
loving, generally submissive to her husband but sometimes,
memorably, rebellious against his authority, and always strongly
protective of her son. Both parents are seen through their son's
dawning sense of their woundedness; they are both survivors
of the Holocaust. As Jason discerns the damage they have sustained, he recognizes also his need to incorporate them both into
his sense of himself as a fully embodied, fully sexualized Jewish
man. His path diverges not only from Portnoy's but also from the
pattern of male gendering with its repudiation of femininity sub-
scribed to by psychoanalysts.

Instead of the sustained collisions between traditional morality and male libido that animate Roth's novels, *Damaged Goods*
allows Jason's growing awareness of the residue of the Holocaust to intersect the comic trajectory of sexual transgressiveness
that the early portion of the novel vigorously sketches. Midway
through this novel the mother, always self-effacing, begins to
vanish slowly, losing weight as her son moves into his first romantic relationship, unburdening herself of memories of her girlhood and her experience in the camps. Eventually she walks into
the ocean and doesn't return. The shadow of her disappearance

darkens the novel; the antics of Jason's friends vanish with her. Friedmann's novel traces in the wake of this mother's disappearance the way in which a boy's gendered and embodied self-realization, desire and sexuality, may be inflected by both parents and by the residue of the "little secrets" they carry away from the Holocaust.

Jason's father—like the paternal figure in many psychoanalytic discussions of gender differentiation—models for his son both authority and desire. He has rescued his wife from Europe after their liberation from the camps; he has determined that they will be Orthodox Jews; his choices and commands define the lives of his wife and son. But he is a silent, withdrawn man, a keeper of secrets. Jason imagines himself pleading with this father, begging to know about his courtship and love for his wife. But the father's emotional life remains entirely masked. His body also, like his suffering during the war and his love for the boy's mother, remains obscured. Even in nightclothes he seems fully dressed, his body encased, as it were, in garments that signify his obedience to the Orthodox discipline of gender. The Orthodox Jewish male body becomes, in this novel, a divided body, its upper and lower, spiritual and earthly parts separated by the twisted black cords observant men wear around their middles on Sabbath mornings (62).

Jason attributes partly to his father's silences, denials, and withdrawals and partly to Orthodoxy his own inability to consummate his relationship with a girlfriend, Rachel. He believes that Orthodoxy not only inhibits sexuality among the unmarried, but masks it even after marriage; he and other waiters at a hotel frequented by Orthodox Jews cannot discern signs of sexual satisfaction among the newlyweds. He thinks that he has been a yeshiva boy for too long, that the part of himself he withholds from his lover is the organ marked by circumcision: the one part of himself "that was unquestionably Jewish" (53). He will not allow himself to consummate the sexual act, but he credits his father as the source of his pleasure in sexual play; as he strokes Rachel's body he tells her: "'I'm a tailor's son. . . . I can't resist touch and textures'" (152). He cannot learn from this father to love. He explains that he cannot find his way into fully sexualized love because "cleavings among the Orthodox are difficult. . . . [T]here are no transitions. . . . I could have made love to Rachel if I had had grandparents to teach me the sweetness of ceremony and the strength in acceptance. But the people who could have smoothed my transition from God to Father and from Father to Rachel have been killed off" (53). His father cannot teach him either to savor the sweetness of ritual life or to accept the burden of responsiveness that love demands. In the wake of the Holocaust the nuances of both religious life and loving sexuality have been obscured.

The pattern of male gendering that psychologists teach us to expect is disrupted here, for, in order to become a man, Jason needs the model his mother provides; he does not repudiate her or the feminine traits that liken him to her. She cannot model agency and desire, for she has never been "quite sure of what she wanted" (96). She cannot even help him to feel at home in his body. She has always been self-effacing except when she put herself between her critical husband and her son; even her own body seems gradually to fade away—partly because she is losing weight, but partly also because Orthodox gender imperatives of dress—for her as for Jason's father—have always rendered it invisible. On the day of her final disappearance she passes among thousands of people on the beach as she moves toward the ocean, but "no one saw her." The search for her is hampered because "no photographs exist of the way she looked with her hair loose and in a bathing suit." Even "Father himself would not have known her, so how could strangers, looking at a photograph of her in long sleeved dress and tucked wig?" (141). Though her body is obscured to her son, he keeps a sense of her as vital, and beautiful, remembering the color and sound that entered with her into his rented room at the beach (87).

Despite her handicaps, Jason is strengthened by the memory of her resolute protectiveness of him, her resistance in the face of his father's demands, her singular power to penetrate the defensive carapace of dignity that encloses her husband. Unlike him, she models openness, sharing with Jason some secrets of the camps that complicate gender after the Holocaust. He becomes "suddenly vulnerable" (101) to his mother's past, remembering her dismay at confusing with men the starving, hairless girls imprisoned in her barracks. In some ways, this mother "remains a victim" (73) to her son; "she, like me, had walked too long the prescribed four paces behind Father" (72). But she has

taught him nonetheless the "sweetness of ceremony," for together they always "draped" their "house with summer," cutting
fragrant branches to prepare for Shevuoth. This ritual becomes
effective for him, leaving him "so softened, so sensitive, so filled
with smells, that I would feel weak, ready for any suggestion. . . .
Such obligations were joys" (57). From the sweetness of these
memories and from her opposition to his father on his behalf he
will draw the power to free himself from obedience and to invent
the Jew he will become.

She also models love for him, for he recalls that as long as he
lived at home, she "would help camouflage [him] in the leaf and
vine of her presence" (30). Her last gift to him is a letter from Rachel that she delivers to his room at the beach before she disappears. From one point of view, this complex final gesture could
be seen as neurotically hostile, retaliatory, turning her anger
against herself instead of her son's love affair. From another
point of view, it could be understood as representing a retreat
from the burden of her own life. The novelist does not clarify this
ambiguity but concentrates instead on the way her death liberates Jason. After her death he conceives a chivalric image of
himself as her "faithful pageboy" who stands when he prays in
shul—despite his father's disapproval—like a "ghostly attendant in my mother's shadow home" (186). Her disappearance also
liberates his sexuality, for he seems to absorb from her memory
the strength to resist the imperatives of tradition and his father,
to act upon his own desire, finally consummating his love for
Rachel. The pattern of gendering that psychologists teach us to
expect is altered here. Instead of denying his mother's characteristics in himself, Jason uses them to render himself capable of
loving, of becoming strong in defense of his own needs, and
ready to become a man. He will become neither the tough fighter,
nor the sexual athlete, nor the gentle, passive scholar; he will be
neither victim nor abuser. He will embody instead a male Jew
who neither assimilates to nor reacts against non-Jewish models
of manliness. Friedmann's novel never attracted much attention;
and it is no longer an object of critical scrutiny. Its portrayal of
characters is sometimes clumsy, sometimes sentimental. In some
ways it appears to try to ameliorate the Oedipal implications of
the family dynamic in Henry Roth's *Call It Sleep,* diminishing the
brutality of the father in that novel without canceling his power

over wife and child, carrying past adolescence into maturity the child protagonist who grows up too close to a too-devoted mother, introducing as his lover a fully embodied and sexualized young woman who bears the mother's name, and eliminating the mother from competition with the younger woman and from interference in her son's romance by having her commit what appears to be suicide. Friedmann's Jason can love his Rachel without feeling unfaithful to his mother. In these and other ways, Friedmann's novel takes up the issues Henry Roth's work set in place. It does not measure up artistically to the earlier work. But it represents an important effort to realign parental roles in the process of gendering. It revises the construction of manliness inherited from generations of European Jews. And it marks the explicit entry of awareness of the Holocaust into American Jewish literary discourse on Jewish masculinity.

In other works, however, the delicate cultural work of rebalancing parental roles and revising inherited constructions of Jewish masculinity gives way to a more anguished awareness of the lasting wounds left by the Holocaust on the bodies of Jewish men. These bodies become both texts—inscribed by suffering— and vessels filled with the unquiet ghosts of the past. Anne Michaels *(Fugitive Pieces)* imagines a seven-year-old survivor struggling up out of the swamp that has hidden him from the Nazis, "stiff as a golem, clay tight behind [his] knees," his "mud mask cracked with tears"; he is "wild with deafness" because his ears are clogged with peat,[17] and he is screaming "in Polish and German and Yiddish, thumping [his] fists on [his] own chest: dirty Jew, dirty Jew" (13). In the caked mud that covers him Michaels represents outwardly the foul inner residue of self-disgust instilled by the Nazis in victims who survived. Rescued from his burial/hiding place in a swamp by a kind, strong, learned Greek geologist, this boy discovers he is filled with ghosts: The "grotesque remains of incomplete lives," his ghosts embody the "complexity of desires eternally denied." "They floated until they grew heavier, and began to walk, heaving into humanness; until they grew more human than phantom and thru their effort began to sweat. Their strain poured from my skin, until I woke dripping with their deaths" (14). The boy's rescuer will turn him away from obsession with his beloved ghosts, "diluting memory" (28) with the more general, more detached stuff of scientific understanding.

But the boy's "body remembers them" (170) and eventually he will become a poet, seeking to exorcise his ghosts by imaginatively recalling them into language.

Bodily mutilation also becomes a primary issue for Joseph Skibell *(A Blessing on the Moon),* whose male protagonist drags himself out of the ditch into which the bodies of all the town's Jews have been thrown, to discover—as he bends over a small pond—that he looks "like a mangled dog carcass": one side of his face "is entirely missing, except for an eye, which has turned completely white. Barely hanging in its socket, it stares at itself in an astonished wonder. My grey beard is matted thick with blood, and broken bits of bone protrude here and there thru the raw patches of my flesh."[18] A half-embodied spirit now, he is mostly invisible to others, but at times his wounds ooze and bleed, marking what's left of his damaged body and also staining, invisibly, the world from which he has been expelled. A "dead and mutilated Jew" (120), he haunts this world, wishing to leave it but unable to let it go. He cannot be healed or restored to life, and before he is released into forgetfulness he will need to wander the earth, listening to the sorrows of others both alive and dead, asking unanswerable questions about forgiveness and responsibility.

Michaels's and Skibell's images of the Jewish male body exhibit outwardly the scars that writers of the second generation will develop as inward wounds, incapable of healing. Ghosts also haunt the fictional world of Thane Rosenbaum's *Second Hand Smoke,* but for its protagonist, Duncan Katz, they have become invisible, inaudible. This novel—by a child of survivors—tangles more directly with the inward damage sustained by those who survived the camps and with the crippling and gendered legacy they pass to their children. Reviving the gender imbalance of Portnoy's parents, this protagonist's father has receded even further into passivity than Mr. Portnoy. "Yankee" Katz is a "former German intellectual" who rarely speaks—except to his typewriter. He shows "the wear and tear not so much of age, but of circumstance and bad luck."[19] He has been "rendered impotent by the violence done to his life" (2). Not a ghost, he is a visible but only marginally audible presence in his son's life; he can express disapproval of his wife's treatment of their son, but he can neither change nor improve it.

Mila, the boy's mother, is even more grievously damaged by
the Holocaust. Imprisoned in Auschwitz-Birkenau at fifteen, she
becomes a "young parent" whose body, though "much-abused,"
is still strong. All her movements are "abrupt and often dangerous" (10); her aggressions have been magnified and unleashed
by her years in Auschwitz. Though her husband protests, she
trains their son to be hard, to fight, to travel light, to leave "behind what you must in order to survive" (73). She is never able to
love this American-born son, and she has left behind—in order
to escape from Poland—another, earlier-born child, an infant boy
whose arm she has branded with the number of her own tattoo—
an "act of disfigurement . . . that defined her parenthood" (174).
In these broken and toxic parental figures Rosenbaum represents
"the true legacy of the Shoah" (2).

This legacy passes to the protagonist of the novel, Duncan,
who "would rather have done without" it. He inherits from these
parents "the splintered, disembodied memories that . . . were
now his alone, as though their two lives couldn't exhaust the outrage. The pain lived on as a family heirloom of unknown origins"
(1). His body is beautiful, unmarked by pain: he "had a handsome but rugged face. The nose small, as though stunted. . . .
Compact body. A full head of thick, dirty, blond hair. Deep, exaggerated blue eyes. . . . Muscular shoulders and arms that seam-
lessly filled in the slack in his clothes. The waistline thick but
hard. A strong jaw that concealed a set of unsmiling, gritting
teeth. Like a box he sat there, unopened and shut tight." (20).
Raised to become "the Samurai son of survivors from Miami
Beach" (30), Duncan Katz knows "I am what I am today because
of my mother. . . . I don't like myself very much. I'm her creation.
A creature. A machine" (55). Imprisoned by an inheritance he can
neither fathom nor cast off, Duncan can neither love nor work.
Abandoned by parents whose deaths come too early, deserted by
his wife who takes with her his beloved child, Duncan roams
New York, making angry love to models, working out, and stalk-
ing a former Nazi whom he is unable to prosecute successfully.

When he travels to Poland to find the half brother his mother
abandoned there, he arrives "like a cargo of petrified rock. . . . On
the outside, Duncan looked like an Adonis; on the inside he was
a car wreck" (215). His intestinal system is fragile and his wife
understands that behind the "cement-block stare" (56) his eyes

reveal what she calls "the look of the Six Million in one fragile, but very frightening face" (145). As Mila's and her abandoned child's bodies are forever marked by the blue digits that line their forearms, Duncan's body is inwardly marked by the legacy of his parents' pain. The novel will attempt to imagine the stresses that have deformed Mila, but the most salient subject of the work is the effect of her deformation on the surviving American son. A magnet for pain, programmed to react violently to any provocation, Duncan is unable to heal himself or to attach securely to another. In his meetings with his child, metaphors of linkage, of their hands (165) and bodies (146) holding each other, of even their dreams (221) fitting one another, of anchoring (137) and—in a later novel—docking,[20] speak the desire for attachment that eludes Rosenbaum's protagonists but figures the most precious achievement their imaginations can conceive. Duncan is wholly baffled by his own failures because he cannot fathom the extent of the inner damage he has sustained.

His ignorance becomes an important issue for the novelist, who writes a hallucinatory scene of imprisonment by Nazis in which Duncan's body finally manifests the damage it has concealed throughout the novel. When he is made powerless, and fouled with his own excrement, he can no longer "not see" the residue of suffering that must be acknowledged before the process of mourning—for his parents as well as for himself—can begin.[21] Only when the classically beautiful body of its protagonist is transformed into a shorn and filthy prisoner in striped, stinking rags does the novel introduce the possibility of self-knowledge and acceptance of the past that has eluded Duncan.[22] His transformation brings to a climax this novel's preoccupation with Duncan's diarrhea—a symptom linked with what theorists since Bakhtin recognize as the "gaps, orifices and symbolic filth"[23] that always attended the introduction of grotesque figures into pre-Enlightenment carnivals.

In carnivals the appearance of such figures not only disrupted customary forms of behavior but also symbolically inverted the values on which culture is predicated. Contemporary theorists believe that "cultures 'think themselves'" through the values they assign to all kinds of phenomena (Stallybrass and White 2–3). Extremes of high and low, of what is exalted and what is base, help people to organize they way they think about things and to order their priorities within a culture (Stallybrass and White 3). Carnivals in pre-Enlightenment Europe inverted these hierarchies, enabling people to see high culture from a low perspective, to critique it, even to liberate it, temporarily, "from the prevailing truth of the established order" (quoting Bakhtin, Stallybrass and White 7). According to two contemporary scholars, "carnival is presented by Bakhtin as a world of topsy-turvy, of heteroglot exuberance, of ceaseless overrunning and excess where all is mixed, hybrid, ritually degraded and defiled" (Stallybrass and White 8).

The human body was transformed by carnival representations from a classical into a grotesque body, for carnival used "the material body—flesh conceptualized as corpulent excess" to represent "fertility, growth and a brimming-over abundance" (Stallybrass and White 9–10). In the activities of carnival—fairs, processions, dancing, masks, and comic shows—the human body was imaged as "multiple, bulging, over- or under-sized, protuberant and incomplete. The openings and orifices of this carnival body are emphasized, not its closure and finish. It is an image of impure corporeal bulk with its orifices (mouth, flared nostrils, anus) yawning wide and its lower regions (belly, legs, feet, buttocks and genitals) given priority over its upper regions (head, 'spirit,' reason)" (Stallybrass and White 9–10). The grotesque body, according to Bakhtin, was not individualized but represented all the people, who "are continually growing and renewed. This is why all that is bodily becomes grandiose, exaggerated, immeasurable" (Stallybrass and White 9–10). Later theorists have suspected that carnival imagery may have served not only to suggest renewal but also to embody social revolt against repressive cultures.

Rosenbaum introduces such imagery for a slightly different purpose. In the grotesque body of carnival, celebrants could recognize the intrusion into the familiar world of impulses usually masked, repressed, regulated, excluded by law, by custom, by propriety, or ordered by conventions that control social behavior. But in Rosenbaum's *Second Hand Smoke* Duncan's transformation reveals instead the residue of his parents' suffering in himself, a legacy that must, theorists insist, be acknowledged, and then mourned.[24] The novel suggests that a similar legacy persists—and must be revealed—within the collective body of American

Jewish culture.[25] To mark the parallel, Rosenbaum fashions communal rituals as transgressive carnivals that shame the cultural memories they seek to preserve. As Duncan's transformation into a befouled and powerless victim reveals the hidden, inherited pain that cripples his life, the transformation of classically beautiful rituals into antic parodies of themselves reveals in Rosenbaum's novels the power of invisible ghosts to drain meaning from the ways in which surviving Jews honor the past and commemorate their losses.

In his first collection of stories, the ritual lighting of a *yahrtzeit* (memorial) candle is transformed into a comic, nearly grotesque seduction ritual—turning into social satire the comic attention Roth had focused on individual sexuality, restoring to American Jewish reconstructions of the male body the antic and transgressive possibilities realized so fully in Roth's fiction. But the effect does not break through ethical restraints that limit individual development. Instead, Rosenbaum wants to make plain in both an individual and a collective context, the crippling aftermath of outrage, the destructive, deforming energy of unmourned ghosts that transforms both sexuality and ritual into parodies of themselves.

As the bodies and sexual interactions of male protagonists throughout his works reveal the crippling effects of the Holocaust's aftermath, every seder in Rosenbaum's works is transformed into a carnival. In *Second Hand Smoke* refugee Russians get "stuffed into slick gray Armani monkey suits with black shirts" (290). At the seder table these petty gangsters ogle non-Jewish models and hunt wildly with them for an *afikoman* worth a thousand dollars; there are no Haggadahs, "just tear sheets from glossy fashion magazines" (291); and spontaneous drunkenness replaces the ritual four cups. Duncan's Polish brother sees the event as "spiritually empty" (292). But within the context of the novel as a whole it suggests the corruption of ritual behavior in a culture gone toxic, like the persona of the novel's protagonist, from the hidden damage left by the Holocaust. A culture full of ghosts, unbidden and unrecognized, who haunt the aftermath.

In Rosenbaum's next novel (*Golems of Gotham*) the element of carnival returns not only in another transgressive seder but also in the antics and destructive rampages of the ghosts themselves: spirits of Holocaust writers who committed suicide years after their "liberation" and who return as golems to help this child of survivors become aware of what he really already knows. He is, like them, a writer. But unlike them he does not know, cannot remember, the destructive past that must be mourned. In comic scenes that allow the golems to act out desires precluded by the Holocaust, they ride carousels, drink and flirt with strippers in bars, and finally, out of control, riot through the city turning things upside down and inside out, disrupting established patterns of behavior and expectation that regulate ordinary life and that mask the deadly residue beneath its familiar surface. Like medieval carnivals, these scenes make manifest what convention would keep hidden. Their satiric edge articulates the rage that always underlies antic behavior in Rosenbaum's novels, as though the energy needed to fuel revelation were generated by the holy anger that rises from pain.

Carnival motifs appear even more centrally in Melvin Bukiet's *After*, where damaged male bodies of just liberated Holocaust survivors testify to the moral, social, and spiritual outrage they have endured, and the entire fictional world of postwar Europe is transformed into a "lethal, shabby domain composed equally of lunacy, misery, pandemonium, and pain."[26] As noted in chapter 3, in the camps, Isaac's teeth have been shattered by a sadistic guard and Marcus, a dentist used by the Nazis to forge American currency, can see "no farther than his knuckles," his "genetic nearsightedness . . . deliberately magnified by those who compelled him to wear too strong a pair of spectacles to accomplish the fine work they required" (38). Alter, Isaac's older brother, wears an eye patch to cover a wound acquired from a prewar antisemite. These men learned in the camps that all their "ideas about life were no longer valid" (12). When liberated they believe only that "the one thing that had more value than gold was blood" (295). Emotionally, spiritually, intellectually, and physically transformed by their years in Nazi concentration camps, these damaged men—once devout and simple Jewish boys—become expert black marketeers. They become grotesque versions of their former selves.

Collective behavior and personal interactions are similarly transformed. Because, as the narrator observes, "holiness was not in them" (192), the seder in one newly liberated camp, gutted by the ignorance of an American rabbi as well as by the bitter cynicism of the survivors, is a sad, satirical travesty of ritual. Sexuality is also reduced in the aftermath to a purely animal exercise: either "they paired like rabbits in a cage" (187) or they use women casually—without engaging in delicate courtship rituals or making emotional commitments. The "grotesque feast" (278–79), which accompanies a costume party held on a large yacht near the end of the novel, becomes an elaborate metaphor for both the transgression of all conventions and the transformation of all characters. At this party, "excess was the only principle" (251). A corrupt American general comes dressed as a baby "in an army mess table cloth that swaddled his bottom and was held together by safety pins" (263); one survivor dresses "as a Nazi kommandant, complete with riding crop with which he slapped his boots" (247). A secretary appears as her typewriter, and her boss wears his secretary's yellow dress. "Fact mingled with fiction; it was all too strange. There was no sense, no proportion" (256); one partygoer says he thinks it is a "dream," and a survivor corrects him: "'Nightmare,'" he says. "'No,'" Isaac responds. "'Neither. You don't wake up and find that you've imagined it. The rest of our life is the dream. Turn over, blink, and maybe we're all back in the *lager. Raus*'" (256). Having lost the ability to differentiate dream from reality, these characters struggle to learn the world again in the postwar European frenzy of carnival that turns everything upside down and inside out.

Schemers and fabulators, accustomed to the world of the *lager* where, like the world of carnival, "everything meant its opposite" (296), the survivors experience at this costume party both the nadir of unreality and the beginning of a new life. Presided over by Annubis, the Egyptian god of death, the party becomes an event from which meaning has entirely departed. "'No books, here,'" the yacht's owner points out: "'nothing to read. Nothing to learn. Nothing to regret. Nothing to forget. Nothing to remember'" (298). But below deck one survivor's wife, Rivka, is giving birth to their baby. "There was blood all over the place, not the blood Isaac was familiar with, leeching life's energy from bodies without count, but blood meant to harken in a new life . . . the reverse of the world he thought he knew" (298). Borne to delivery not only by his mother's tears and blood, but also by the story of the Jews, told to Rivka while she labors by another survivor of the *lager*, this baby figures the emergence of energies directed not toward survival alone but also toward the renewal of meaning.[27] The baby, a boy, can appear only after the story has been retold, evoking finally the response it requires. Rivka gives herself to the story: as she listens she imagines herself "removed from everything, not only the tombs of her grandparents and the tombless, disembodied souls of her parents, but from history itself. Her memory was washing away with the waves." Finally she weeps—her tears performing the act of mourning that will allow the future to be born. "'For three years I didn't make a sound,'" she cries: "'not when they shot my father . . . not when they dragged away my mother . . . not when I dreamed about what they did to my sisters'" (301). Her grief and pain as she labors both to mourn the past and give birth to the future are the pivot on which the scene turns—an image of the work awaiting Jews in the aftermath of the Holocaust.[28]

In the stories of yet another child of survivors, that work embraces not only the new birth or reconstruction of the Jewish male body but also the effort to reanimate a sense of what it means to be a Jew. The two tasks are interwoven. For both Rosenbaum and Bukiet, the bodies of Jewish men are damaged and Jewish ritual practice is moribund—weakened by ignorance and contaminated by worldliness. Bodily scars and corrupt rituals articulate the residue of Holocaust damage in both personal and collective Jewish life. In the world of the aftermath where seders become carnivals, their protagonists cannot remember how to be Jews—or even why they ought to perform Jewish rituals. "'Did Jews survive?'" Bukiet's Isaac, newly liberated, asks himself. "'I don't know what a Jew is anymore. I don't think that I bear any resemblance to my father or my grandfather or some ancestor with camels. Things are different now.'" And his friend Marcus adds: "'Did they really say the same things in Babylonia and after Spain? Or is there a difference in the way we speak because of what happened to us?'" (156–57). These survivors have lost the language of belief spoken by their fathers.

Lev Raphael's stories (*Dancing on Tisha B'Av*) try to restore that language through male protagonists who must reinvent themselves as Jews. Many of the young men in his stories are children of survivors, often left uncircumcised by fearful parents who learned from the Nazis the cost of that ethnic marking. The bodily defect signals deeper deprivations. Some of Raphael's young men have been raised as Reform Jews; others have even less awareness of the tradition their parents have abandoned. They speak virtually no Hebrew, they understand little of the residual rituals they still perform. But they are either searching for or moving toward deeper Jewish commitments, more fully informed and observant Jewish lives.

As the stories follow protagonists through their college years—sometimes in Hillel cooperatives, sometimes in Orthodox shuls—these young men speak of Jewish commitments "as fierce and sullen as the clutch of a baby's hand on a stolen toy"[29] for they are still too new at Jewish observance to feel entirely at home with it. Having longed for "some authentic way to be Jewish" (52), having worked toward a "commitment that filled as well as bound" (55), Raphael's protagonists are savoring the Jewish practices that Friedmann's Jason is rebelling against, that Rosenbaum's and Bukiet's protagonists experience as corrupted by the aftereffects of the Holocaust. In part, Raphael's protagonists seek in Jewish observance what their parents have withheld. In one case, a young man desires to learn about Judaism in order to fit the fragments of his parents' lives "into something larger" (77). They are both survivors, but his father is particularly remote and the boy wishes to penetrate his father's silences and anger through "our shared Jewish past, the tradition he had completely abandoned and refused to pass on to me" (78). One of several sons of silent, withdrawn fathers in these stories, this boy seeks in Jewish practice a path toward an understanding of his father, who was—before the Holocaust—a learned and observant Jew.

That Raphael's protagonists are all homosexuals deepens and complicates their spiritual quests. As Jews they sometimes suffer the hostility of tradition to their sexuality. One boy and his lover are asked to leave the Orthodox minyan in which they have been *davening* when the community discovers their relationship and sexual orientation. But in many stories the aura of Jewish learning and practice lends glamour and power to male characters who are magnified both by its privileges and by its accouterments. Raphael's protagonists are always sensitive to the ways in which Orthodoxy favors its men; he develops this awareness through sisters who note, bitterly, their dismissal as functional members of Orthodox minyanim. The title story begins with one sister's observation that Orthodox men say "they needed one

more 'person' to make the minyan of ten, while she and sometimes as many as six other women might be there" (1). She will
say at this story's end, "'it's not my minyan'" (13) and both her
brother and his lover will understand her sense of exclusion. In a
later story when a protagonist says that he likes the "remnant of
the Temple hierarchy even though [as a Levite] he was at the bottom," his sister says, "'Well then, that leaves *me* underground!'"
(117). Her presence on the other side of the *mehitza* allows her
brother to feel "more anchored" (119) in congregations whose
tradition frames him, because of his homosexuality, as an "abom-
ination." Like some of the mothers in these stories, this sister's
loving acceptance seems to offset the boy's uneasy awareness of
his questionable status within traditional Judaism.

But sisters and mothers cannot validate their sons and brothers as Jews. Raphael's women are mostly supportive of their
homosexual brothers and sons. But they are ultimately hampered by their secondariness within the family and the congregation; they cannot insulate these young men from fathers whose
disapproval—silent or voiced—and whose power to exclude is
so damaging. One boy remembers his survivor father peering
down at him, "hands clenched, as if wishing they were equals
and could fight" (2). Another recalls that in "his father's presence" he "often felt as if he had to excuse himself; one look of
those narrow dark eyes would put him so much on the defensive
that even a hello could come out apologetically. Ten minutes
alone with his father could exhaust" this boy (23). In response to
his desire to ride with his taxi-driver father in the front seat his
father says: "'What're you . . . a *baby*?'" The boy will remember
that "those cool, dismissive questions" would pounce on him at
night, "just as he was falling asleep. Strap marks would at least
have faded" (26). These protagonists will long as deeply for their
father's affirmation and love as they long for a living sense that
they are Jews, living Jewish lives. They feel the residue of pain
carried by these angry, withdrawn fathers and sometimes damaged mothers who have survived the Nazis. At times they waver
between fearing the silent fathers and resenting the mothers who
do speak of a past their sons cannot bear to hear, whose ruined
faces hurt their children (23). Raphael—like Friedmann—works
with the problem of gendering in families where paternal affirmation is wanting and maternal support is insufficient to validate

either gender or ethnic identity. Both novelists write large the obstacles that add a new layer of complexity to patterns of gender differentiation conceived by psychologists without regard to the legacy of the Holocaust.

In some ways, however, the mantle of Jewish practice seems to gather into itself the affirming comfort and strength that the damaged fathers in these stories cannot confer upon their sons. To the protagonists of these stories, men who appear "unexceptional" in other circumstances look "costumed and exotic in prayer shawls and skullcaps" (118). One man's "strong shoulders inside the black-striped prayer shawl . . . [and] beautiful large hands flat on the lectern" provoke the narrator to imagine him "in the Temple, strong feet bare, curly hair and beard fragrantly oiled. With those deepset blue eyes, beard growing high on his cheeks, and the muscular frame, he looked distant, romantic, like someone's burly wild grandfather in an old photograph" (121). This man's ritual "gestures were smooth and authentic expressions of a certainty" that the narrator finds seductive. In one scene the narrator gazes at his "long hands on the swelling, shiny challah" (121); in another, he gazes in a mirror at the same hands that render the younger boy's body, for the first time, sexual. The struggle to love, to allow himself to be loved and to respond in kind accompanies in these stories descriptions of male bodies seen as erotic objects of desire. And in most cases the beauty of these men's bodies is highlighted by their participation in Jewish ritual: "I was surprised," one protagonist remarks of his lover, "at how seriously he took services. . . . I saw him *shokeling*—the swaying back and forth that intensely religious Jews do, which I had always found a bit alien and repulsive. But in Jeff it was very sexy, imbued with all the power of his beautiful body. I suppose it also made him more unknowable, almost romantic . . . at that moment no longer an individual, but an expression of faith and tradition" (98). Though the stories repeatedly demonstrate painful obstacles to fully realized homosexual love, they reconstruct the Jewish male body as powerful, beautiful, particularly desirable as it moves into the aura of Jewish ritual life.

In Raphael's work the superficial, cosmetic healing of the damaged Jewish male body occurs partly through the disciplines of running and weight lifting, and partly through participation in traditional Jewish observance. Gender is only slightly bent

in these stories, allowing the development of mature, fully sexualized love between men but not transgressing any other conventional boundaries. Raphael acknowledges the psychological
damage that passes as a legacy from survivor parents to their
sons; he knows the silent anger of outraged fathers and the vulnerabilities of victimized mothers. But the ghosts that haunt
so deeply the world of the aftermath in other works by children
of survivors make no demands in Raphael's work; these stories
avoid the larger, cultural issues raised by Rosenbaum and Bukiet
and the enraged despair these issues provoke. Instead, Raphael's
stories suggest—more optimistically than realistically—that the
legacy of the Holocaust is susceptible to healing by love and the
renewal of religious observance.

Awareness of damage beyond the reach of healing returns,
however, in Aryeh Lev Stollman's first novel about a boy whose
sense of himself as a Jewish man is deeply marked by ancient as
well as recent Jewish experience. In *The Far Euphrates* Alexander
struggles to become a man in a world ruinously scarred both by
the Holocaust and by long exile from the "impossibly remote and
primordial" home of humankind, the Garden of Eden. Schooled
by the expulsion and exile that came as punishment to Adam and
Eve, characters in this novel tend to understand their sufferings
as punishments inflicted by God. The mother of a dying child
believes she is being punished because her husband profited
from jewelry received from Hitler's Jewish victims.[30] Alexander's mother believes that sharing the care of her only son with
her friend, Berenice, might insure the vitality of her next pregnancy (73). But the novel radically questions these readings of
human pain, holding up against them the suffering of innocents.
As I noted above (chapter 4), two non-Jewish children die suddenly when a car drives into the garden where they play. And
twin survivors of the Holocaust bear on their bodies and in their
souls the legacy of sadistic Nazi experimentation. One, the cantor
of Alexander's father's congregation, cannot father a child because the Nazis sterilized him. His twin, born male—now living
as a Christian female—has been similarly damaged, her sense of
her self as a gendered creature altered as radically by her psychic
inability to remain male as by the Nazi scalpels that mutilated her.

The problem of the novel—which becomes the problem of its
protagonist, the boy, Alexander—is to find a way to live in a

world like this one: to become a man, and to remain a Jew, in a world where innocents suffer without cause. Hampered by his mother's anxieties about him, scarred by her withdrawals from him and by her efforts to shape him nearer to her own desire, Alexander becomes peculiarly sensitive to the suffering of others, needing to find a way to become himself and to remain faithful to his collective identity as well, without minimizing or falsifying the pain of human life within the world of exile.

From the beginning, true to theoretical insights into the process of gender differentiation, Alexander will depend mainly upon his father to liberate himself from his mother's power.[31] He has learned from this father's retreats into scholarly work the power of creative energy to accomplish by withdrawal from domestic life a "necessary rearrangement of the hierarchy that exists in every breathing soul, the structure that mirrors the mystical shape of the living God Himself" (7). Alexander will imagine his own withdrawal from daylight and the life of the family as a kind of *"tsimtsum"*: a "self-contraction, retreat"; like "God's withdrawal into Himself to make a space in which He might place the physical universe" (147). During the year of his isolation Alexander's father becomes the boy's only link to the life of the family. He visits Alexander, speaks to him of his own scholarly projects, and leaves books that develop the subjects the boy seems to be interested in. They are committed intellectuals.

But the chief subject of Alexander's study is the body. Alone, Alexander studies his own body and the systems that sustain it, "the nourishing arteries and the veins that run like a sieve through . . . our corporeal selves"; he studies the brain and the nervous system until he feels he "could see the great axonal network that housed our souls and wove our dreams" (154–55). His erotic dreams of a beautiful young man confirm his untroubled awareness of his own homosexuality, even as his readings confirm his awareness of the body as an envelope of the soul. Study and isolation confirm his sense of his own inner strength so that, when his period of withdrawal is over, he cares only for "clear statement, the unobstructed, even if tormenting, truth" (188). He can allow himself for the first time to contemplate his father's beauty (169); he can consider that the soul may be "no more lasting or real than the watery matrix of our bodies" (186); he begins to feel "a warm sense of pleasure at the sight of my man's body lying there on the bed" even though the sight terrifies him (186). Eventually, as he accepts himself, he moves also toward acceptance of the world as it is. Both through understanding and through submission to conditions he cannot understand, he becomes a man, returns to the world, and resolves the problem that the novel has formulated.

Stollman's patience with the mystery of loss and suffering underlies the logic of the boy's development and fashions the deep emotional and philosophical undertone that grounds this fictional world, permeated by the presence of an unfathomable God and by the "tormenting" awareness of all the suffering that flesh is heir to. The adult narrator of this work already knows at the beginning two important things that the boy will need to learn. He knows that "God's sweet letters" are "powerful tools" that bring forth "not only the universe" but, to his even "greater astonishment," his "very own existence" (3). He also knows that "our souls . . . our accumulated knowledge and memory, are locked away, held prisoner within the disintegrating vault that is our corporeal selves" (4). The work itself honors and affirms these dual understandings of enduring symbols and perishable, embodied experience. Letters, from which symbolic words take shape, are given material form in little cakes. Which he eats. Trees become symbolic figures that represent the attributes of God or the branching pathways through which blood moves within our bodies. One tree represents an ancient pagan goddess to the boy's father, but it is also a great giver of real shade beyond the window where the boy's father studies. And it is eventually cut down. The dual nature of the created world, its intricacy both as symbol and as "reality," baffles and intrigues the mind. The work refuses to minimize the generosity and complexity of phenomena, but it also insists on the threats that erode them. All the promises of our collective past, and all the ghosts that haunt the post-Holocaust world are present here, together with the power and beauty of the human body—and the irresistible disintegration that time works upon it.

Neither aggression nor sexuality, neither rage nor mourning, can resolve here the problem of becoming an adult male Jew in such a world. Only deliberate attentiveness to the details and logic of one's own and others' experience addresses the needs this novel formulates. The marks of that attentiveness are everywhere in the novel. Inconsequential observations by unimportant characters become metaphors for significant actions. When a physician explains that the body can heal itself by expelling infection, his explication suggests a way of understanding Alexander's anger at his mother. The narrator also models unusual attentiveness to detail, seeking always accurate description even when understanding isn't possible. This narrator carefully analyzes his own motivations, acknowledging his limitations (4), probing the inexplicable motives that underlie his sometimes eccentric behavior (62), accumulating data about himself and others in a narrative process that gradually reveals a pattern. Sometimes the boy intuits a false or inadequate pattern, as when he imagines that his mother's mentally ill brother is like an insane criminal who mutilated the eyes and genitals of dogs (51). In these moments he resembles the characters who try, mistakenly, to understand suffering as punishment from God. But the work of gathering data enlightens and ultimately transforms him. The process itself, like the narrative process that engages the reader, drawing one through a maze of terror and tenderness, of beauty and belief on one hand and pain on the other, becomes a metaphor for what Alexander's father understands as a search for the imprint of God's hand in worldly experience. "'It's human nature to seek out patterns wherever they may present themselves,'" his father has told him; "'This seeking after patterns is nothing more than man's natural yearning to know God. It underlies every pursuit of knowledge'" (43). To be a man and a Jew in this novel, then, is not to perform rituals, but to search for God within the baffling and unlikely circumstances of corporeal, emotional, worldly experience.

In the end, Alexander will be man enough to accept the death of his father and to assume responsibility for his mother; he will be able to reconcile himself to innocent suffering without forgiving—like his grandparents—those who caused it, or cursing God—like his mother—because of it. He repudiates nothing and no one. The novel concludes, as we have seen, with a scene at his father's graveside in which his multiple acceptances become explicit. Here, in full awareness of the dangers, and losses, and savage cruelties of "time and this earth," the boy is reconciled to life and chooses "to bless God's Holy Name forevermore" (206). In Alexander's acceptance of that apparent paradox, as in his refusal to repudiate any of the figures who have both loved and failed him, the novel confronts the "little secrets" of the post-Holocaust world and refuses to simplify the passage through adolescence that enables boys to become men. Alexander embodies at the end a gendered image of the male Jew that depends upon neither aggression, nor sexuality, nor ritualized obedience for its achievement. Instead, the novel updates a rabbinic model of maleness in which emotional and spiritual strengths are reunited with acceptance—even joy—of the body, and the power—limited but significant—of the mind.

6

Becoming Rubies

Engendering Jewish Women

There is much that we still need to learn about the specific effects of the Holocaust on Jewish women.[1] But our literature
has long been replete with data that can help us to understand
the little secrets that existed before the Holocaust—and that survived it, to shape Jewish women's sense of themselves as gendered and embodied creatures. When Tillie Olsen's Eva in "Tell
Me a Riddle" turns off her hearing aid to listen to her own inner
voices, she embodies a conflict that has both enriched and distressed the lives of Jewish women since Genesis. Tuning out her
husband's demands, her children's memories and expectations,
even her grandchildren's whispers, sorting through the sounds
of her revolutionary and immigrant past beneath the still resonant babble of her marital and family life, Eva struggles to
recover—but cannot reconcile—the separate strands of being
that have met in her. Before she yields to the cancer that enfeebles
and finally kills her, she becomes an emblem of tensions that
have constructed the figure of the Jewish woman, tensions that
can be traced partly to biblical and rabbinic representations and
partly to contemporary cultural imperatives that continue to inscribe themselves upon women's bodies.

Like the rubies whose worth the psalmist says she excels, the
Jewish woman has been formed by both intense pressure and intense heat: the pressure of male-authored imperatives and the
heat of her responses to them. In contemporary American Jewish
literature she is often marked by her exposure to these tensions.

She is sometimes damaged, sometimes strengthened by them. But whether she appears eroded by illness or anorexia, whether she is withered by postmenopausal depletion or blooming with the hormonal flush of youth, pregnancy, or sexual arousal, her embodiments reflect the conflicted legacy that formed and hardened her. In contemporary works by Jewish writers of the new wave, she inhabits a literature that honors the tensions it remembers, even as it moves beyond them.

According to contemporary Jewish feminists such tensions rise initially from what one biblical scholar calls the "gapped and dialogical" text we call Torah.[2] This text preserves both "consent to and dissent from existing power structures,"[3] which were inarguably patriarchal; women in this text belong to the men who father or husband them. But because the dominant culture from which the text emerged "was neither monolithic nor utterly self-confident,"[4] "subversive alternatives," as David Biale points out, survive within it. On one hand, scholars agree that our Bible often figures women as beautiful and strong, sometimes granting them initiative, resourcefulness and power; one feminist scholar even argues that women's images in this foundational text are "consistently the same as [those] of men."[5] But on the other hand, scholars point out, there are narratives here that silence and punish such women or remove them from active roles in the plot. Sarah has the audacity to laugh at God's messengers when told she will bear a child so late in life; she names a son for that laughter, and she protects him from a threatening stepbrother. But she is absent from the narrative when Isaac's life is threatened by his father and his father's God; her death, which banishes her "from before the face" of Abraham and denies her a role in his story, follows hard upon the report of Isaac's rescue. Eve defies God's command in Eden, and she boasts of her own generative power after Cain and Abel are born. But the loss of these children punishes her pride, and by the time her third son is born she has learned to give God credit rather than take it herself.[6] Ilana Pardes sees in these biblical women the residue of earlier, mythical female figures powerful enough to challenge patriarchal assumptions common to monotheism—and potentially subversive or hubristic enough to be disciplined into subordination to the will of God.

Motherhood, which was to remain a defining imperative for Jewish women, becomes the site of terrific struggle in the biblical text. The central issue of generative power that energizes the stories of Eve and Sarah as well as the competition between Rachel and Leah, Pardes argues, also fuels the revisionary Book of Ruth, which grants primary roles to two women who bond with one another instead of competing, who even manage, together, to "build the house of Israel," continuing the family line by seducing a kinsman to replace a dead son and husband (Pardes 98–117). But if generative strength flowers in some biblical women, procreation eventually becomes "primarily a male issue" in the resonant genealogies that mark the succession of biblical generations. From these passages the names of daughters and mothers simply disappear; fathers are presented instead as "primary agents of the divine blessing" (Pardes 56). Adrienne Rich has taught us that "ancient motherhood was filled with a *mana* (supernatural force)"; nowhere else in life, Rich observes, "does a woman possess such literal power over life and death."[7] In the Bible one sees the consequences to self-esteem of the bodily capacity or incapacity to conceive and bear a child in both the rejoicing of mothers and the suffering of "barren women." But from the beginning, female fecundity is a site of tension as fruitfulness comes to depend on a (male) God and as paternity takes genealogical precedence over motherhood.

The friction or tension that Pardes and other biblical scholars have discerned within the Bible among differing "patriarchal figurations of femininity" (Pardes 95) gives way in rabbinic literature[8] to a perspective even more problematical for women. Different scholars offer different reasons for this change. But there is some agreement that as the rabbis worked to construct an ideal society by interpreting the biblical texts and laws they had inherited, sexuality became a site of considerable conflict for them. Mary Douglas taught us long ago that all cultures construct themselves by ordering the chaos of experience in characteristic ways. By drawing boundaries between the permissible and the forbidden, between the sacred and profane, between the clean and the unclean, a society organizes and stabilizes itself, imposing "system on an inherently untidy" world of experience.[9] As the rabbis performed this task they found that it was, as Howard Eilberg-Schwartz points out, "difficult, if not impossible, to reconcile aspects of human embodiment, particularly human sexual relations, with the idea of being made in the divine image."[10] They resolved this conflict to some extent by constructing women as other than and inferior to men,[11] as incapable of generative power,[12] and as potential sources of contamination for men. In rabbinic literature women are more sexually avid and less sexually controllable than men,[13] and they remain attractive to men even though female bodies are regularly capable of polluting male bodies by contact.[14] Always desirous, always dangerously attractive, rendered "unclean" at regular intervals by the biological process that equips her for motherhood, her most important function, she was seen as threatening to men at all times, in all seasons.

To be sure, one needs to see the work of the rabbis as both a continuation of the earlier biblical texts and as part of the wider cultural fabric of their time. Judith Hauptman argues persuasively that the clearly patriarchal elements of rabbinic legal thinking need to be compared with "their Greco-Roman counterparts."[15] Even more pertinent, she believes, is comparison with Jewish legal practices that preceded the rabbinic system, for their work was "bound by a commitment to maintain continuity with the practices of the past and accept the authority of the texts of the past" (4). Even so, she finds that although the rabbis "upheld patriarchy" and "thus perpetuated women's second-class, subordinate status" as the Torah had dictated, they began nevertheless to "introduce numerous, significant, and occasionally bold corrective measures to ameliorate the lot of women" (4). She believes that, "from their own perspective, the rabbis were seeking to close the gap that had developed over time between more enlightened social thinking and women's more subordinate status as defined by the received texts . . . without openly opposing such texts" (4). What they achieved, she suggests, is a "more nuanced patriarchy than is generally assumed," a "'benevolent patriarchy'" (5).

Nevertheless, the social arrangements that the rabbis constructed to control women's sexuality and to protect men from it became in time serious sources of Jewish women's malaise. Daniel Boyarin has argued that rabbinic "exclusion of women from the study of Torah" protected male concentration on texts but also constructed a fraternity and a social system within which a group of men (the rabbis) held power over "the actual practices and pleasures of female bodies."[16] In women's exclusion from study of the Torah Boyarin finds "the clearest structural, ritual expression" of their "inferiority" (156). Torah study was "the functional modality by which male dominance over women is secured in rabbinic discourse" (156), he points out, insisting that through the exclusion of women "from the [study of] Torah as the most valued practice of the society" (169), the rabbis achieved a "generally compassionate and humane (but absolute) control of female subjects through maintaining them in virtual ignorance of the practices that enable ritual decision making" (154). One can only speculate upon the effects this exclusion from textual study would have had on a woman's sense of her own capacity for intellectual work.[17] But when one remembers that rabbinic texts come from a time when all practices connected with marriage and divorce, with sexual behavior, domestic arrangements and conjugal rights, with the power to inherit and control property—when all these aspects of ordinary life were regulated by what Boyarin calls here "ritual decision making"—the nature of women's dependence upon male control in rabbinic literature becomes painfully clear.

Born into virtually absolute dependence upon rulings devised entirely by men, women would probably have absorbed an image of themselves profoundly marked by the rabbi's anxieties about them. Those anxieties marked most deeply the image of women's bodies. Men's bodies entered a state of ritual impurity after seminal discharges, but such events were understood by the rabbis to be "unusual and sporadic." For women, however, as Howard Eilberg-Schwartz has pointed out, "discharges are characteristic" (qtd. in Baskin 24). Or, at least, regular and predictable. Unlike the blood of circumcision, which was "associated with fecundity, the blood of menstruation may be linked with defilement, estrangement from God, and death" (Baskin 24). The Bible had forbidden sexual relations with a menstruating woman during her period; the rabbis lengthened that separation between husbands and wives by seven days. Sexual separation, moreover, was only part of the menstrual woman's enforced alienation. Shaye Cohen observes that "'in Judaism (at least until recently) public sacred space is male space, and the exclusion of menstruants from that space confirms that women, because they are women, are not its natural occupants'" (qtd. in Baskin 28). It may very well be true that many ancient peoples were as mystified and repelled as the rabbis by bloody discharges whose function in the reproductive process was hardly understood. But biology becomes destiny in a culture that projects onto women its anxieties about gender, sexuality, and bodily readiness for the bearing and birthing of children, and that orders both domestic and ritual life and space according to those projections.

Even motherhood was further emptied by the rabbis of its ancient creative power. For the most part, rabbinic culture considered woman's role in procreation a passive one, obligating men, not women, to reproduce after their own kind and attributing to men the active, generative power to create a child. Judith Baskin notes "that the majority of the rabbis distinguished between procreation as an active male role . . . and bearing children as the female's designated passive purpose" (119). For these rabbis, "procreation is a masculine act of potency quite different from the feminine role of bearing and birthing the fruit of male seed" (126). As rabbinic commentary revisioned the matriarchs to affirm the greater power of male seed and divine dispensation in the vital, ongoing work of building the house of Israel, women were stripped of the pride and power that swell with the body as it brings new life into the world.

Again, we can only imagine the effects of these cultural constructions of women's bodies and social role upon their sense of themselves; virtually no texts record women's experiences or conversations in this period.[18] And we need to remember that rabbinic opinion is not single but multivocal. Nevertheless, excluded from marital contact and from sacred spaces during menstruation, forbidden to study holy texts or to sit beside men at prayer in communal sacred spaces, denied an active role even within the processes of reproduction, Jewish women would have confronted an image of themselves saturated with negative implications about their nature, their bodies, their status in the community. "The rabbinic remark that woman is 'a pitcher full of filth with its mouth full of blood, yet all run after her' (B. Shabbat 152a) is in its own terms," Judith Baskin points out, "less a misogynistic opinion than a bewildered statement of fact. A similar expression of corporeal repugnance is the tradition that female pubic hair is a divine punishment for women's transgressions" (34). Even her voice, the rabbis believed, needed to be silenced lest it distract men from prayer or study. Unable to hear the voices of women who first experienced this culture, we have only the word of today's scholars and writers to sketch the ways in which Jewish women's sense of themselves may have been affected by these ancient constructions of their bodies, of their effects upon men, and of their social roles. One such scholar observes that "women have been made in historical Judaism to experience themselves as impure, dangerous, and devalued" (Boyarin, *Unheroic Conduct* 153).

In time, the power of the rabbis to regulate all of Jewish life was eroded by the coming of the Enlightenment—called "the *Haskalah*"—to Jewish communities in Europe. Collective historical experience during this period and the time of immigration that followed it both exacerbated and ameliorated the images of women constructed by ancient texts and rabbinical commentary. Before the *Haskalah* women were active primarily in the home and in the marketplace. Either sharing with men or carrying by themselves responsibility for the economic sustenance of their families, "women's work, economic and domestic, was acknowledged as an essential component of physical and cultural survival, but women as a sex were considered inferior to men."[19] Denied the right to study, "the bread-winning partnership gave Jewish wives some family authority, a knowledge of the marketplace, and a certain worldliness" (Glenn 14). In the carping, kvetching wives of stories by Sholom Aleichem and other Yiddish writers one sees such qualities refracted, as it were, through the eyes of male writers.[20]

But when the Enlightenment came to Eastern Europe it brought first the impulse toward secularization that weakened the control of the rabbis and drew young Jewish women into secular schools. Paula Hyman reports that by 1890 about forty percent of Jewish girls in Galicia were enrolled in public primary schools.[21] Although few of them were exposed to formal Jewish learning, they read European texts taught in a non-Jewish social context (Hyman 58). The *Haskalah* also spread radical political ideas that drew many women into revolutionary work. Naomi Shepherd observes that "Jewish women had all been excluded from [the] intellectual inheritance which was the mainstay of Jewish life, while much of the responsibility for family and communal survival had been placed on women's shoulders. From about 1870 the radical ideas current in Eastern Europe were immensely seductive for young Jews of both sexes. But the limitations accepted almost unquestioningly for so long by Jewish women now intensified their motives for rebellion, just as their practical energies, approved by tradition, sought fresh outlets."[22] Young Jewish women's participation in secular learning and their work for the Bund, the Zionist movement, and other collective enterprises drew them away from their traditional families and into the cities, radically altering the image of femaleness that had long been dominant in Jewish culture.

The *Haskalah,* revolutionary experience, and the uprootings of immigration lie between the women who had struggled in Europe with life as the rabbis ordained it and who had learned to see themselves principally through rabbinical constructions and the women who left Europe and who wrote early-twentieth-century Yiddish stories. But the dilemma of gender remains haunted in these stories by the resonance of ancient restrictions and perceptions. In the stories one sees, from a woman's point of view, the residual shadow of rabbinic contempt for and fear of women's bodies. In Miriam Raskin's "Zlatke," the protagonist embodies conflicts between sexuality and ambition that will persist in later female characters. She knows herself to be "passionate," but her desire for Zavel, her male companion in the Bund, has become entwined with the secret political ambitions that they share. The greatest hindrance to those ambitions is her sense of her own body. She "didn't like her own appearance. Her pale face was still too round, her lips too red, her light brown hair too curly and unmanageable. When she was alone in [her] room she would stand in front of the mirror critically examining herself. She was angry at her full, round body—'round like a pumpkin'—she scowled to herself grimacing at the mirror. She tried hard to walk hunched over, hoping to hide her full, high breasts."[23] She longs for Zavel, she also dreams of "rising in the movement, of girding herself with knowledge, perhaps becoming one of the leaders," and she envies her roommate who is thin, flat-chested and severely dressed. This roommate is said to have "an intelligent look" (*Found Treasures* 121). As Zlatke's abundant and blooming femaleness conflicts here with both her political and her intellectual aspirations, one remembers the old roots of such conflict in the rabbis' distrust of women's bodies and denial of women's intellectuality.[24] This sense of conflict or split between woman's sexual and physical self and her intellectual self will continue into literature by writers of the new wave.

An equally problematic source of tension that appears in Yiddish stories and also continues into new wave writings reflects the conflict between a woman's sense of herself as a sexual being, capable of agency and desire, and her role as a mother. Celia Dropkin's Gysia in "A Dancer" is at first fragile, impetuous, her girlish body "agile, young and slender, her legs slim and lively" as she moves to the "rhythm of her body and the summer life around her" (*Found Treasures* 195). A part of her continues to identify with her light, girlish self; she knows herself best as a dancer who can leap into air. After she marries, repeated pregnancies alienate her from her now heavy, clumsy, maternal body. She begins to live within the memory of her younger, thinner, self. Ultimately she loses touch with the life outside the memory; she stops eating because she fears she will be too heavy to dance. Confined to a sanitorium, she imagines that "her body, unnaturally thin, seems to float in the air" while a "smile plays on her withered lips" (200–01). In this story the split between a maternal and a sexual/artistic sense of self deepens into pathology that will recur in the bodies of anorexics and the obsession with size and fitness in later literature.

Rikuda Potash's mother and daughter in "G'ula and Shulamit" develop a similar sense of division between the maternal and the younger, still sexual, female self that recalls both the ancient discomfort with women's sexuality and the diminishing of generative power within the figure of the Jewish mother. In this story the eldest daughter, one of many children, asks her mother for a kind of nurturance that will dignify the gender they share. Shulamit complains that Hadase, worn out with mothering, never has time to talk with her: "I want that so much," she says; "Your face is tired; maybe I should help you? I know you're always too busy. When I grow up, I won't let you have any more children. They're the reason you never have time. A mother should be beautiful and not tired." In response, "A fear [that] could be seen in her eyes took hold of Hadase." She "understood full well what Shulamit had just said. She washed her hands and dried them on a piece of a child's woolen undershirt. . . . She drew on her prettiest blouse; she buttoned it crooked, so tired were her hands. But her eyes now cleared of all shadows." Instead of the

talk that her daughter asked for, Hadase sat "down beside Shulamit, unbraided and combed her hair, rebraided it and tied it
with a fresh ribbon. 'Take your father's mirror and look at your-
self!'" she says. Shulamit "understood her mother was offering
compensation for something owed her, something she should
have given her and hadn't" (*Found Treasures* 342). In the combing
of her daughter's hair, as in the hasty grooming of her own body,
this woman not only masks her own deprivations but also substitutes for talk—a social/intellectual interaction that might validate both women as subjects—a performance of femaleness that
encourages the child to seek validation, instead, as an object for
the eyes of men. As she performs what Nancy Chodorow has
called "the reproduction of mothering" she fashions her daughter's appearance so that it will be acceptable in her father's mirror. By reflection in his eyes the girl can learn to see her female
self as a desirable object, briefly flowering before maternity and
domesticity wear out her youth and turn her into her mother.

In the wake of the American feminist movement of the sixties,
Jewish women writers of the seventies like Erica Jong, Phyllis
Chesler, E. M. Broner, and Alix Kates Shulman, among others,
developed in memorable protagonists the conflicts among sexuality, intellectuality, maternity, and ambition that appeared earlier in Yiddish women's writing.[25] In the nineties, however, Pearl
Abraham's novels carry these familiar conflicts into writings of
the new wave and reconnect them explicitly to the traditional
imperatives that continue to energize them.

The spirit of defection and rebellion against traditional imperatives comes to life in Abraham's Rachel in *The Romance Reader*.
She watches her "Ma" and "Father" as though they were characters in one of the novels she is forbidden to read. From their
interactions she learns the gendered imbalance of the Chasidic
family. Her mother's frantic scolding and threats disturb the
family but make nothing happen. Her father, a scholarly rebbe
who dreams of having his own shul, is socially and financially
inept. But within the family his word is law. And his silences are
as powerful as his words. When his wife threatens to leave him
and return to her parents in Israel if he commits himself to building a shul they cannot afford, he says nothing to her. Instead, he
"starts to sing" the blessings for the end of the meal. She "gets up
and shoves her chair back with her leg. It falls. She leaves it there

on its side on the floor and goes to her room." After she has left, Rachel and her sister "start humming along with Father, first softly, then louder." Their brother looks warningly at them and says, "sha. No girls singing." When the sisters persist, raising their voices, "Father stops singing and slams his hand down on the table."[26] and Rachel, following her mother's example, gets up "hard, pushing my chair back noisily, not daring to throw it down the way Ma did" (23). The silencing and ineffectuality of women's voices within the power structure of a traditional family is impressed here upon two generations of women; behind it, the brother's warning and the father's angry, violent gesture make explicit the rabbinic prohibition against the raising of female voices.

Rachel's response in this scene foreshadows her later, even more rebellious anger at male authority. She is attracted to men, susceptible not only to their strengths but to their vulnerabilities: it upsets her to see her "Father so needy" (8) and she comforts, when he is punished, the brother whose assumptions of male authority she resents. But she defies parental attempts to control her appearance and behavior. They assert the imperatives of the rabbis, and she resists them. She fights their restrictions on dress; she steals and reads forbidden books. Her mother often appears to be her primary antagonist, but Rachel sees past her to the real source of her authority—wondering at the weakness that paradoxically reinforces her father's power. Her mother is the hands-on disciplinarian, the "bad tongue" (207) of the parental "team," but Rachel's father is always the final authority: "She's my mother, but also a woman, who isn't allowed to hand things to another man directly. To avoid temptation. To avoid spilling seed. Men must be so easily tempted" (244–45). One hears both wonder and contempt in Rachel's attitude toward these parents, especially toward her mother, so loud, vital, and energetic, yet also neutralized by a tradition that empowers its men by disempowering its women.

Rachel's attitude toward her father is similarly complex, for she sees his vulnerabilities yet struggles against his power to constrain her. Believing that "married is the only way I can be on my own," Rachel allows herself to be coerced into a marriage she does not desire. She will feel at her wedding the full weight of male-authored tradition when the grandfather who treated her mother badly when she was a bride, "puts his hands on my head heavily." She bends to protect her hairdo, but "his heavy hands drop lower with me, weighing me down" (245). Within days she learns that her husband will assume her father's authority over her; he will continue to referee her behavior, allowing her to buy a small radio only if she agrees to wear the seamed, opaque stockings that she detests. And he is sexually impotent. Thoroughly alienated by several generations of authoritative Jewish men, she will divorce him. "I want to just be and do, with no one saying they're letting me" (280) she says. The novels she has read, the domestic imbalance and maternal frustration she has witnessed, her family's refusal to let her satisfy her own intellectual and social needs, and her lack of sexual satisfaction in marriage have alienated her from a traditional culture that offers young women only one, limited, domestic role to grow into.

Rachel's aversion to the gender arrangements first conceived by the rabbis and still imposed upon traditional Jewish women by authoritative men is intensified by her awareness of both her own young body and the bodies of women like her mother. Forbidden to swim in the ocean unclothed, she wades in, her underpants getting wet, cold, and heavy while her father and brother undress and return to the family refreshed by their swim (84–85). Wanting to live near the ocean, to spend "most of our day undressed, near our bodies" (169), she enrolls—in her mother's absence—in a course for lifeguards. She exults in the exercise and the sensuality of swimming: "inhaling and exhaling, using my arms and legs to move me through the water, feeling every inch of my body, the water knowing every inch of my body, I'm more alive than ever" (176). But her mother is horrified to learn that Rachel wears a bathing suit in public. "'Aren't you ashamed?' she says, 'showing everything you've got to these children.'" "Everything I've got," Rachel thinks: "Breasts, hips, and thighs, the body of a woman. . . . She and Mrs. Lender . . . leave me there in my life-guard's chair feeling ugly, disgustingly grown-up and naked, fat and ugly" (185). As Abraham traces in such experiences the systole and diastole, the contraction and expansion of Rachel's confidence, the novel delineates the roles of both parents in the insistent covering and shaming of her young body.

Rachel is also aware of—and horrified by—both her mother's body and the changes after marriage in the body of her friend. At the beginning she watches her always-pregnant mother lowering herself heavily into a taxi, using "her arms to help bring her legs in" as she leaves for the hospital to deliver her seventh child (4–5). She has seen her mother's nipples; they "looked funny, and her breasts were long and stretched," and she prays, "please God, my breasts don't grow that way" (21). She has also seen her mother's shaven, stubbled head under the kerchief she always wears: "It was a ball, round and white, something you kick around on a playground." She remembers that in a photograph taken before marriage her mother's hair was "light golden brown . . . [,] braided around her head like a crown" (239). She sees a comparable change in her newly married friend Elke, whose hair was shorn after she was married: "Her once smooth skin is red and pimply, and in her wig she looks ten years older. It's been five months, and already she looks like an old married woman" (280). Rachel knows sexual desire; she hopes that marriage will satisfy it. But when she looks at the married girls in her class "they look different" to her, "not like themselves" (244). To remain, to become, herself, she leaves her husband.

The Romance Reader moves a giant step beyond the gendered and bodily malaise of Yiddish women's stories, even beyond the generalized rage against male authority and bad mothering and the demand for sexual freedom of the seventies. The novel identifies the traditional sources of gender imbalance and women's bodily shame within the malaise of a contemporary Chasidic family—without sacrificing its sympathy for the fathers who wield power, and without simplifying the condition of mothers who submit to the authority of their husbands, who love them and raise their children. Abraham's next novel, *Giving Up America*, continues Rachel's quest "to just be and do, with no one saying they're letting me." This novel's protagonist, Deena, has married an American man of her own choosing. But their marriage is faltering and the novel traces Deena's efforts to clarify—and then to remedy—the sources of her distress.

As she and her husband, Daniel, work to repair and reconstruct an old house they have bought to live in, the house and the work it requires become a metaphor for the labor of relationship. As Deena's impatience shatters the cloudy mirrored surface she wants to remove from the old leaded windows and doors, as the burglar alarm shrills every time they return home, the house responds to them in ways that signal this couple's distress. She will don gloves to work with the shattered glass; he will try to remember to disarm the alarm system. But their efforts to make things work fail to address the sources of stress in this marriage. He is drawn to another woman, a beautiful gentile who seems to represent his own rebellion against the authority of his parents and his Orthodoxy. Deena is uneasy with his inability to share tasks with her, annoyed by his ready assumption of superiority when they try to work together. Because she is accustomed to the warmth and spontaneity of Chasidic spirituality, Daniel's religious practices (as her father predicted) seem cold to her. And she is gradually, finally, alienated by his pursuit of another woman.

These issues come clear very slowly in the novel as Deena struggles to sort out her own reactions, to identify her own needs. Clarity comes to her partly through her work on the house and partly through running—physical activities that embody her need both to be free of constraint, to feel her own power, and to move constructively through accretions that distort the original form and purpose of the house. As she liberates its structure and freshens its appearance, she does the same thing with her own body, moving toward growth rather than lapsing into stasis. While she tears down old partitions with a crowbar, listening to the wood splinter and crack, she also increases the time she spends running, feeling her muscles respond, "shedding slag and emerging minus the dross."[27] Gradually she emerges from distressed confusion: "This was the cure for everything," she thinks: "A body stripped of extras, a body you could live in without shame made up for a lot that was missing" (174). She will use the pain of running to "fight" the "half-living" of her marriage (58). She will confront the disappointments of her domestic relationship as fully as she once confronted her earliest images of her own body:

> She hadn't grown up with the knowledge that looks matter. She didn't treat herself as if she deserved the best. She tended if anything toward punishment. It seemed there were women who were goddesses on pedestals, and then there were the others: she and her mother and grandmothers before her, women born to be wives and mothers. They didn't have their coffee brought to bed because

they were out of bed before anyone else. They made beds, washed laundry and dishes, saw the hamper and sink fill again before they were entirely empty. The men had to eat. The children couldn't be sent to school without breakfast. . . . These were the women who'd given birth to her, and she was destined to be one of them." (159)

Running, now, she reshapes that destiny, purchasing a too-small leather skirt that will redefine her as sexually available, different from the women "who'd given birth to her."

Ultimately she will find in another man the sexual pleasure that had gone "missing" from her marriage. She will give up her job in New York and return, briefly, to her family in Jerusalem before starting the next chapter of her life. But the energy of the novel lies not in the choices she makes but in the labor of clarifying her options. In housework that doesn't merely keep up with a family's needs but rebuilds and reshapes the very structure that may outlive the human life it shelters. In bodily pleasure and exercise that restore to her a sense of herself as both desirable and powerful. This work must penetrate layers of old constructions— of gender arrangements and women's bodies—before Rachel can either discern her own "first intentions" (28) or begin to grow again. The stylistic spareness of the narrative, the reader's sense of enclosure within the uncertainties of this protagonist, speak to the nature of the work that Rachel undertakes: to the determined peeling away of whatever obscures her self and to the refusal of whatever influences would distract her from that essential task.[28]

As Abraham's writings refresh the sense of woman's ancient struggle against male authority and traditional Jewish images of the gendered female body, two other writers of the new wave suggest the ways in which contemporary thought and culture bear upon that conflict—without losing sight of its ancient roots. Jonathan Rosen's 1998 novel, *Eve's Apple*, explores the connections between a contemporary woman's struggle with anorexia, her lover's obsession with her illness, the power of late-twentieth-century Western culture to inscribe its own confusions on the bodies of women, and the contemporary echoes of rabbinical preoccupations that project onto women the uneasiness of men. In Ruth Simon, Rosen's female protagonist, the novel portrays a beautiful yet radically insecure young woman, whose anxieties focus on the image of her body. Ruth had been institutionalized for anorexia as a teenager. By the time she meets Joseph, Rosen's male protagonist, she is—as one therapist says—"inching toward happiness,"[29] her fear of food and her obsession with her own body more or less under control. But like most contemporary American women—exposed continually to the objectification and commodification of the female body[30]—Ruth has "no inner sense of her body at all" (8). She is so thin that she has ceased to menstruate. Yet she lives "by the scale, regulating herself not by appetite but by sheer will." Her fear of the effect on her weight of one chocolate chip cookie—provided by her mother—is sufficient to render her bulimic.

Such fears reflect, on one hand, the coding inscribed on contemporary Western female bodies. Anorexia, of course, is not a disease that afflicts only Jews;[31] it was not uncommon for American girls of Ruth's postfeminist era to realize that the independent lives they desired—not as mothers, but as working women in a man's world—would require them to suppress appetite. Feminist scholars observe that most contemporary women assume they will need to "embody a 'masculine language and values' that belong to the professional area . . . now open to them."[32] They learn to adopt quasimasculine values—"self-control, determination, cool, emotional discipline, mastery"—which will dictate the size of ambitious women's bodies, shaping them "slender" and "spare" (Bordo 19) like the bodies of boys or adolescents. In the course of the novel Joseph will study the literature of anorexia that develops in horrifying psychological and historical detail the efforts of young, privileged women to master their appetite and thus control, if not eliminate, the fleshly swellings that would mark them "female." Under what Kim Chernin called "the tyranny of slenderness," these swellings betray a woman's connection to the natural, rather than the intellectual, or professional, or artistic world; they reveal her "uneasiness about what is expected of women in this culture" (Chernin 73); and they remind her that she will one day become a woman like her mother.

Rosen's novel suggests that contemporary Western culture demands of women not only the regulation of appetite but also submission of the body to a hard discipline, for without constant vigilance and effort, without working hard at diet, dress, makeup, and hair removal they never look good enough. Always minutely self-conscious and radically dissatisfied with her body,

Ruth processes and costumes it from the skin out—performing gender as she modifies the flesh. "She favored lacy underthings, stockings that rose to the upper thigh—but not beyond. The flesh above had been waxed smooth by the strong hands of Russian refugees—they were, she felt, the best—who tore off the hot waxed strips with savage speed and then slapped the skin to prevent pain. Her underpants arched up to the thigh's hollow, courting the hair beyond, which was tamed and tweezed as if for the beach. . . . She mistrusted the natural packaging of the flesh, lovely though hers was. The first time I undressed her," Joseph recalls, "the vision of her body, not merely given but gift-wrapped, nearly knocked me out" (15). In Ruth's work on her body Rosen develops an articulate symbol of what Foucault called "the disciplinary project" that, as Sandra Lee Bartky explains, "requires such radical and extensive measures of bodily transformation that virtually every woman who gives herself to it is destined in some degree to fail." Thus, one theorist argues, "a measure of shame is added to a woman's sense that the body she inhabits is deficient" (Bartky, "Foucault, Feminity and the Modernization of Patriarchal Power" 71).

For a Jewish woman like Ruth this obsessive care of the body and the shame that accompanies the felt failure ever to be clean enough (she takes very long showers) or hairless enough may recall what Judith Baskin describes as rabbinic "repugnance" toward the female body in general and pubic hair in particular. Within the fluid and murky ebb and flow of cultural attitudes toward women in the West, rabbinic attitudes may also continue to play a part. Descended from a long line of women whose hair needed to be shorn or covered, whose biological processes were considered capable of contaminating others, and whose sexuality was seen as a problem rather than a gift, Ruth's insecurities may suggest that she sees herself—in Jonathan Boyarin's words—as "impure, dangerous, and devalued."

Ruth's hostility to her mother, Carol, reveals another site of conflict that is engendered by both contemporary and ancient cultural imperatives. Carol has divorced her husband, taken many lovers, secured an education and a career. Ruth is proud of her feminist mother's education and independent career; "after all, she wanted these things for herself." But she also longs for a "storybook mother . . . who would fill the kitchen with warm food smells, who would . . . convert her own suffering into love energy" (5). She cannot forgive her mother for abandoning her to "frozen dinners . . . public transportation . . . an empty house when school was over. And she could not forgive herself for not forgiving her mother" (5). Her ambivalence and her mother's resistance to maternal imperatives problematize the consequences of what one contemporary theorist calls "the domestic conception of femininity . . . with woman as chief emotional and physical nurturer. The rules require that [domestic] women feed others, not [themselves], and construe any desires for self-nurturance as greedy and excessive" (Bordo 18). For feminists it has long been common to trace this conception of the self-denying mother to nineteenth-century Western ideas about femininity and the family. But the notion also rises from more ancient roots. As Shulamit's mother and the prideful, punished, and excluded women of the biblical and rabbinic texts that lie behind her suggest, mothering women have long been taught to set aside their own ambitions in order to nurture others and to defer to higher authorities.

As they do this, however, they both experience conflict and pass it on to their daughters. Whether mothers long, like Carol Simon, for social, sexual, and professional gratification, or whether they desire social status, artistic or political power, like Miriam Raskin's Zlatke and Celia Dropkin's Gysia, they discover that these appetites are inconsistent with the maternal roles for which their biology, their tradition, and their womanly bodies equip them. Ruth's mother, Carol, rebels against these imperatives, indulging and satisfying her own hungers. Ruth both admires and resents her. At the other extreme, Joseph and Evelyn's mother meets cultural expectations of the self-denying mother. She has sacrificed her own desire for a career in order to serve the needs of her family. But the effects of maternal self-sacrifice are not entirely silenced in her; her daughter, Evelyn, can hear the "secret note of grief" that haunts her mother's voice (61). Daughters of both women seem to suffer, then, from their mothers' very different choices. Ruth becomes anorexic; Evelyn commits suicide.

Motherhood has become a deadly problem in Rosen's novel, where the ideal of maternal service that is biblically and rabbinically imperative for Jewish women, and is still sanctioned by

contemporary Western culture, has lost its power both to reconcile mothers to their prescribed social roles and to reconcile
daughters to their mothers.[33] Emptied long ago, in both biblical
and rabbinic texts, of the creative force that once lived in motherhood, reduced in contemporary culture to the endless work of
emotional nurturance and support, "mothering" is figured in
this novel by images of hovering over and filling open mouths—
a labor performed here more often by male than by female characters. The appropriation of maternal creative power in ancient
texts—first by God and then by human fathers—is ironically recalled in this novel by male doctors, dentists, therapists, and
teachers. In some cases their nurturing or healing power is eroti-
cally tinged: the doctor who treats Ruth's anorexia takes her
"pulse the way gentlemen used to kiss a lady's hand . . . as if he
wanted to press my hand to his heart" (33). In other cases, it remains sexually neutral: Joseph's father, a dentist, tends to "the
open mouths of his patients," hearing there "a ceaseless transmission of the misery of the world" (61). Joseph, a teacher of
English to Russian immigrants, echoes his father's neutral role
as he stands before "a roomful of open mouths," and he "had
to drop English" into every one (39). But his tendance of Ruth is
maternally charged. In one scene she simply holds her empty
teacup out to him to fill (49), but in another she lies at his "breast
like an infant" even though "it was a man's breast, empty and
unprepared" (12). Despite Joseph's zeal as caregiver, despite the
professional commitment of male therapists, teachers, and doctors to tending and healing, the novel figures in the labor of these
male nurturers the futility of their efforts to nourish or to ease the
suffering of women. "If someone wants to be sick," Ruth tells
him, "there's nothing you can do" (216).

Joseph will need to learn that the "sickness" he desires to heal
is not just Ruth's but his as well. He is obsessed with Ruth's
body as a symbol he must labor to decipher.[34] Like the rabbis
whose preoccupation with women's bodies may mask their anxiety about the mystery and potentially anarchic disruptiveness
of human—perhaps even their own—sexuality, Joseph's anxious
concentration on Ruth masks an old anxiety about the suicide
of his sister and his own responsibility for it. He had teased his
sister—"always dieting, exercising, and fretting over clothes"
(70)—about her weight; he had been insensitive to her needs and

envious of her attempts to draw her parents into closer emotional attachments; he had ridiculed her nostalgia for the immigrant past and its supposedly warmer, closer family life. He had even found and kept secret from their parents her desperate letter written months before her suicide. His sins of omission and commission overwhelm him after her death. He begins to suffer from migraine headaches. He puts on Evelyn's nightgown and sleeps in her bed, expressing in this way both anguish at her loss, and guilt, and a desire to take on the burden of her suffering. He transfers these feelings to his relationship with Ruth. As he slyly reads her diary, researches her "condition" at the public library, examines her body for evidence of wasting, and worries—constantly worries—about her health, he becomes a kind of rabbinical midrashist: compulsively probing the mystery of the "other" as text, filling in the gaps left by the resistance of Ruth's body to his rational penetration and control.[35] His sexual and emotional rapport with Ruth wanes as his anxious research increases.

The novel gradually exposes the nexus of Ruth's illness and Joseph's neurotic anxieties. In the web that entangles them the novel also reveals a post-Holocaust malaise that bears upon their discomfort. The structure of the novel juxtaposes Joseph, Ruth, and Evelyn with a series of other characters: the Russian immigrants whom Joseph teaches, the immigrant principal of the language school who escaped the Nazis, the even earlier immigrants who fled European pogroms, and Anne Frank (11). All of them targets of murderous oppression, these characters suggest both the resilience of human beings and the reactive strength that grows out of what the novel will call opposition to "powerful negatives" (40).

Oppositional strength like theirs appears also in the biblical Eve, whose eating of divinely prohibited food is recalled both by the title and by frequent references throughout the work. Dr. Fleck, a psychiatrist, understands this kind of strength, for he knows firsthand the power of defiance to elicit, from sick despair, the urge to live. Stricken with polio in adolescence, he once rolled his wheel chair into a swimming pool and discovered in himself, as his heavy leg braces dragged him beneath the water, the power to swim for his life. Defiance of "powerful negatives" animates all the other structural counterparts to the novel's protagonists as well. The Russian immigrants, drawn together by their defiance of communism and their struggle to assimilate, are clearly life-oriented: always eating, warmly furred, their still-warm though domesticated sexuality defies even Joseph's authority, for when he separates husbands from wives in class, they invariably work "their way back to each other" (37). Defiance animates also the school's principal, Blitstein, who mastered seven languages in order to escape the Nazis. Evelyn is attracted to the way in which earlier immigrants, as she imagines them, tightened family bonds to defy pogroms and to adjust to a new country; she is also drawn to the image of Anne Frank, closed in with her family in opposition to the Nazis. Vital oppositional energy animates finally the image of Eve herself, the disobedient progenitress of women for whom food will become the site of defiant struggle against the imperatives of self-denial.

Lacking in this affluent, comparatively unharried, post-Holocaust culture the "powerful negatives" that defined the lives of earlier Jews, Joseph, Ruth, Evelyn, and their parents do not enjoy the "clean distinctions" that can work like a prism in reverse: drawing energy from multiple sources and focusing in opposition to a single antagonist. Their energies are unfocused. Their family lives are eroded by the pressure to achieve individualized, unheroic self-centered or self-denying goals. Like Ruth, they feel "tiny in the cathedral" (268) of larger purposes as they struggle with personal agendas that are incompatible with domestic and collective imperatives. The children of such families inherit this malaise but don't know whom to blame for the conflict it produces. Ruth, for example, is trapped by her inability to resolve the conflicted cultural imperatives that blur distinctions between a mother's desire and her maternal responsibilities—between nourishing others and satisfying her own appetite for life. Ruth demonizes her mother partly because she cannot clarify the cultural values that intersect in her. Evelyn's mother—depriving herself to provide for her husband and children—presents a similar conflict that bewilders the daughter who, like Ruth, can't find a way to be happy partly because her energies remain confused, unfocused. Both daughters will turn their negative energies against themselves, as will Joseph who suffers from recurrent, disabling headaches.

In general cultural terms, the malaise of young women who hate themselves is linked, Flek explains, to what de Tocqueville

called "the strange melancholy which often haunts the inhabi-
tants of democratic countries in the midst of their abundance"
(276). Deprived of the clear distinctions that can organize us into
defiance of powerful opponents, young women in this culture
fight themselves instead of other adversaries, feeling in their
bodies the vexed uncertainties of appetite denied, starving or
killing their bodies to articulate their malaise. Both "the weapon
and the wound" (169), Flek points out, the bodies of women become the texts upon which the suppression and resurgence of
powerful appetites get inscribed. Contemporary theorists have
unearthed the cultural roots of his argument.[36] Anorexia is not a
particularly Jewish problem, but Rosen not only marks it ethni-
cally as belonging to contemporary American Jews, he also connects it—in Joseph's obsession with Ruth's body—to a more ancient cultural malaise: the unconscious contribution to women's
suffering made by men who seek, by analyzing and controlling
women, to heal themselves.[37] Like the rabbis who projected onto
women's bodies anxieties about sexuality that they could not
identify or control within themselves, Joseph, ignorant of his own
neurotic burden, unconsciously allies himself with the malaise in
his beloved that he thinks he desires to heal.

In both Joseph's obsessive analysis and Ruth's bodily malaise,
then, this novel links contemporary and ancient cultural imperatives that afflict women's bodies. In the distress of these and other
characters the novel also formulates the situation of contemporary American Jews, caught in the wake of the Holocaust. Joseph's father, for example, desperately grieves his daughter's
death, listening while he sleeps, eats, and works, to both news reports of the world's misery and to the passionate drama of grand
opera. In him Rosen embodies the dilemma of a culture trying to
move forward when it is handicapped by a half-conscious awareness of—and a need to mourn—terrible losses. In Evelyn and
Ruth, Rosen suggests the dilemma of a culture that cannot legitimate its own desires. These women punish themselves because
they have no goal larger than what Evelyn calls her own happiness. Rosen's novel introduces these cultural and historical issues
into the literature of the new wave as it figures the embodying of
Jewish women. In its wide symbolic embrace, however, the novel
never muffles its primary care for the pathos of Joseph's and
Ruth's struggle to know themselves and to hold onto one another.

Like Rosen, Rebecca Goldstein considers the ways in which both contemporary and traditional cultural imperatives inflect the gendering and embodying of Jewish women. But her emphasis is philosophical: she shows us how the habit of thinking in binaries—male/female; body/mind; past/present; death/life; good/evil—both reflects traditional patterns of thought and restricts our awareness of the fullness of experiential reality. She concentrates particularly, in several important novels, on the power that long-standing habits of thought exercise over our images of ourselves, of our bodies, and of one another. Because Goldstein has been enchanted since childhood by both fiction and philosophy, her novels characteristically embrace both ways of looking at, thinking about, and representing human experience. But she is not unaware of—and her novels always recognize—the profound difference between them. Indeed, differences of many kinds become issues for her as various dualities begin to mirror the dichotomous habits of thought that also shape our sense of what it means to be male or female.[38]

For contemporary theorists, the word "difference" is shorthand for a binary way of thinking that first divides phenomena into opposites, and then valorizes one over the other.[39] We construct such a binary when we first conceive "human" as "male" or "female." Goldstein, raised in an Orthodox Jewish family, knows that our earliest and most lasting conceptions of gender are not innocent. She knows how Jewish tradition differentiates men from women. Her first novel embodies in its female protagonist the gendered consequences of that cultural differentiation. Renee Feuer, also raised as an Orthodox Jew, learns very early that men matter, but women do not. Though she has—like the writer herself—finessed her tradition's reluctance to educate its women, though she has won academic honors as a student of philosophy, she feels only a "deepening sense of guilty failure" because her mother has taught her that a woman is only "who she marries":[40] "This is why God gave you such good brains," her mother tells her when she attracts the romantic interest of a mathematical genius, "so that you could make such a man like this love you" (57). Her mother's shame at Renee's budding adolescent body (67) has left her so detached from her own physical appetites and satisfactions that she experiences sex only in her head (19); thus ancient rabbinical anxiety about women's

sexuality finds its way through a traditional mother to this rebel-
liously rational, antireligious contemporary daughter.

Not sex but vanity drives Renee's interactions with men.
After Noam, the genius, first makes love to Renee she remembers mostly how she must have "appeared to him, lit up against
the brilliant blue sky . . . while inside my head sang the triumphant thought: I am making love to . . . the genius" (41). Not bodily pleasure but narcissistic reassurance is what Noam's attention
provides. A later, adulterous, lover will teach her deeper acceptance of her body by making love to her during her menstrual
period—an act abhorrent to and prohibited by rabbinic law.
Through this lover's defiance of rabbinical imperative Renee will
both confront and overcome her "Jewish distaste for the body"
(251), her fear of male "revulsion at the state of being female"
(253). But her sexual escapades before and during marriage articulate her efforts to matter to someone rather than to express or to
satisfy bodily desire. In Renee one sees clearly the interweaving
of gendered and bodily self-awareness, as the insecurities constructed by traditional Jewish culture in this woman interfere
with her access to her own sexuality.

Goldstein juxtaposes with Renee another woman, her sister-in-
law Tzippy, who fulfills—instead of defying—traditional requirements of Jewish women. When Renee's beloved father lies dying
and his family, numbed by the smell of death, has withdrawn
from him, Tzippy draws him close, holds and talks to him "as she
always had" (172–73) and receives his last smile. She bears a child
to carry this father-in-law's name, and she is "happy," "completely absorbed in her maternity" (172). Other Orthodox women
in the novel, like Renee's former friend, Fruma, are also "happy"
within their traditional roles: "More than anything else I want to
be a good mother . . . just as I wanted to be a good daughter,"
Fruma says (177); but "deep down," she feels she is "not really an
adult yet. . . . Someone just handed me the script and I started
reading" (177). These women accept the gendered limits set
by the "script" that honors traditional imperatives. They grew
up understanding that "it is God's way for women to wait on
men" (135), that men get served first at dinner, and that men's
portions—even of education—will always be larger than their
sisters' portions. These women, like Renee's mother and aunts,
stay within the boundaries constructed for them by tradition.

Confined by those boundaries, their bodies grow soft and shapeless while Renee remains thin and beautiful. But Renee's psyche is disturbed: "permanently disfigured—encrusted with the oozing scabs of ancient bruises" (169). Like Rosen's Ruth and Evelyn, confused about the nature and essential value of their adversaries, Renee is both defiant of tradition and nostalgic for what she defies; she continues to love the tradition that oppresses her. In Rome with Noam at an academic conference she wanders into a shabby Jewish restaurant and meets there survivors of the Holocaust sharing a Sabbath meal. Leaving them, she weeps: "the longing in me—for my father and his world—had risen to my eyes and was blurring my vision. And then suddenly I was back inside it, inside Shabbos. The world had that different feel, that closed-off, restful, floating calm. I was back inside its space, enfolded in its distances, feeling the enforced but real sense of serenity, bounded round by prohibitions" (123). Like Rosen's more thoroughly secular American Jewish women, Goldstein's Renee struggles against an antagonist whose value she cannot entirely deny.

Throughout the novel she will remain divided: between mind and body, between religiosity and rational secularism, between marital faithfulness and adultery. These differences split her persona; the binary split itself achieves formal representation in the divided narrative voice that often edits or contradicts itself from within parentheses (74, 76–78, 110,135, 169, etc.).

The end of the novel attempts to resolve this split, but the problem of difference that has arisen from the site of Jewish women's bodies and gendered self-images persists and will be enlarged within her subsequent novel, *The Dark Sister*. Wider cultural tendencies to bifurcate and valorize one side of an opposition over the other complicate in this novel the gender issues alive in the earlier one. Narrated by Hedda, a Jewish woman writer who sees herself as her sister's opposite, and who tells the story of two other supposed sisters, two brothers, and three women named "Alice," this novel "gets at . . . truth" by working on what the narrator calls "a little system of two mirrors. A Parallel Plot . . . two stories played off against each other."[41] The novel thus embodies a binary construct in which many kinds of difference reflect one another. Within the doubled plot—as in a mirrored room—Goldstein envisions a multiplicity of characters and family groups. Hedda's family story mirrors the stories of several nineteenth-century figures: philosopher William and novelist Henry James, their repressed sister Alice, William's domesticated wife Alice, astronomer Vivianna and housekeeper Alice Bonnet, and two spiritual mediums. Differences of many kinds—among science, philosophy, and art, between domestic and romantic love—all familiar components of Goldstein's earlier fiction, intersect here with speculation about ghosts and spirits, who belong to a world at once different from and connected to the quotidian social world more familiar to contemporary fictional characters.

Divided by time, geography, ethnicity, and family, many characters and places in this novel share, nonetheless, significant characteristics. Such repetitions emphasize relationships, suggesting that affinities, likenesses, connections exist despite and beneath apparent differences. Irascible blue eyes appear in Hedda's twentieth-century father, in the Bonnet women's father, and in Doctors William James and Austin Sloper a hundred years earlier. Probing or chastising index fingers belong to both the predatory man who deflowered Hedda when she was sixteen and the pointedly rational, analytical men, William James and Dr. Sloper. Several characters live in towered places, the tower itself becoming not only a phallic pointer asserting itself against the mystery of heaven, but also a womblike space of enclosure where art is made—and science too. Doubleness and replication become formative presences within this work, for the novel not only uses reflective parallels to "get at truth" but also takes multiplicity as its theme, suggesting that conventional assumptions about difference limit experience, dividing it arbitrarily into binaries when in fact reality is always multiple, various: containing differences instead of polarizing them·

It's useful to remember that Jewish law—like foundational social and legal structures in many other cultures—is itself constructed, as Mary Douglas pointed out, by a system of binaries that divide the permitted from the forbidden.[42] In this novel, Goldstein works toward a more capacious, more fluid, less rigidly divided sense of reality, not only by mirroring in many characters and settings features that would ordinarily be ascribed to only one or another but also by subverting conventional habits of thought that conceive as monstrous any phenomenon too complex, too vast, or too amorphous to be narrowly defined. Women, their gender and their bodies, demonstrate this idea as Goldstein counts the ways in which the conventional idea of "femaleness" limits and deforms the human beings it tries to define. She quotes repeatedly Adrienne Rich's lines: "A woman in the shape of a monster / a monster in the shape of a woman / the skies are full of them." And she draws in this novel several women characters who reflect Rich's insight into female monstrosity. The narrator, Hedda, outgrows conventional limits of female size: "She stood six feet two . . . she weighed one hundred and forty-two pounds. She was thirty-eight years old and was still waiting to need a bra" (9). Bodily overgrowth is linked in Hedda with emotional excess: "She felt sometimes that her anger could not be contained within the precincts of her person. . . . She felt herself the repository of all the unowned anger of all the gently smiling females of all the unenlightened (that is, of all) times. And as she sopped up this floating feminine fury, it seemed to her that she grew still huger (for what else was it that had deformed her in the first place if not the unowned fury of her own grotesque mother, the Saint of West End Avenue?)" (7). Emotional and bodily overgrowth signal in Hedda the problem with rigid boundaries that constrict women's emotional range.

It's hard for women themselves to conceive the fluid, changeful nature of the emotional life they experience in this novel. Hedda sees her mother as grotesque because she is changeable beneath her gendered social mask: she could "be soft and silky— and then, in an instant, become deadly, choking off all air" (184). She has both a public and private face. In public she is "righteous and forbearing, slow to anger and full of great mercy" (103), because she lives for the "approbation" (11) of others. But in private her children can perceive the emotional damage caused by their father's abandonment of his wife and children. The pain and rage of the abandoned woman, condemned by convention to mask itself in public as self-righteousness and forbearance but rushing out of hiding behind the closed door of their apartment, terrifies and alienates her daughters.

Goldstein embodies the distress of women, shrink-wrapped in public personae too restrictive to articulate the real fullness and complexity of their being, in two memorable images of female flesh pouring out of its restraining undergarments—to the horror of male onlookers. When clothed, William James's wife Alice is "an example of the no-nonsense, invincibly healthy-minded female, over whom morbidity had no hold. She practiced the gentle art of domesticity with a calm and patient hand" (122). But one evening William watches, unseen, as Alice undresses before her mirror: "The female flesh of her came pouring out from its brutal encasement, bruised red and purple where the stays had cut most cruelly into her. Her drooping maternal abdomen was mottled and puckered. A fiendish riot of female flesh—of eddying swirls and dimpling swells. The great white mounds that had had the shape long ago sucked out of them by the five infant mouths. Falling down, down, melting into the tumbling abdomen that was falling down, down. . . .William stood and stared. . . . He stood and stared, paralyzed by his mounting horror" (120). Behind this epiphany of maternal female flesh[43] one senses Goldstein's awareness of rabbinic horror at the messy mystery of woman's body. In this novel, as in the *Mind-Body Problem,* something like that horror is also felt by women, who have been taught to see their bodies in their fathers' mirrors.

More important, however, is the novel's suggestion that female shame and male horror rise directly from dualistic tendencies of thought that may be common now to many cultures that define gender rigidly and harshly—like the corsets and stays that "brutally encase" the flesh they bruise, reshape, restrict. In the figures of two other women Goldstein develops this facet of the novel's wider argument against binary thinking about gender. Hedda's gigantic size and the outpouring of Alice James's abdomen and breasts call attention through the flesh to the vagaries of human feeling—that flows where it will, into new and entirely unsuspected channels if necessary, ignoring at flood tide whatever banks or boundaries ordinarily restrain it.

In the Bonnet sisters, however, intellectual rather than emotional or physical development drives one character beyond the boundaries set for women so that she becomes not gigantic, and not duplicitous—but her own double. Because, as Hedda knows, "women of genius . . . have always been seen as . . . freaks . . . of nature," because "the kinds of gifts that are . . . celebrated in men . . . are seen as . . . ghastly and . . . monstrous . . . in women" (217), the novelist splits a single female person into two personae: putative sisters—one of whom is pinched and repressed into conventional, domestic female shape and attitude while the other, uncorseted, develops into a gifted astronomer who seeks a "darkened star," hidden because of its own immensity in the night sky (92–93, 242).

In the end the two "sisters" will be revealed as one persona so complex, so deviant from the conventional pattern of woman, that even William James will be unable to understand that both "sisters" inhabit with equal right a single body. Analysts in the novel hypothesize a pathology called "Schizotypal Personality Disorder" (212)—William James will fail to recognize each "sister" as part of a whole female person, and his wife Alice will suspect "that the female state is in itself a most horrible deviation" (245) from the male norm that we call "human." But the novel will insist that rigidly defined, gender-differentiated "norms" and "roles" not only "brutally encase" women's minds, bodies, and feelings but cruelly impoverish the disorderly abundance of experiential reality.

As a feminist Goldstein is profoundly sensitive to the damage that women sustain when culture allows them to be only part of who they are, when they must fit themselves as tightly as possible into the role marked "female." But as a novelist and philosopher Goldstein is also aware of the more general harm worked by restrictive misrepresentations of what "human" is and means. Benign and sympathetic men of science in this novel cannot grasp any better than the rabbis the real complexity of human experience. As the rabbis sought to limit, to order, and control awareness of mysterious and potentially anarchic processes, so William James, watching one "sister" become another, assumes there can be only one "rightful resident" of the body they actually share (250). But Hedda, the writer/narrator, senses the real interconnectedness of disparate phenomena that the habit of binary thinking in this novel presses into categories and polarizes into difference. She always knows what William James will ultimately discover just before he dies: that "there is a buried place in the psyche, where the boundaries between us all dissolve. . . . We with our lives are like islands in the sea, or like trees in the forest. The maple and the pine may whisper to each other with their leaves. . . . But the trees also commingle their roots in the darkness underground, and the islands also hang together through the ocean's bottom" (264). This image of life and self as continuum, unboundaried and unconfined, defies the regulatory differentiations of the rabbis even as it opposes the centuries of Western thought that first divide and then polarizemale and female, valorizing the former over the latter.

The sense that boundaries and binaries restrictively misrepresent reality becomes even more pronounced in Goldstein's latest novel *Properties of Light* (2000). The title itself denounces binary thinking by calling attention to the "paradoxical duality" of light: "both wave- and particle-like."[44] The work again undercuts our sense of boundaried individuality by repeating identical features in several characters. Narrative structure subverts conventionally rigid, linear temporal distinctions by moving back and forth among historic, cultural, and personal moments instead of dividing time into "before" and "after." There are no parallel plots or mirrored spaces here. Instead, there is a vast continuum— contained by time like water in a glass.

In all these ways this novel subverts habits of thought that rigidly differentiate human experience, ordering and stabilizing phenomena so deeply intermixed that mind and body, past and present, science and poetry appear connected rather than divided.[45] Scraps of Yeats and Blake illuminate science here. Samuel Mallach and his daughter, Dana, both physicists, not only think but also feel the physics within them, within the muscles of their own bodies (46, 172); their bodies can dance the abstract truths their minds perceive. Instead of differentiating sexual from intellectual energy, this novel connects them—philosophically through the discipline of Tantrism that "identifies eros . . . as the source of all creation" (110–111) and fictionally through the marriage of Samuel Mallach to a woman whose erotic intensity once made vital his scientific work. Mallach's daughter, Dana, and her lover, the mathematician Justin Childs, will practice the Tantric discipline of sexual ecstasy, rising from their bed in the morning to work with Dana's father on equations that will ground his theory. "All Things linked are," this novel asserts in multiple ways: "thou can'st not stir a flower, without troubling of a star" (95). The novel embodies continuity and connection as its vital principles.

It looks in a new way at human behaviors that seemed, in Goldstein's earlier novels, to be flaws in character. Changefulness in women appeared to be a flaw in the earlier novels when characters needed to define themselves and others in stable

ways. Like the rabbis who sought to order collective life, to
steady it within an uncertain world, even Hedda—like William
James—was troubled by configurations of her mother's character that seemed to shift as she looked at them. In this novel, however, the protagonist Dana is "a girl hammered out of furious
gold" (58) whose name links her to the mythical Danae, a human
girl beloved of the changeful god Zeus who made love to her in a
shower of golden rain. In Dana the novel develops most fully its
interest in the ways in which women actually model by their
changefulness the fluid, indivisible, defiantly uncategorical nature of reality. We see her through her lover Justin's eyes as the
complex, many-sided woman she actually is. Scarred, aged, and
limping when the novel opens, she appears to us also as she was
when Justin met her: graceful and lovely—her "light was of
some different world, striking imbalance and wild awe wherever
it fell" (67). Children of mixed Jewish and Anglo Irish parentage,
they share also the love of intellectual work—though Justin is at
first put off by Dana's brilliance, surprised that genius should
surface in a lovely girl. He finds even more unsettling Dana's
power both to change and to keep hidden the "inner life" (21)
that he needs to understand.

Like Dr. William James and Dr. Austin Sloper in *The Dark Sister*, needing to analyze and theorize the hidden variables that
animate women, recoiling from epiphanic moments in which the
fluid complexity of women reveals itself beneath its rigid social
masks, Justin is profoundly disturbed by the variety and richness
he senses but cannot see clearly in the woman he loves: "She had
an inner life. . . . She had a mind. . . . It was a torment to need so
desperately to know the contents of her mind, the hidden variables behind her words and silences, and laughter" (80). He is
even more troubled by the way her body and face seem always
to be caught in process, as though they existed, like light itself,
in a state of continual becoming. When they first make love he
records this capacity for changefulness that will continue to haunt
him: "She turned her back to him then . . . one arm cast back over
her head, slightly altering the shape of her breasts. . . . Only minutes ago, sitting astride him, she had seemed almost terrifying in
what she knew. Now he . . . saw that she was smiling, her lips
playfully curved. . . . He could read the intent out of her mouth.
Sometimes she was like this, childish and charming, and other

times she terrified him by what she knew" (25–26). He sees "the expression on her face changing . . . so that the little girl who had been present just a moment before, asking me her naive questions, instantaneously vanished" (136).

Most terrifying are the passages in which he connects the sexual woman who first took him, open-eyed and pitiless, into the tenderness and ferocity of her lovemaking, with the apparently vengeful woman who seemed to watch, similarly still and staring, as he burned to death in the car she had just crashed (76–77). Not until her own death and their reunion will he understand that stillness; she will reveal that she had meant to kill herself, not him, that her surprise at being alive delayed her response to his peril. Seeing her scars, he remembers that she had crawled back into the fire—too late to pull him out (233). The ambiguity of these revelatory moments is recorded in both his loving idealizations of her and his daunted recognitions of her anger and suffering when he sees the "shudder rising up through her, pulling all her features along with it, so that she was for one single instant a ghastly ugly woman . . . recognizably the same Dana Mallach, but she was ugly" (232). Justin too will change in the course of the novel. Though he has died before the novel opens, he narrates for us, kept present in time by the power of his attachment to Dana. He describes himself at the beginning as a thing that hates (3) but recognizes himself eventually as "a thing that loves" (187). Both are true. But Dana, like the god Zeus, master of metamorphosis who loved her namesake, embodies more dramatically the principle of continuity within change: multiple truths pass vividly through her body and across her face, appearing to transform her but actually just making visible the rich possibilities of selfhood that lie within a single persona.

The boundary between the writer and the authorial persona demands—like all boundaries—respect. But in Goldstein's case it seems peculiarly permeable. To some extent, the rabbis seem to furnish the ground from which her fictional visions of human experience rise. Her early awareness of herself as what she has called a "yiddishe maidel of questionable worth"[46] appears to lie coiled beneath the insecurities, defiances, and oscillations of Renee Feuer. Her sense of the ways in which cultural imperatives limit and misrepresent women appears to owe something to both the tradition in which she was raised and the philosophical culture she has studied; her response to those limits and misrepresentations persists within the emotional, physical, and intellectual burgeonings of Hedda, Vivianna, and their mothers, and within the memorable metamorphoses of Dana Mallach. All of Goldstein's fictions might be seen to wrestle with the problem of too-limited embodiments—like those the rabbis first projected onto Jewish women—and with the possibility of understanding that our gendered bodies, which seem to define us to ourselves and others, are actually inadequate constructs that reflect only partial truths about the nature of human beings. These challenging and beautiful novels extend awareness beyond conventional limits in much the same way as Hedda, and Vivianna, and Dana outgrow the physical, emotional, and intellectual limits that restrict them as women of genius.

Recent work on the gendering and embodying of women in American Jewish writings, then, distinguishes the lasting effects of ancient assumptions and ways of thinking that have shaped women's sense of themselves since long before the Holocaust. Abraham's work demonstrates that these assumptions may impoverish our sense of what "female" means and cripple the ways in which we learn to address what appears different from ourselves. Rosen's novel suggests that in a time when we wrestle not with aggressors against the Jews but with adversarial impulses within ourselves, perhaps women's struggle to fulfill ancient collective expectations, to become more precious than rubies, takes second place to another kind of struggle: to see how cultural imperatives limit—and persistent anxieties about sexuality and desire obscure—our sense of ourselves and others. And Goldstein's work sees beneath traditional and contemporary efforts to rigidly gender the female body a persistent, underlying instability that threatens all our certainties. Her novels encourage us to imagine that the profound disturbance of change may, if we will let it, speak to an unsuspected richness of human experience, in which the "other" both is and is not us. Finally, in the wake of massive cultural and human losses, perhaps it will seem appropriate that all these writers, looking through the lens of women's continuing struggle with ancient conflicts, are clarifying the residual power of our earliest ideas to tell us who we are and who we may become.

7

Midrash as Undertow
Looking Back and Moving On

Near the end of Aryeh Lev Stollman's *The Far Euphrates* an adolescent boy watches from the deck of a boat as the ashes of his friend's body, just emptied from their urn, gather "themselves like a pillar of cloud over the water. A brilliant shaft of sunlight drove through the cloud, and for an instant it seemed on fire. The marvelous pillar stood still a moment, hesitated, then moved slowly away from our boat. 'Don't look back,'" the boy calls out. And the pillar disappeared."[1] A song composed for this ceremony reinforces the boy's command as a Cantor sings words drawn from the last line of the biblical Book of Daniel: "*V'atah lech l'kaytz.* . . . And go thou on thy way" (136). Against the insistent forward thrust of these instructions, however, the novel as a whole really does "look back." It reconstructs the boy's family past. And its references to pillars of cloud and fire "look back" even further—to the guidance lent by a biblical God to a people wandering in a wilderness. As one unwraps the implications of this passage, looking back and moving on become two facets of a single, complex process—like the undertow that accompanies a breaking wave.

American Jewish writing of the eighties and after is shaped by such a process. In my earlier chapters I discussed some of the ways in which writers respond to this doubled trajectory. Second-generation writers "look back" as they take on the cultural task of reckoning massive losses; they also mourn—and move on. Other writers yield to the undertow of the past as they

174

reconstruct the image of "home" or confront historic images of Jewish maleness and femaleness and then move beyond those images. Nowhere in contemporary writing is this profoundly ambivalent sense of how we move through time more evident than in works formed by what one could call "the midrashic impulse":[2] the interpretive effort to re-connect with textual sources. This effort has a long, distinguished history, but in contemporary American Jewish writing it serves a distinctive cultural purpose. It instructs collective memory, highlighting by reflection the "little secrets" that are "still there" and that seem most crucial to our experience in these decades.

According to most accounts the earliest midrashists, interpreters of the Hebrew Bible, were rabbinical scholars of the first five centuries.[3] Gerald L. Bruns has argued that the Scriptures themselves had participated in an even earlier hermeneutical process "in which biblical materials" were "rewritten" in order "to make them intelligible, applicable to later situations."[4] Intelligibility and applicability became the twin desiderata of midrashic work. Rabbis took up this work of interpretation, Bruns suggests, partly to clarify meaning; they wanted to overcome the distance between the text and themselves (629). They cared also about the moral, behavioral consequences of scriptural teaching. They were "concerned everywhere with the force of the text as well as with its form and meaning . . . the sense in which it is binding upon life . . . the way it bears upon human action and the quality of conduct in the everyday world" (628).[5] In the beginning, then, interpreters sought both to clarify and to reinforce the moral resonance of their foundational text within contemporary experience.

These intentions persist into writings of our own time. But now the impulse to "look back" even as we move on produces texts that also perform the work of collective memory. The notion that memory can be collective is counterintuitive, for we know how deeply private an act it is to remember. A facial expression—the lifted eyebrow or crooked smile—the warm pressure of a familiar hand, or the sound of laughter that memory recalls can tighten the throat, disturb the rhythm of the breath. But we also know that groups of people share a sense of a common past. In her last work Susan Sontag connects these insights: "All memory," she writes, "is individual, unreproducible—it dies with each person. What is called collective memory is not a remembering but a stipulating:

that *this* is important, and this is the story about how it happened."[6] We "instruct" memory, Sontag suggests, by telling stories, using narrative to "make us understand" (89) the sometimes harrowing, singular images of our shared past. For her, visual images are only "freeze-frames" that narrative makes coherent, meaningful, persistent in memory.

Sontag's emphasis on our need to make the past understandable, and thus memorable for one another, is foreshadowed in the work of Maurice Halbwachs, an earlier theorist who also believed that we do—together—the work of memory. We depend on other people, he explains, to keep remembrances alive.[7] Only individuals actually remember. But as they pass memories back and forth (31) they create collective memory that "endures and draws its strength from its base in a coherent body of people" (48). Fragments alone will not be memorable; they need to be connected in a meaningful way in order to be remembered. In Halbwachs's view, Mary Douglas explains, we remember collectively only "when some new reminder helps us to piece together small scattered, and indistinct bits of the past" (5). The "meaning" of these "bits of the past" needs to be made clear (61), for time becomes "real" to us "only insofar as it . . . offers events as material for thought" (127). As these theorists describe the social and cultural processes that allow us to recall a shared past, they suggest the nature of the cultural work performed by much contemporary writing. Animated by the midrashic impulse, contemporary writings speak to us of what has been important, reinforcing our awareness of significant events, characters, promises, and warnings by embedding them in narratives that develop their meaning.

The motives from which this impulse springs are as complex as the writings they provoke.[8] Thomas Mann's massive *Joseph and His Brothers* may serve as a paradigmatic modern literary example of several important motives—chief among them, the desire to sustain in collective memory what Sontag called the "important" things that contemporary experience threatened to obliterate. Mann wrote this work during the "turbulent" years between 1921 and 1942, years in which he feared that Western culture might be annihilated by the savagery set loose upon the world by Nazi Germany. He believed that German antisemitism was directed not only against Jews but also "against Europe and against that higher Germanism itself . . . against the Christian and classical foundations of Western morality."[9] Fearful that this cultural inheritance would be lost, he drew from the Hebrew Bible the story of Joseph, elaborating and embedding it within a fictional context that also included vital elements of other ancient systems of belief and practice. He was shoring up against the imminent ruin of Western culture a collective memory of its classical, Christian, and Hebraic roots. *"This,"* to quote Sontag again, was "important" to him; to sustain its memory he made a "story of how it happened" (86). "Descending," Mann's narrator says, into what he saw as "the deep well" of the past, he drew to the surface an image of Jewish culture bearers and their God, to instruct collective memory in a new wilderness.[10]

The threat of imminent loss that provoked Mann's long work has been displaced in contemporary American Jewish writing by awareness of losses that have already occurred. Jewish writers know what Mann could only anticipate, for Jewish losses have been various and manifold. As writers remember them, they make a kind of mirrored chamber in which contemporary experience identifies its precursors. Remembering the rabbinic sense of distance from textual beginnings, contemporary writers can apprehend more deeply their own distance from scriptural events and behavioral norms. Remembering the slow accretion of meaning around biblical texts, a contemporary writer can appreciate the resonance that belongs to a community of voices—and hear the comparative thinness of the individual voice. Remembering the distinctively Jewish features of European life that were gradually shaped by the rabbis and violently erased, contemporary writers can see more clearly their own susceptibility to the seductions of non-Jewish culture.

In light of these recollections and reflections, the process of "looking back" and "moving on" becomes for contemporary American Jewish writers a deeply ironic process that acknowledges loss and looks beyond it—even as it recuperates in memory and imagination what has disappeared from experience. It seems peculiarly ironic, for example, that so many of the first contemporary American Jewish writers to "look back" toward ancient texts were women. Despite their traditional exclusion from textual study, women writers of the late eighties and early nineties carried back to their reading of biblical texts a traditional midrashic interest in searching out meaning, in "seizing upon" what Norma Rosen in *Biblical Women Unbound* calls "improbabilities" and "gaps" in the original narratives.[11] Like the rabbinical midrashists, women writers sought to diminish the distance between the Scriptures and themselves. Rosen wants to give voice to the matriarchs, to bring them into contemporary perspective, to ask questions and "to argue . . . with the text, trying to draw closer to it" (x, xi, xiv). But, like other women writing on biblical texts at this time, Rosen's work also brings to bear on her sources a politically edged, feminist intention. Energized partly by her awareness of Jewish women's long-standing deprivations but also, more deeply, by the destruction of European Jewry, Rosen and other women writers sought in the work of midrash "some new way to express the human cry of loss" (25). That "ongoing task, both terrible and radiant" (28), assumed cultural importance as narrative rendered collective losses meaningful—memorable.

In Rosen's work as in two contemporaneous collections of women's writing on biblical texts[12] the midrashic impulse turns up vividly in personal essays: short, discursive narratives that suggest the ways in which writers bring to a text not only what they are taught by tradition to see there[13] but also what their own experience and imagination enable them to see.[14] From the beginning, the midrashic impulse in contemporary writing follows the double curve of wave and undertow, looking back toward powerful figures of the far past, drawing forward narrative strands of meaning that keep their images—"shadows" of those significant predecessors—sharp, vital. In the hands of contemporary writers the work of midrash becomes what one critic calls a "labor of remembrance"[15]—a partly originary process, like that of giving birth, but partly also a work of recovery. Writers weave new meaning into the fabric of ancient narrative as they recover and then tell, in their own fresh voices, the "little secrets" of the collective past.

Many of these first women's essays move predictably forward, giving voice to intricacies of female experience largely silent in the ancient text. But the essays also look back, recovering a nuanced sense of the text and the rabbinic commentary that accompanies it. They intend on one hand to recuperate loss by imagining the significant "givens" of women's lives that are often obscured in scripture. But they also attend closely to particulars of classical rabbinic commentary that may once, ironically, have thickened the obscurity that contemporary writers seek to penetrate. This doubled trajectory is embodied in Rebecca Goldstein's contemporary midrash on Lot's wife. Goldstein approaches the dilemma of Lot's wife first through the lens of traditional teaching. Ordered by God not to look back, this woman disobeys, looks back, and is turned into a pillar of salt as punishment for her disobedience. Goldstein's traditional teacher emphasizes the woman's disobedience and its swift punishment, but she doesn't explain why Lot's wife looked back. Goldstein seeks the meaning of this behavior within her own experience: she knows the lure of rebelliousness, the attraction of the forbidden, of nostalgia, of voyeuristic curiosity. But she knows also the love of family and the fear of loss that emerge from her father's ambivalent response to this text. Unlike the righteous teacher who emphasizes disobedience and punishment, he finds a rabbinical midrash that names Lot's wife and explains that she looked back in pity for her two daughters who couldn't flee the doomed city because they were already married to Sodomite men. Goldstein's father's "confusion" as he tells her this midrash teaches his daughter that he, too, might have disobeyed the command to move on without looking back; he too might have turned "to see if all his daughters were following" ("Looking Back at Lot's Wife," *Out of the Garden*).

From the text and the traditional teacher, from the ancient rabbis and from her rabbinical father, then, Goldstein draws multiple possibilities of meanings, complicated further by her own experience as a rebellious student of philosophy and as a writer whose curiosity dwells on salient psychological detail. She is moved by her father's "confusion," comparing him gratefully with more "righteous" biblical parents: the obedient fathers who were willing to sacrifice their children, and the obedient mothers—like her namesake Rebekah—who could withdraw "love and loyalty" from one child for the sake of another ("Looking Back at Lot's Wife" 6–7). She also compares the emotionally dense family context within which righteousness lives in the Bible with the cool impersonality of transcendence and truth—paramount values in the Greek philosophy she studies professionally. Ultimately she discovers another rabbinic midrash that explains that the people of Sodom were also turned to salt (11)—like Lot's wife. And then, as meaning gathers around this harrowing image of the past, Goldstein suddenly understands. When Lot's wife "looked back" to discover that her eldest daughters were not following, she knew "only one desire: to follow after [her] child, to experience what she's experienced, to be one with her. . . . Only to be one with her." Instead of punishing this grieving mother, Goldstein suggests, God may have granted her desire (12) by turning her, like her daughters, into salt. The essay "instructs" collective memory by discerning in the old story a meaning that honors not only the classical rabbinic commentary, and the ancient, persistent, textual tenderness toward parental attachment, but also a contemporary feminist respect for womanly desire: one may look back, Goldstein's midrash suggests, not because of "voyeurism or skepticism, nostalgia or bravado," but because of "the backward pull of love" (8) for what one has lost.

A harrowing sense of loss is everywhere in these essays; in some cases it even reshapes the form of the personal essay itself as the writer struggles to recover voices silenced for generations.[16] Norma Rosen, for example, refashions the personal essay as dialogue in order to give those voices a hearing. Aware that the matriarchs were often muted by a culture that continued to silence and subordinate women, Rosen engages both her characters and their rabbinic interpreters dialogically, wanting to name and thus to remove questions that "stand between me and the text" (x). She imagines her way into biblical women's stories, considering the speculations of the early midrashists but bringing to bear upon them the "ironies, skepticisms, scruples" and also the "spiritual longings" of her own, contemporary, female experience (xi). Writing new midrash becomes Rosen's "activist response to existential despair" (27), recalling Mann's work on the Joseph narrative not only in the complexity of its intention and the ironic modern emphasis of its interpretive perspective but also in its need to respond to the sense of loss that Mann anticipated—and that now haunts contemporary memory.

In Rosen's midrash on the marriage of Rebekah and Isaac, loss is an old, inherited theme. Before their marriage takes place, Hagar and Ishmael have lost their places in Abraham's family, and the near loss of Isaac, kept secret from his bride, casts a deep shadow over his relationship with his new wife. Rosen allows Rebekah to enter a dialogue with the narrative of these inherited losses. Ignorant of Isaac's near sacrifice when she married him, childless and discontented with her traumatized husband, she invites Hagar to return to Abraham's tent. She wants to substitute this tough, resilient woman for the apparently more compliant Sarah, who was ninety before she bore a child and who died before she could learn that her son's sacrifice had been prevented. Rebekah also welcomes Ishmael to her own tent, for she wants to substitute this other son of Abraham for the traumatized Isaac who has been unable to give her a child. She fails in both attempts; Isaac impregnates her and the original plot reasserts itself. Rebekah's narrative is framed by two meditative sections that reflect upon other, midrashic, "alternative drafts" (25) of the story; these meditations reflect as well upon the failure of the rabbis to consider the effects of the *Akedah* on Rebekah. Throughout this piece, ancient and contemporary voices speak and respond to one another as the modern writer engages in dialogue the text, its characters, and its commentators. Instead of "descending" like Mann's narrator into "the well of the past," Rosen speaks into it from her own place and time, recuperating what has been lost in the voices that answer hers.

The dialogical form that Rosen develops in this and other essays on biblical texts reflects the intertexuality that Daniel Boyarin and other scholars have identified as a feature of both midrash and the Bible.[17] In Boyarin's view, all literature is "ultimately dialogical in that it cannot but record the traces of its contentions and doubling of earlier discourses." For him, "reality is always represented through texts that refer to other texts" (14). The Bible is particularly "dialogical" because its "fractured and unsystematic surface" encodes "its own intertextuality" (15)—its own effort to record early and later cultural and social awarenesses within a single text. Boyarin understands "the dialogue and dialectic of the midrashic rabbis" as "readings of the dialogue and dialectic of the biblical text. The intertextuality of midrash is thus an outgrowth of intertextuality within the Bible itself" (15).[18] Within both scripture and the writings that seek to interpret it, then, time becomes a kind of echo chamber, in which no voice is ever stilled.

This scriptural and midrashic sense of time as a hollow space in which past and present voices can connect, shapes as dialogue not only the personal essay but also the contemporary novel. In

Todd Gitlin's *Sacrifice* the ancient story of the *Akedah* informs a dialogue between a contemporary father, dead when the novel opens, and his estranged son. Behind them, Gitlin hears the voices of Abraham and Isaac, Jacob and Esau. To evoke the chamber of echoes these voices inhabit, Gitlin's novel develops several lines of narrative: the son's quest for insight into the father who betrayed and abandoned him; the father's multiple efforts to understand himself and to tell his son both the personal secrets that shadow their mutual past, and the collective secrets—the ancient and repeated sacrifices apparently demanded of fathers and sons—that inform the filial story this father and son have lived out. Gitlin has said that for him, being a Jew "entails not so much the comfort of an achieved wisdom or a promised land, but the anxiety of trying always to see a bit more clearly, even or especially when what you're seeing includes your own shadow."[19] In this novel, the shadows of fathers and sons thicken between the generations as characters try, and fail, and try again to love and to understand themselves and one another.

The father, Chester Garland—a psychiatrist, a writer, and an apparent suicide when the novel begins—speaks through his articles, his book, and three handwritten notebooks that contain the private journal he leaves for his son. He is the protagonist of this novel. Neither time nor death stills his voice or diminishes the ancient, persistent mystery his experience replicates. Unable to understand why he has abandoned one son and irreparably damaged another—the beloved, illegitimate child of a young woman Chester falls in love with when he has left his wife—this man probes not only the Freudian wisdoms of his profession but the more ancient wisdom of scripture.

Aware of the rabbinical midrashim that attempt to explain Abraham's response to God's demand that Isaac be sacrificed, Garland—the name itself suggests the flowering branches woven by pagans around the heads of sacrificial offerings—concentrates on two overlooked elements of the scriptural narrative. Remembering his own father's coldness, knowing that "distant, controlling fathers" beget "estranged" sons,[20] he imagines that Abraham may also have been a sacrifice to the will of God (44). Indeed, as he considers the lives of other fathers and sons in scripture—Abraham and Ishmael, Jacob and Esau, God and Jesus—and, in classical texts, Laius and Oedipus, he begins to believe that fear and cruelty, betrayal and punishment (211) are implicit within the world of the family. He sees these forces alive in the wider world as well, for the novel remembers the Holocaust, which enters the current experience of this protagonist not only as he sits in a peaceful park in France but also as he works with survivors in his practice. Then too, he is painfully aware of contemporary suffering, in the places where political prisoners still endure torture and powerful nations maim and kill without respect for the dignity and fragility of human beings. In his own brief, but terrifying impulses toward suicide he sees the "wish to be done with the self who suffers" (75). The weight of the suffering—repeated generation after generation of fathers and sons—becomes, at times, too heavy for him to bear.

Having fallen out of love with a wife whose long barrenness, echoing the matriarch Sarah's, finally yielded a child but destroyed the joy and spontaneity of her sexual, emotional connection to him, he finds love in a fragrant, European garden: Edenic, filled with apple trees. But even there he encounters the sense of a cruelly ruined world as his lover recalls her home village, transformed now into a Soviet military dump so contaminated that "the birds are dying" and "the trees have no leaves" (155). After an accident that maims his lover's child, Garland returns to the chaos and cacophony of New York City and divorce. He knows that he has not found the secret of healing he sought in psychiatry, or scripture, or romantic adventure. Though he has entered deeply into the dialogue they offered, though he has heard and tried to obey the command to love, he cannot heal either his own anguish, or the suffering he has caused, or the pain of the world. Nor can he justify their persistence.

Looking back at the *Akedah* through the eyes of Isaac, Garland perceives in both himself and his son the child's loss of trust after the father's betrayal. The perception shows him the "helplessness of both generations" (207). He looks at the scriptural record and its rabbinical interpretations and he imagines "Here is what Isaac thought: From the altar on Mount Moriah I came. I am the son of cruelty. . . . Thus did the God of Abraham beget betrayal upon betrayal, cruelty upon cruelty, punishment upon punishment. His altars do not crumble" (211). Garland sees those altars and the willing and unwilling sacrifices exacted on them everywhere in the world.

His son, Paul, comes to share this vision but embeds it in a larger perception of the suffering necessarily rooted in mortality: he knows that "all will lose those whom they love, or will be lost to them" (227–28). He listens to his father's former lover, who tells him that "bitterness is a luxury. Forgiveness, if you will forgive me for saying so, is practical" (227). The novel ends with this son, like Esau after his father's funeral, "poised at the edge of a wilderness . . . alert with hope" (227–28). From the multiple dialogues he has entered into, from the interwoven texts of his father's journals and publications, this abandoned, untrusting child learns that "you could love the man who wrote those words. Even if he were your father" (211). Paul begins to identify with his father's suffering—and to understand the relief it may have given his father to turn away from the tangle of damage in his own family toward the study of Abraham and Isaac and the social activism of his later years. Though the novel offers no promise that the cycle of filial pain can be interrupted, it draws from its characters' willingness to enter into dialogue with one another and with the narratives of the collective past a shred of hope for the human future. The "little secrets" that midrash recovers, the novel suggests, instruct collective memory: they help us to know that one may leap, laughing, upon the altar—and that we are not the first to hurt what we would love.

Pearl Abraham's most recent novel offers a darker vision of failed dialogues—both among characters and between them and the wisdoms of the past. *The Seventh Beggar* also chronicles a series of generational and textual dialogues. Members of a single family try and fail three times to engage one another in dialogue. First, a Chasidic boy, Joel, secretly defies his parents in order to engage in dialogue with a storyteller who belonged to an earlier generation and a different Chasidic dynasty. In a vision, Nachman of Bratslav—the storyteller Joel has sought—slaps his face. Second, after Joel's death, his sister, Ada, winds her way through flooded underground tunnels, looking for a message from him. But she recovers only scraps of his writing, fragments of an incoherent alphabet, many of which the rats have used to make their nests. In her search she confronts flight of steps that will not allow her to go either up or down. Finally, her son, Jakob Joel—a student of computer science at MIT—will engage in an extended dialogue with the uncle who died before he was born. But their communications—like the earlier attempts at dialogue in this novel—are frustrated by the different values and spiritual commitments particular to uncle and nephew. Every generation departs from the path of the one before it as this novel traces the disjunctive pattern that frustrates dialogue within this family and, to some extent, within the larger community as well.

Only stories speak easily to one another in this work. Through his nephew, Joel begins to finish the story of the seventh beggar, left unfinished by Nachman. Joel's midrash on Nachman's text is narrated by a beggar without feet who nonetheless travels "farther and deeper" than all the other beggars because he dreams "another tale, another dream" at every step. He knows that even a prince who has stumbled into "heresy" will be "restrained" as long as he "listened and believed the tales."[21] The nephew's response to his uncle Joel's midrash on Nachman's story will become another, less hopeful, narrative about a new creator, a computer called Cog—a powerful being, both male and female—capable of outthinking human beings and of making an alternative world of ones and zeros that is different from but deeply reflective of the world created by God in Genesis. Like the original Creator, Cog brings order to chaos, replicates "later generations of his machine in his own image" (345) and insures that the generations will be instructed only by prescribed procedures—called "handshakings" (345)—which limit sources of information. Cog also eliminates the first two generations of descendants who have been engaged in a quasisibling rivalry for primacy.

The story of Cog works midrashically with the early chapters of Genesis as it replicates the creation story and several family narratives; it ends with Babel and the deliberate baffling of communication by Cog's confusing languages and interfaces. Thus this novel offers an image of a brave new world in which disjunctive patterns repeatedly mark failures of dialogue. Here, human generations fail to understand one another, and the stories people create replicate even in the minds of their computers the oblique, frustrated attempts at dialogical connection that have long been part of both scriptural and Yiddish texts.

As Abraham's skepticism finds its counterpart in its biblical antecedent, the midrashic impulse turns the mind back to its foundational texts, bending contemporary literature into a shape that responds to specific contemporary tensions that seem always new and particular to us but reveal uncanny resemblances to earlier collective experience. Abraham's novel addresses the loss of early bonds that depend on what we share, bonds between parents and children, and students and teachers, formed by what they have in common. But the work substitutes for dialogue an ironic echo that affirms similarity only within difference. We see the power of difference to alienate generations from one another and to keep even our computers from making the effortless interfaces we always expect of them. And we see that our predecessors knew the same failure and the losses—of shared understanding—that accompany it.

The problem of difference—cultural, rather than generational or personal—becomes a second crux of contemporary writings shaped by the midrashic impulse. Mann's *Joseph,* again, may be paradigmatic, for it acknowledges abundantly the multitudinousness of cultural differences—the fragrant, colorful bazaar of options that animate our passage through contemporary life. Mann gives us a protagonist who embodies and exploits many such options simultaneously. He is mythic as well as biblical—only a step removed in time from the cultures that preceded and still surround his own. Because Mann believed that "religious symbolism" was a "cultural treasure-house, wherein we have a perfect right to dip when we need to use the familiar image to make visible and tangible some general aspect of spirit" (Heilbut 552–53), the biblical Joseph became for this writer a "Typhonic Tammuz-Osiris-Adonis-Dionysus figure" (Hayman 367, quoting Mann's letter to Ernst Bertram) in whom the wisdoms of many cultures are mixed.

Mann found "something marvelously enticing and mysterious in this world of cultural multiplicity—or 'correspondences'" (Kerényi 46). The word suggests that we know ourselves and understand our experiences partly by grasping their correspondence—their qualified likenesses—to earlier figures and events. In the Joseph story, Mann said, "the various mythologies—Jewish Egyptian, Greek—mix so freely that one license more or less will make no difference."[22] He allowed his characters not only to correspond to earlier mythic figures but even to resemble beings who would come much later in history: "Anachronism no longer bothers me in the least" he wrote; "Egyptian, Jewish, Greek, even medieval elements, both linguistic and mythological, make a colorful mixture" (Kerényi 67). As he descended into the deep well of the past, Mann freed himself from the sense of time as a line moving always forward. He fashioned instead a fictional world in which mythic, historic, and biblical elements were comfortably—if ironically—mixed.

Mann's deft, mischievous mixture of differing cultural influences within his fictional world undergoes a sea change in some contemporary American Jewish writings that confront cultural difference and that are moved by a midrashic impulse. As Cynthia Ozick's "The Pagan Rabbi" (1966) foresaw, contemporary awareness of cultural difference may be as vivid as Mann's work suggests, but it can affirm dichotomy and polarity rather than dialogue or intertextuality. Upon the biblical moment in which Rebakah comes upon Isaac walking in the field,[23] Ozick builds a narrative that divides its protagonist between irreconcilable alternatives that have existed in us, and in the world, from the beginning. Images of gates, fences, and divisions are everywhere in Ozick's story. From Isaac Kornfeld's dining table, divided by a "crocheted lace runner"[24] that becomes first a "boundary line" (11) and then a "divider" (18), to the barbed wire fence that scarred the face of his wife (7), to the "fence" danced around this bride by ladies at her wedding, the story's preoccupation with divisions and boundaries is clearly marked.

This stream of images culminates in "the Fence of the Law" (20) that has always confined Ozick's rabbi within an observant Jewish life. Preparing to transgress that boundary, Isaac begins to read Romantic poetry and to seek out the "free spirits" of the natural world, abandoning the sacred texts, his wife and daughters. He knows that faithfulness to the Law obliges him to turn away from the beauty of nature and the storied wealth of Western culture. He will learn that "freedom" to become intimate with spirits of the natural world will mean the loss of family love, of spiritual comfort, of moral and psychological integrity within the multiple boundaries that regulate life in his own culture.

He falls in love with the heartless, conscienceless spirit of a tree and discovers in her a being who embodies boundarylessness. Different species merge in her. She can, like an animal, move and make love; like a human, she can speak. But she is also part vegetable: her skin is like an "eggplant's"; her fingers

"like the ligula of a leaf"; her breasts are like "velvety color-
less pear[s]." Though "human in aspect," she is "unmistakably
flowerlike" (30). He discovers in conversation that, for her, words
become things that can be played with or bruise the skin. In her
world "ugliness" replaces pain and "immorality" (33). The symbolic and the literal, the aesthetic and the moral are thoroughly
confused in her.

The confusion is powerfully seductive—partly because it is
forbidden. Jews are biblically taught to avoid mixtures.[25] Responsive to that teaching, Ozick has insisted that "right conduct
can emerge only out of the stringent will toward distinction-
making"; "the rabbinic way is to refuse blur, to see how one thing
is not another thing."[26] But Ozick's rabbi yields to the "freedom"
from distinction making promised by the tree nymph. He loves
his Jewish life: his wife and daughters, his study of holy books.
But he leaps the Fence of Rabbinic Law, clings to the anomalous
creature he finds on the other side, and loses his soul. His profound ambivalence as he struggles with the restraints and dualities of his world shows us ourselves—always working on the
limits of our own freedoms.

In the fictional world of Mann's Joseph, classical, Christian,
and Hebraic influences swirl congenially within the dense linguistic medium the writer devised for them. In his work, time no
longer silences ancient voices that remain vital long after the
speakers themselves have disappeared. Characters hear, and listen, to them all. But in the world of Ozick's fictional rabbi—which
is, after all, much like our own—the persistence of those seductive voices presents a problem that Ozick's later fictions and essays work—both formally and thematically—to represent and
resolve. As she writes large the problem of post-Enlightenment
Jewish life in a Diaspora replete with the philosophical, theological, aesthetic, and moral seductions of different cultures, her representations will emphasize deliberate differentiation and choice.
Jewish ideas and texts[27] will become the touchstones that clarify
choices as her work develops the sense of contemporary American Jewish experience as divided between unreconcilable, mutually exclusive cultural options.

In the contemporary world of Ozick's fictions, diverse cultural
influences—thoroughly mixed for Mann's Joseph—will become
polarized. In *The Cannibal Galaxy*, Naomi Sokoloff observes,

"Enlightenment values and Jewish primacy" oppose one another; "art and Jewish identity do seem to remain warring forces."[28] Mann's Joseph could move fluidly within the thick, rich cultural medium of classical, Christian, and Hebrew beliefs and practices. But Ozick's characters of this American Diaspora, exposed to cultural options every bit as diverse—and as seductive—as Joseph's, must learn first to differentiate among them. Then they must find and choose the ways in which a Jewish life can be sustained.

Ozick's personal essays chart the progress of this enterprise. She saw how far we had come from our Jewish texts, how plentifully we and our culture had absorbed the influences of the non-Jewish world. Confronting the powerful ambiguities of contemporary Diaspora experience, Ozick suggested in 1983 that Jewish writers might keep faith with their own culture by "compos[ing] *midrashim*"[29] or by trying to transform English "into the language of a culture that is centrally Jewish in its concerns and thereby liturgical in nature" ("Notes toward a New Yiddish" 174). In a later essay ("Bialik's Hint") she considered a different strategy, suggesting that contemporary Jewish writers in the Diaspora might court instead "the high muse of fusion." They might keep faith with both "Jewish primacy"—"the Sinaitic challenge of distinctive restraint and responsibility that the rabbis held out" (227)—and "the offerings of the Enlightenment—which, in any case we cannot avoid, forgo, or escape" (236–37). She imagined that the dual heritage of the Jewish tradition and the Enlightenment might "learn to commingle" (239).[30] But she wasn't sure "what we are to become" when that happens (239).

The possibilities of dialogue and intertextuality don't arise in these essays. Instead, Ozick's nonfiction formulates another—a different—response to the cultural dilemma she perceives so clearly. First, she turns the idea of "fusion" into a formal rather than a cultural option. She reconceives the genre of the essay itself as a mixed thing—belonging both to the mode of "argument or . . . history" (Forewarning, *Memory and Metaphor* xii) and to the imaginative mode of fiction. She knows that the personal essay can both argue and persuade. But it can also, like a story, "invent, burn, guess, try out, hurtle forward, succumb to that flood of sign and nuance that adds up to intuition, disclosure, discovery" (Foreword, *Art and Ardor* xi). A writer of essays that dazzle by their verbal elegance and inventiveness, Ozick demonstrates that essays move along the path of fictions—uncovering the surprise of truth rather than targeting it beforehand.

Second, however, within the personal essay that she conceives as a mixed literary form, the movement of her mind avoids mixtures. Her speakers discover and sustain boundaries between differences rather than fusing or reconciling them. Ozick's non-fictional writings are shaped by an awareness of duality that becomes in every essay sharper and clearer, that leads to choices rather than to dialogue or to fusion. She calls this strategy of the essay "polemics": "thinking in the furnace of antithesis" ("Remembering Maurice Samuel," *Art and Ardor* 214). She first identified this quality of the personal essay's rhetoric in the work of Maurice Samuel, but it applies as well to her own nonfiction. The essential gift of the "argumentative explainer," whose "living voice," she would later explain, "takes us in" to a personal essay,[31] is the power to identify with both sides of every argument. This is the storyteller's gift, transferred to the writer of essays. An "explainer hurls himself into his story," Ozick tells us: "He becomes the story. . . . By joining himself with its elements, by taking sides with its various parts. By sorting out. By setting aside error and misapprehension—only after first entering into their spirit" (214). The last sentence is crucial. Imagination allows the writer to identify with different "sides" of every argument. But "polemics" moves the writer through these various identifications; it becomes the strategy by which error may be set aside, confusion may be clarified, and choices may be made.

In most of the essays of her 1983 collection, *Art and Ardor,* one can see this strategy at work. Her thought characteristically proceeds by differentiating among apparent antitheses. But she makes herself at home on both sides of every question. She differentiates essays from fictions. But she also insists that "the only non-fiction worth writing—at least for me"—is the one in which "knowledge swims up from invention and imagination," as it does in stories (Introduction xi). She contrasts Edith Wharton with Henry James to uncover, by identifying with both of them, their differing virtues and flaws. She sees the saintliness of Leonard Woolf and then, from Virginia's point of view, the guilt he induced in her (47). She contrasts Freud ("a peephole into a dark chamber") with Gershom Scholem ("a radiotelescope monitoring the universe" [1939]) in order to clarify the magnitude and value of each man's work; but her choice between them is clear. She contrasts Abraham with Terach, knowing that both belong to the "chimera" known as "a 'Jewish writer'"; but she sees as well that both are "icily, elegiacally, at war" (198). She does not bring differences into dialogue. Neither does she interweave differences with one another. Instead, she approaches understanding by way of antithesis. Always, as she gives herself to each side of every opposition, the essays move her—and the reader—toward a richer, more intense clarity. And toward the possibility of choosing among the options she has offered.[32]

In her capacity to differentiate, to sustain tension among differences, and to allow the writer's identificatory embrace to provoke insight into both sides of every polarity, Ozick has produced a body of personal essays whose cultural importance transcends their particular subjects. Even for readers who do not care about the relative merits of Henry James and Edith Wharton, Ozick's essay formulates a way of thinking that is profoundly appropriate to a cultural condition like our own. She shows us that difference—between us and them, between then and now, between what is forbidden and what is sanctioned—can become a "furnace of antithesis" from which understanding may emerge, drawn out by the living voice of the writer who sets "aside error and misapprehension—only after first entering into their spirit." Like Thomas Mann, Ozick employs in the essays the artist's power of "entering in" to different cultural and literary possibilities. But unlike Mann, who rests easy in the cultural mélange he portrays, Ozick uses the artist's power of "entering in" to "coerce assent" to a particular end. The essay, Ozick wrote in her most recent collection (*Quarrel and Quandary* 2000), is "not a hidden principle or a thesis or a construct: she is *there,* a living voice"—warmed, edged, and modulated, in Ozick's case, by the powerful undertow of her Jewish sources ("The Essay as Warm Body" 181, 187).

The sense of moving through alternatives, living out their implications before attempting to achieve clarity, resolution, or choice, guided by the remembered presence of a powerful, transcendent force and by its traces in foundational texts and teachings is as vivid in contemporary fiction as in Ozick's brilliant essays. Allegra Goodman's *Paradise Park* recounts the stages of its young protagonist's path through such a process. Drawn to the past from her earliest years, she has always wanted "to live in the old days."[33] But she moves always forward, searching in each new spiritual, philosophical location for the sense that she "might actually be resting in the palm of God" (31), a momentary awareness that she experienced first on a scientific expedition off the coast of Hawaii but that seems to her "like something from the old days" (49–50). Though her parents were Jewish secularists (48), she longs to experience the kind of revelatory "breakthrough" (75) that actually comes to her when a great whale, like Job's Leviathan, rises out of the ocean beside her boat. "I saw something," she reports: "The world was big, not little. The place was deep. The sky swung back in liquid gold, the air mixed with the water. I saw something. It was a whale, but not just the whale. It was a vision. It was a vision of God . . . all of a sudden I'd seen it—all the power under the world, all this presence and wisdom that wasn't human" (81). This vision animates her journey through Christian fundamentalism and Jewish Orthodoxy, Buddhism, university courses in religion, a yeshiva in Jerusalem and a Hasidic community in the states. She will be reconciled with her mother, marry and bear a child before she decides to stop looking for God "because God was actually looking for me!" (358).

Many critics have praised Goodman's ability to enter into the different stages of her protagonist's spiritual pilgrimage.[34] But it is the form of this novel, rather than the depth or complexity of the protagonist's experience within each cultural situation, that seems particularly interesting to me. As Goodman sympathetically moves her quixotic adolescent through the alternatives offered by this culture one sees, like Ozick, the rich confusion that dazzles post-Enlightenment Jews—and also the profound spiritual hunger that drives the quest. The novel restores its protagonist to her sense of herself as a Jew, but that self-designation seems arbitrary, provisional, beside the vision of Leviathan, drawn from an ancient source to sustain the sense of divine power and presence in a confusing world. The midrashic impulse that drives this novel recovers for collective memory a sense of origins that remains fresh in a fictional world littered with the debris of many cultures and dusty with the effort of sorting through and choosing among them.

For several other writers of the new wave, the world we know is neither littered nor dusty. It is, rather, alive with fresh voices that remain distinct but connected with one another. In it, the consciousness and memory of contemporary American Jews can experience the resonance of these voices without mixing or reconciling them with one another. Representing neither dialogue, nor fusion, nor choice among dichotomous alternatives, Jonathan Rosen's *The Talmud and the Internet: A Journey between Worlds* is formed like a great web. The long essay immerses itself in the undertow of Midrash as it turns toward ancient Jewish texts to consider—like Ozick's nonfiction—the condition and the imperatives of Jewish life in this Diaspora. Rosen's work merges verbal simplicity and informality with structural complexity and intellectual depth. The moral and spiritual emphases of the earliest midrashists come second, here, to the cultural/existential issues formulated in different ways by Thomas Mann and Cynthia Ozick. Not "how should one behave" or "what should one believe," but rather "how can one best apprehend and respond to" the multiplicity of contemporary cultural experience becomes the root question here, as the writer looks back to the sources—both cultural and personal—that shaped him. Jonathan Rosen's response to this question is formally innovative, "carefully shaped," as Frank Kermode observed.[35] The essay draws bits of ancient and contemporary, collective and individual experience—like drops of last night's rain, hung upon a silken web—into a pattern at whose center is the writer's mind at work. This long essay develops in six parts—each one radiating from a common center, like spokes in a wheel, or petals on a sunflower. Each part takes up an aspect of the complex, astonishingly parallel situations in which Jews, then and now, have found themselves.

All but one of the six sections begin within the personal space of the writer—as if to ground us in the place where experience always begins, to which understanding, if we are lucky and work hard at it, ultimately comes. But whether a section opens with the death of his grandmother, his father's boyhood in Vienna, his own life at graduate school in Berkeley, his wedding, or his trip to Scotland, each one weaves into and around the center of Rosen's personal life an extended meditation on the particular theme embedded in it. Part 1, on loss and translation, moves from the death of a beloved grandmother, to the writer's loss of his computer notes on her dying, to the loss of print culture—of "the book as object, as body"[36]—and finally to the loss of the ancient "Temple service of fire and blood" (15). Various and manifold, as I have suggested, loss remains a threshold issue for contemporary Jewish writers. But Jonathan Rosen sets beside the recognition of loss—poignant, personal as well as historic—the recuperative strategy of translation. Also various and manifold, translation is both what the writer does when he takes notes on his grandmother's dying—translating "into words the physical intimacy of her death" (4)—and what Jochanan ben Zakkai did when he had himself carried away from the ruins of Jerusalem in a coffin to found the Talmudic enterprise that allowed the Jews to be "reborn" as a people not of "land" and Temple services but as "the people of the book" (15). The "Talmud was also born of loss," Rosen points out, insisting that while loss is final, translation carries forward a version of the past, a sense of what was important, what needs to be remembered.

One is struck by the aptness of the term "translation" for the deep, complex work of both individual and collective memory. Able to keep in mind only what we can select and translate out of what William James called "the blooming, buzzing confusion"[37] of raw experience, we know this process from the moment we begin to think. Rosen's work gives the process historical depth and dignity as he demonstrates its cultural power to sustain what might otherwise be lost in the confusion of time and change. But that power is limited, as part 2 of this book-length essay suggests. Rosen acknowledges that as Temple worship became the Rabbinic Judaism of the Oral Law, and as the Oral Law was transcribed and codified, the "gigantic, unfolding act of translation" revealed that in such a process "things are always lost" (34). No translation, however careful, can exactly replicate the original that inspired it.

Some modern writers, he argues, believe that one such loss is the sense of wholeness that once characterized human experience. But, he insists, "wholeness has always been a fantasy" (36). As this section develops the theme of fragmentation and wholeness, Rosen discovers that the cultural process he has been calling "translation" is itself a "mixture of endless proliferation mingled with endless loss" (32). Like a living organism, like collective memory itself, this process carries forward fragments of what has been important to it, and the work of contemporary

Jews is not to choose among them but to find "a way to make each fragment feel whole" (32). Different from dialogue, and differentiation, and choice, "this notion" allows Rosen "to feel a connection to a vast body of knowledge of which I am not master" (32). Study becomes for him what the midrashic enterprise was for the first rabbis: a way of bridging the gap between ancient text—itself a collection of fragments—and contemporary self-awareness.

By meditating on ways in which a modern Jew addresses the different elements of personal and collective, contemporary and historical Jewish experience, part 3 considers the problem of connecting oneself to precious fragments of one's cultural past. The dilemma is twofold: "how can I stop trying to connect myself in some way to the past?" (63) Rosen asks first, remembering his failures to preserve or recapture it. Second, he wonders, how "do I live inside the comfortable life" of a contemporary American Jew "without feeling I am somehow betraying history?" (58). Instead of affirming one of these existential questions at the expense of the other, he moves—like Ozick—into both sides of the problem. But unlike her polemical strategy—which always arrives at clarification by ultimately validating one possibility over another—he sustains his identificatory embrace of both alternatives. His maternal grandmother, American born, lived comfortably and at peace, surviving to attend his wedding. His paternal grandmother, European born, was murdered early by the Nazis. "Each embodies a world that pulls on my life with equal gravity" (66), he decides, refusing to choose between the dual heritage of Europe and America, between the tragic past and the pragmatic present.

Part 4 sustains and enlarges this awareness of persistent, potentially conflictual differences that underlie his—and our— American Jewish experience by suggesting that one may—like Henry Adams—remain torn between opposing cultural forces (77). Or, instructed by the Talmud, one may recognize instead the "invisible linkages" between apparently dichotomous forces; one may even remain open to them both. Judaism, he points out, "borrowed and transformed images from Christianity" and vice versa (83). Even Rashi, our most precious midrashist, "incorporated Old French into his Hebrew commentaries." Honoring these models, Rosen avoids both Thomas Mann's sense of cultural mélange in which awareness of difference virtually disappears, and also Cynthia Ozick's insistence on differentiating and choosing Jewishly among alternatives. Instead, he praises the "willingness to assimilate outside cultures into your own without worrying that they will corrupt your beliefs" (84). He discerns this tendency in the Talmud itself, whose "unlikely joinings" seem to him to invite "openness" (91).

He knows himself to be a creature of "unlikely joinings." Child of a European father who was taught to spit when he walked by a Church and an American mother who was taught to sing Christmas carols, he remembers the mixed icons within the house of his childhood: a mezuzah on every doorpost and a "small blue square of stained glass depicting an angel blowing a trumpet—a replica of a pane from Chartres Cathedral" that leaned against the kitchen window (70). He carries within him the dual legacy of those parents; he studied Milton in graduate school and Talmud afterward. But he is neither torn between the contradictions embedded within these influences nor, like Thomas Mann, ironically or mischievously indifferent to them.

Instead, in part 5, he imagines it might be possible to live in the "intersection" (104), to conceive himself as an "unlikely joining" between different but not necessarily oppositional cultural forces. He considers two very different Jews: Josephus—who wrote in Greek a secular history of the destruction of the Temple—and ben Zakkai—who founded the academy that produced the Talmud after that destruction. Both become emblems for him of cultural regeneration. Both die symbolic deaths; both remain Jews; both carry forward what they treasure from the destruction of their culture. Perhaps, Rosen muses, "reconciliation" between them and what they represent "isn't necessary"; perhaps they can continue to live side by side within his mind, like different opinions upon a page of the Talmud. Or, like different sites on the web of the Internet joined by links that connect them without reconciling them to one another. Analogies like this one have troubled reviewers who are offended by the significant differences between Talmud and Internet.[38] These readers fail to appreciate the point of the analogy—which links differences without merging, or fusing, or synthesizing, or reconciling, or identifying one with another. And without constructing a dialogue between them.

The midrashic impulse alive in this work draws Rosen instead toward the desire to "do justice" (123) to the differing forces that have shaped him and continue to attract him, to the differing voices that speak to him of the collective and the personal past as he translates them into the vernacular of contemporary experience. Part 6 of his essay hears those voices as parental and collectively historical, describes those forces as secular and religious, and represents the writer wanting to find "a kind of disjointed harmony" among them as he seeks "a home inside exile," a sense of "self inside a sea of competing voices" (131). Like Mann and Ozick, he uses the persona of the writer as culture bearer to serve as an emblem of this enterprise. As he looks through the narrow window of his own personal experience into the vast reaches of ancient texts and ancient history his work resembles as well the midrashic writings by women of the nineties, his mother— Norma Rosen—among them, who wove their contemporary, womanly insights into the ancient fabric of biblical literature. But Rosen's small book develops its own distinctive form beside the other rhetorical strategies in personal essays that honor the midrashic impulse. Neither dialogue nor "polemic," *The Talmud and the Internet* imitates the form of the web to represent the condition of contemporary American Jews—centered among the plentiful influences and attractions of multiple cultures, each of which remains distinct and asserts its own influence on us.

I know of only two contemporary novels whose sense of time and whose vision of our exposure to multiple, unreconciled, cultural influences resemble those in Rosen's essay. For Rebecca Goldstein and Aryeh Lev Stollman, distinctive shadows cast by manifold "little secrets" of the cultural past become vital presences in our own world—without dialogically engaging, or becoming indistinguishable from, one another and without provoking judgments about their comparative value. In these two novels the representation of time encourages one to perceive events as layered or interwoven, rather than strung out upon a narrative line that moves predictably from "before" to "after." And the dilemma of character is to forge a singular, coherent sense of self without slighting the disparate influences that have shaped it.

Differences of many kinds enrich the fictional world of Rebecca Goldstein's *Properties of Light*, gilding the experience of characters able to conceive a world in which ancient wisdoms

and contemporary insights coexist. I want to call this work "midrashic" not because it seeks to interpret specifically Jewish
sources. And not because it advocates a particular behavioral
code. But because it replicates the midrashic sense of time. It
frames in a new way the impulse to both look back and move
forward by suggesting that we conceive time as Einstein and the
original midrashists did: as a space in which the old voices continue to speak, and everything that was once vital is held in
being and remains accessible to us. Because we age as we grow,
because we conceive our lives as journeys with beginnings and
ends, because narratives since *Don Quixote* have reinforced our
awareness of time as movement from one place or event to another, we conceive time in terms of progression or regression. But
real time, Goldstein's novel insists, is—as Einstein understood—
"static, the flow unreal."[39] In Einstein's physics, the narrator informs us, "the passage of time is nothing real. . . . The flow of moments, which seems so relentless and so real, which seems to
carry off one's every treasure, leaving one like a chest spilled
open on the waves: unreal, unreal" (57). Instead, for Einstein,
time was "as stilled as spread space" (57). The novel moves at
will within that space: like memory itself—selecting, connecting
events that illuminate one another, disclosing what one physicist
in the novel calls the "hidden variables" that shape human behavior though they themselves remain invisible.

In this fictional world where time is static, many sources of
wisdom intersect: physicists recite Romantic poetry and practice
erotic Tantric exercises as a prelude to scientific inspiration; two
scientists can translate highly abstract theories into dance movements, feeling "the physics within . . . the muscles" (46) of their
bodies. The sometimes difficult language of the novel—lyrical at
one moment, theoretical and abstract the next—insists upon the
drawing together of different ways of knowing and of saying
what we know. Here, insights from many cultures remain vital
long after the people who conceived them have passed from the
earth. Their contemporary value is neither dimmed nor replaced
by the work of later cultures. They speak, still, to those who can
hear them.

Although two principal characters are born of what we call
"mixed" parentage, both Jewish and non-Jewish, mixture—as
Mann understood it in *Joseph*—is not the defining characteristic

of their natures or of the fictional world Goldstein constructs for them. Different also from Ozick's world of "either . . . or," it is, like the world constructed by Rosen's long essay, a world of "both . . . and." One physicist insists that both Romantic poetry and his wife's passion for occult studies have been as helpful to his scientific career as his own work in physics. Instead of dialogue among differing cultural systems or practices, the novel suggests the possibility of parallel wisdoms that remain accessible—alive in the hollow chamber of time like the voices of generations of rabbis whose commentary survives on the pages of the Talmud.

The cultural perspective of this novel shapes its romantic element as well, for the narrator has burned to death in an auto accident before the novel begins, yet his voice delivers to us the entire story; he is kept present, one might say, by the energy of his continuing passionate attachment to the woman responsible for his death. Like the moths he watches, drawn by the dazzling eruption of unloosed light from within her house, "immobilized by love" of the light within (20), he will watch her until she joins him on the far side of the boundary that divides life on earth from what comes after. "I am and am and am," he says, insisting on the undying energy and will that hold him both to her and to himself. Though much is lost in the course of the novel, though parents and lovers exploit and betray one another, though characters lose what they love best and reputations suffer from brutal collegial competitiveness, what has been vital—remains. The image of fire, so thoroughly contaminated by the Holocaust past and so painfully associated with the violent deaths of several characters in this novel, is linked here to images of sun and stars that illuminate but don't destroy. Even the fire that devours is connected mythically here to the "ancient dream of fire and divinity" that could transform a mortal into a god (22, 46). The poet Delmore Schwartz wrote that "time is the fire in which we burn."[40] But when time ceases to be constrained by linearity, its destructive power is vitiated. Instead, collective memory gathers up "ancient dreams" of renewal and transformation, together with more harrowing, more familiar images of the recent personal and historical past, acknowledging difference among them, suggesting that all live, still, within the repertoire of human experience. There is more than acknowledgment of loss in this way of conceiving time; there is consolation as well.

Aryeh Lev Stollman's *The Illuminated Soul* (2002) is similarly clear about the painful losses common to human experience—and similarly consoling. As I suggested (in chapter 4), this novel emphasizes the power of memory, rather than the shape of time, as the source of consolation, the keeper of what is most precious. The work is layered and intricate—like a Chopin nocturne or a Bach fugue—like the human brain itself, in which discrete moments, awarenesses, complex emotional attachments, and cultural wisdoms are interwoven. The world of the work is so deeply informed by memory and interpretive energy that virtually every significant insight, action, or event evokes an allusion to an ancient text.

In this deceptively simple story of a beautiful refugee whose wanderings bring her to the home of a Canadian widow and her two sons, every movement forward is made resonant by virtue of its biblical or midrashic accompaniment. When Eva Laquedem Higashi, the refugee, finds herself homeless in Canada, the appearance of clouds in the sky reassures her. They call up not only her father's scholarly fascination with clouds, and his published work on them, and not only her actress-mother's first appearance—seated upon an artificial cloud in a light opera—but also the pillar of cloud that guided the ancient Israelites in the wilderness. Time would appear to have separated Eva from all these associations, for when the novel opens, Eva's father has already been murdered by the Nazis. And her mother is long gone, having abandoned her when she was only four. Many centuries, moreover, lie between all these characters and the wilderness remembered by scripture, in which the reassuring presence of divine guidance could be perceived in the atmosphere. But the midrashic impulse in this novel responds to and links these experiences of loss, suggesting that memories stay—while everything else seems to move on.

Many years after Eva has disappeared from the narrator's life, his memory brings her back as he begins his lectures. She is "still the astonishing figure she was more than fifty years ago. . . . in the dimmest halls and auditoriums, there is a shimmer to her silken clothes. . . . when I look up, she is gone. I do not care that she is a phantom. A conjuring trick from an aging brain. I am grateful to see her again. I am glad to imagine that after all this time she has come back to me."[41] Memory restores here what he has loved, and lost, and longed for, becoming a deep and persistent source of reassurance in a fictional world where illness, ordinary mortality, historic exile, and the violent killings of the Holocaust are all recognizable parts.

Narrative structure emphasizes the power of recollection in this work by encapsulating, rendering virtually simultaneous, events widely separated in time as we live it. The first two chapters describe in different ways the events that enclose, like parentheses or the frame on which a weaving is made, everything else that happens in the novel. The work describes twice, in slightly different ways, the moments in which Eva enters and then leaves the narrator's life, signaling this novel's preoccupation with the layering in consciousness and in memory of everything that comes to—and then leaves—us. Subsequent chapters explain and interpret Eva's behavior and the narrator's responses to it. We learn to understand the logic of her movements in the world as the narrator, Joseph, fills in the gaps between her past and her arrival—like a midrashic scholar explicating a significant text. We learn also to understand the logic of Joseph's persona—so that we can appreciate the nature of Eva's effect upon him. The novel moves backward and forward in dramatic time, like a weaver's shuttle, carrying the narrative thread from Eva's life to Joseph's, linking the moments they share to the ones in which they are separate—and back again. Narrative structure allows us—like characters within the novel—to experience the nature of connectedness: the dance-like movement of connecting and disconnecting, holding on and letting go, that characterizes human relationships.

In the world itself, this novel suggests, phenomena also may become briefly, intermittently, linked with one another. Like Aciman, discovering the "remanence" of beloved places, remembering Paris and Egypt as he sits in a New York City park, Stollman demonstrates the nature of a world in which one river, one castle, calls up memory of another; in which parts of the human body resemble elements of the natural world (39, 152); in which the growth of a human embryo echoes the development of the language and literature of the Bible (61); in which "even seemingly unrelated creatures teach about each other and about our human selves" (120) as the vision of bees can suggest to us the limits of our own eyes (167, 186). What Mann knew as "the

mysterious . . . world of correspondences," and what Jonathan
Rosen represented both structurally and thematically as a vast
web in which we can—if we will—function as links, becomes in
this novel an underlying sense of connection that may or may
not liken things to one another but that does embrace them
within what Enoch Laquedem called *"das Netz der Wirklichkeit*—
the net of reality" (196).

The power to envision this "'net of reality,'" which "weaves
seemingly disparate things together and makes of them whole
cloth" (196), has been, like many precious things and people in
this work, largely lost. Thus vision and blindness become prominent motifs. Joseph's brother gradually loses his eyesight; Eva
has cared for a refugee girl who also goes blind. To discern the
limits of human vision, Joseph and Eva study the eyesight of
birds and insects. But scientific study yields only partial success.
Because we come after the loss of "the true prophets and their
prophecy," Laquedem teaches, we cannot learn to "see the holy
patterns and make sense" of the "endless confusions" of the
"present world' (195). We experience this world as a "chaos of unrelated events" (195) that make no sense to us. But Eva's father—
and eventually Joseph as well, who gives his life to the study of
the brain—believes that beneath the apparent chaos of "human
endeavors and cultures . . . revered literatures and apprehended
sciences, lies a unifying pattern, a structure too vast and too subtle to be seen" (8). Like Jonathan Rosen's sense of both Talmud
and Internet as phenomena too vast for any single mind to comprehend, Stollman's novel insists on the inadequacy of human
knowledge: "There is too much to know," Joseph says (119); the
"infinite complexity" (157) of the human body and the created
world hides itself from our limited understanding. But "sometimes . . . one's eyes are suddenly opened like those of the heav-
enly hosts. . . . one sees far beyond anything ever seen before by
humans, back into the far reaches of time" (158). This novel attempts to deliver such a vision.

Eva—and the illuminations in the ancient miscellany she
carries—become agents that "'open our eyes'" (172). In one of her
small, dazzling, performances she displays to Joseph and his family a miniature painting in an old and precious book, the *Augsberg
Miscellany*, that shows the emblem of the artist: an "aleph . . .
transfigured into a strange bird, its two eagle-clawed feet on

the ground, its upper extremities gilded wings, folded forward, protecting itself" (109). Around the figure of the bird, the novel weaves a rich assortment of interpretive suggestions. Birds are everywhere in this novel: sometimes their eyes teach about human vision; sometimes their iridescent feathers are likened to Eva's shimmering clothes (109).[42] She wears in her hair silver pins decorated with the heads of birds, pins that recall the silver ornaments on Torah scrolls. Scattered throughout the text, which will associate with Hebrew letters all the promises and memories alive in our past, the winged aleph acquires its deepest resonance when Eva explicates it midrashically: "Perhaps they are the wings of the Divine Presence, the holy Shekhinah, or the wings of eagles which will carry God's people back to Jerusalem when the Messiah comes" (110). As the novel multiplies such images and draws out their implications, Stollman deepens the sense of overlapping experiences, layered and mutually resonant in time. One gathers them, to perceive not only the net of reality in which all are held but also the textual allusions that enlarge their suggestiveness.

Eva's arrival is itself a midrashic moment, for her entry into the novel—as we have seen—is associated with the biblical passage that describes "the silvery trumpets that God commanded Moses to make for the calling of assemblies and for the journeying of the camps in the wilderness" (65). Eva's great beauty and dazzling clothes, her dramatic performances of exotic narratives—like her sudden appearance and her power to know the minds of Joseph and his family—suggest to him that she has come to them across "a narrow bridge from a mysterious and enchanted world we knew nothing about" (68). "I had the strange notion that she and the unknown world she came from were more real than we were" (112), he will think later, as though she were a holy messenger, an angel, or a soul made visible. In some respects she could be the collective soul of the Jewish people for she wanders like them, homeless, bearing—like the enameled and jeweled cases that contain the precious *Miscellany*—the learning of Judaic texts she acquired from her father and also bits of wisdom from other cultures. Like Joseph's mother, taught Torah by her father, Eva becomes a vessel in which the past survives. Her wanderings become emblematic not only of the vast journeys in time that Jewish learning survives but also of the historic aftermath of violent historical expulsions and oppressions. Because she has experienced Asian as well as European and Hebrew cultures, homelessness becomes here a simple, painful given of human experience. The last pages of this novel link this perception directly to collective Jewish experience, for Joseph must recite in shul the Torah passages that tell of endless, ancient journeying: "from Ramses . . . they encamped . . . in Sukkos. . . . And they traveled . . . from Sukkos . . . and encamped . . . in Eisom . . . which is at the edge of the desert" (269). Desolate, now, weeping because Eva has left them, he can neither see clearly nor understand the letters that swim before his eyes in "the great parchment sea" of the Torah. But he hears his mother's voice from the women's gallery— which is also "the voice of her father before her"—and "slowly, slowly, my mother fed me the words of the Torah one by one" (269). At first he can only repeat what he hears. But then the "holy letters began to swim back into view. . . .[T]hey told of themselves and of their ancient story, a story carried on from former times, born over and over again in our world, preserved in every generation and in the life of all created things. And they told of Eva, of her wandering soul with its storehouse of knowledge and garments of splendor, with its unbearable longings and moments of sorrow" (270). Though she cannot stay, and though the loss of her remains for Joseph "the most terrible pain" (271), she has summoned into the small world of the novel the drama and the beauty of a wide past, demonstrating its persistence within this long exile.

For Joseph, as for all the writers in this chapter, the work of mind is crucial to the uncovering and telling of obscure truths, little secrets. Among those—like Norma Rosen and Todd Gitlin— who conceive as dialogue our connection with our origins, the effort to imagine what is not ourselves, to address it, and then to listen hard as it responds, is fundamental to encountering the past. Reconnection with the fore-mothers and fathers, as with one's own parents and children, depends entirely on one's capacity for such work. For writers like Cynthia Ozick and Allegra Goodman, the labor of reconnection requires not only the power to imagine and to identify with what is not oneself but also the learning that enables one to make distinctions based upon awareness of what "Jewish" means, to choose among the seductive cultural options always open to contemporary Jews. And for writers like Jonathan Rosen, Rebecca Goldstein, and Aryeh Lev

Stollman, the mind must work to hold in tension apparently divergent, profoundly different ways of understanding and telling human experience—without forgetting the peculiar shape of one's own nature and history. One must wrestle with the language of science, in Goldstein's novel, to appreciate its relevance to the human dilemma of her characters. One must learn something of Josephus as well as Henry Adams, in Rosen's essay, to appreciate the ways in which they may teach us to move easily among our alternatives. And in Aryeh Stollman's novel one needs to consider both the foundational texts that have shaped Jewish culture and the scientific insights that reveal us to ourselves—if we would find consolation for our separations and losses in the promise that we can never lose what has touched, or loved, enlightened or changed us.

Beyond the mental work of learning, thinking, and imagining, memory becomes in these works the crucial faculty that unearths and connects us to the old secrets, that keeps alive in us whatever has mattered. In all the works of this chapter, the contemporary midrashic impulse is performing the work of collective memory. It draws awareness back to our sources. It remembers for us: that we are not the first of our kind to suffer loss, to risk looking backward, to hurt what we would love, to confront irreconcilable differences, to struggle against ourselves and the boundaries that seem to contain us, and to wander in this wilderness of time with only the stories of a collective past and a promised future to strengthen our hearts.

Epilogue
Moving from the Mirror to the Window

Almost at the moment we learn to speak, we learn to keep secrets. Are there reasons to tell them?

This study begins at the mirror. And although I believe the works examined here speak to all kinds of readers, I want to locate myself clearly, through my pronouns, among Americans and Jews: within the cultural community reflected in and by these writings. Early chapters show contemporary writers unearthing the secrets of our recent past: "working through" the aftermath of the Holocaust to consider the ways in which it has shaped our sense of ourselves and the homes from which we came. Two middle chapters suggest that our longer history may both constrict and empower us as it constructs our sense of gender. And the last chapter calls up textual precursors to our collective awareness of ourselves: our conflicts, our faulty loves, our losses. By clarifying the forces that have worked upon us, new wave writings show us some sources of ourselves.

But helping American Jews to know who we are, and how we got to be who we are, is only part of the cultural work these writings accomplish. I want to suggest that this study turns, at the end, from mirror to window. As writers encourage us to count our blessings and bind our wounds, mourn our losses and seek consolation for them, they also turn attention to the multiple seductions and threats of a world of people different from us. And not always friendly. Often preoccupied with the formative catastrophes of their own experience, calling for responses that are not yet clear to us.

In this early spring of 2004 American Jews confront hostility again: in war, in terrorism, as well as in the darkness of their collective memories. With the reading of every morning's news I wonder whether our responses to cultural difference and to hostility will be sufficient. The task of this moment may be to find a way between problematical alternatives. Between a belief on one hand that we can and should make things better for other people. And a fearful, angry wish on the other: to punish or to change what doesn't resemble or love us, what may even threaten instead of embracing us.

In the writings this study has considered, both sides of that ambivalence are muted. Largely by the effort to see more clearly. The attempt to uncover and to tell what may have been obscured by the great trauma of the Holocaust moves these writings toward clarification—rather than toward judgment or reaction. Perhaps there is in this effort a suggestion for readers who would attend now to what may be obscured by the troubles of this time.

Perhaps, within this noisy and distracting place of manifold differences, the necessary work for American Jews will be not only to speak from what we know of our old wounds and promises, but also to listen to those who can speak from their own hurt and hopeful places. To hear the human voices barely audible outside our windows. Some voices of other cultures can be heard in writings of the last chapter, which open a perceptual window onto the world in which we freely move. Those voices articulate visions that differ from our own. Our writers have opened our imaginations to them. Strong as we are now we need to learn from them, to listen. Listening, we may find in ourselves—or invent—responses that will honor not only the stories of our becoming, but also those of people who, like us, are working to uncover and to tell their own little secrets.

Notes

Preface

1. "Eli, the Fanatic" is a character in Philip Roth's first, prize-winning book of stories, *Goodbye, Columbus* (1959). Eli's struggle first to deny and then—astonishingly—to affirm his connection to a yeshiva full of black-hatted and suited survivors who have come to settle in his pleasant, largely gentile suburb has become, for many readers, representative of the attitudes of postwar American Jews.

2. In *Sensational Designs: The Cultural Work of American Fiction 1790–1860* (New York: Oxford UP, 1985) xvii, xi.

3. One is always mindful of the slipperiness of what we mean by "culture." For all serious scholars, as John Hollander pointed out, "the very idea of culture is as problematic as the idea of Jewishness" ("The Question of American Jewish Poetry" 36). For Hollander, the term might call up the Arnoldian sense, carried whole into the work of Lionel Trilling, that culture "involves a relation among texts, moral ideas, and the way in which they affect institutions" (36). But Hollander and others understand that culture is also "what happens every day, culture is normality" (Cynthia Ozick, "America: Toward Yavneh" 25)—like the taste of "Judaized versions of Balto-Slavic or Austro-Hungarian peasant cooking" (Hollander, "The Question of American Jewish Poetry" 36) or like the buried memories of "dark corners . . . secret alleys . . . shuttered windows . . . squalid courtyards" that preserved the old Jewish quarter of Prague within Kafka's mind so that, even as he walked the streets of the modern city, he was haunted by the "ghost of a vanished age" (Robert Alter, "Jewish Dreams and Nightmares" 62). All citations here are from essays gathered and reprinted in Hana Wirth-Nesher's *What Is Jewish Literature?* (Philadelphia: Jewish Publication Society, 1994).

4. Andrew Furman observes that "although assimilation will continue . . . to 'Americanize' its fair share of Jews in this country, I believe
we are in the midst of a powerful countervailing trend toward rediscov-
ery" of the ethnic heritage (*Contemporary Jewish American Writers and the
Multicultural Dilemma: The Return of the Exiled* [Syracuse, NY: Syracuse
UP, 2000] 17).

5. "Forewarning," *Metaphor and Memory* (New York: Knopf, 1989)
x–xi.

Introduction

1. In just the last few years, Jewish scholars have produced the fol-
lowing studies: Alan L. Mintz, *Popular Culture and the Shaping of Holo-
caust Memory in America* (Seattle: U of Washington P, 2001); Hilene
Flanzbaum, ed., *The Americanization of the Holocaust* (Baltimore: Johns
Hopkins UP, 1999); Julia Epstein and Lori Hope Lefkovitz, eds., *Shaping
Losses: Cultural Memory and the Holocaust* (Urbana: U of Illinois P, 2001),
and Alvin H. Rosenfeld, "The Americanization of the Holocaust,"
Thinking about the Holocaust after Half a Century, ed. Alvin H. Rosenfeld
(Bloomington: Indiana UP, 1997) 119–50.

2. *The Ghost Writer,* in *Zuckerman Bound: A Trilogy and Epilogue* (New
York: Farrar, Straus, and Giroux, 1985) 106.

3. Freedman's work explains why it is so hard to conceive a boundary between the dominant, gentile culture and the cultural lives of
Jews. Jewish identity is itself constructed by "reciprocal relations between Jewish and gentile culture" (*The Temple of Culture: Assimilation
and Anti-Semitism in Literary Anglo-America* [Oxford, UK: Oxford UP]
27); a Jew's own understanding of him- or herself, he points out—
remembering the work of Alain Finkielkraut—"is always connected to
a non-Jewish imaginary that itself was partially imagined by Jews" (29).
Thus, Phillip Roth's construction of the Patimkins' materialism surely
owes something to generations of gentile representations of Jews,
whose putative passion for money articulated the gentile writer's own
"ambivalence about the social, cultural, and affective consequences of
capitalism" (59). Nevertheless, the complexity of differentiating among
ethnic experiences of self and other doesn't entirely extinguish the felt
awareness of ethnic particularity that animates Roth's work, for example, as well as the work of many other American Jewish writers.

4. Peter Novick's *The Holocaust in American Life* (New York: Houghton Mifflin, 1999) and Norman Finkelstein's *The Holocaust Industry*
(London: Verso, 2000) belong to this polemic; my chapters two and
three—on writings of the second generation—will address the issues
raised by their work.

5. This label was first applied to American Jewish writers of the eighties and nineties by Morris Dickstein in "Ghost Stories: The New Wave of Jewish Writing," *Tikkun* 12.6 (1997): 33–36. Andrew Furman had used the term earlier (1995), but in a more general way, to refer to postimmigrant writers; Furman recalled Irving Howe's belief—which was common in that time among other critics, like Robert Alter—that Jewish "life after the immigrant experience . . . would prove too sterile and unrecognizably Jewish to inspire a new wave of American Jewish literature" ("A New 'Other' Emerges in American Jewish Literature: Philip Roth's Israel Fiction," *Contemporary Literature* 36.4 [1995]: 635).

6. Both Morris Dickstein ("Never Goodbye, Columbus: The Complex Fate of the Jewish-American Writer," *Nation,* 21 October 2001, 31) and Andrew Furman (*Contemporary Jewish American Writers and the Multicultural Dilemma: Return of the Exiled* [Syracuse, NY: Syracuse UP, 2000]) have described what Rosenbaum calls "new wave writings" as a literature of "return." But I am arguing here for a more complex, more conflicted reading of the ways in which current writers reengage with the collective past. I believe their reengagement speaks more directly to what Freud and several contemporary writers have called the cultural work of *"trauerarbeit,"* of delayed mourning rather than to the comparatively sentimental "retrieval" by the grandsons of what their fathers rejected. Perhaps it is even time to unpack the Oedipal assumptions of Marcus Hansen's sociological thesis that "what the son wishes to forget the grandson wishes to remember"?

7. In Sidra DeKoven Ezrahi's view, however, "the culture of nostalgia is manifest in American Jewish writing ranging from the more sentimental to the more ironic, eclectic efforts at recovery and projection" (*Booking Passage: Exile and Homecoming in the Modern Jewish Imagination* [Berkeley: U of California P, 2000] 228). At the opposite end of this continuum, Ruth Wisse has recently excluded most of the contemporary American Jewish writers from what she calls "the modern Jewish canon" because she sees them as largely "deracinated": without the specifically "Jewish energy" or access, through language, to the "heart of the Jewish polity" that entry into the canon would require (*The Modern Jewish Canon: A Journey through Language and Culture* [New York: Free P, 2000] 25).

8. "The Question of American Jewish Poetry," *What Is Jewish Literature,* ed. Hana Wirth-Nesher (Philadelphia: Jewish Publication Society, 1994) 46.

9. In making this distinction I am following Menachem Z. Rosensaft, who notes that "we are the first generation and we are the last generation: the first to be born after the Holocaust, and the last to have a direct link with that Eastern European Jewish existence that was so brutally

annihilated" ("Reflections of a Child of Holocaust Survivors," *Mid-stream* 27.9 (1981): 31.

10. *The War After: Living with the Holocaust* (London: Heinemann, 1996) 293. Karpf is a British writer included here because her work both echoes and develops many of the issues raised by American writers.

11. Ezrahi's *Booking Passage* furnishes the literary ancestry of this issue.

12. In *Of Woman Born*, Rich described one area of general cultural malaise when she insisted that we had lost awareness of "the full complexity and political significance of the woman's body, the full spectrum of power and powerlessness it represents." She asked women to begin "at last, to think through the body" ([1976; New York: Bantam, 1977] 289–90).

13. Though they don't seem to constitute what Dickstein calls a "complete inventory" of "new wave" issues, "the past," "identity," "gender," and "strict religious observance" have been present, with other issues, for a long time in American Jewish writings. What distinguishes their presence in new wave writing, I believe, is the particular cultural work that they perform in these texts.

14. Trans. Kevin O'Neill and David Suchoff (Lincoln: U of Nebraska P, 1994), originally published as *Le Juif Imaginaire* (Paris: Seuil, 1980).

1. Riddling Identity

1. Hannah Wirth-Nesher, "From Newark to Prague: Roth's Place in the American-Jewish Literary Tradition," *Reading Philip Roth,* ed. Asher Z. Milbauer and Donald G. Watson (New York: St. Martin's P, 1988) 31.

2. In a series of recent essays on Roth's work, Debra Shostak has argued that "throughout his career, Roth's concern has been subjectivity—usually the subjectivity of the Jew, who is usually male, usually a breaker of taboos, and usually both source and target of a comic perspective—a subjectivity constituted and exposed by desires and by embeddedness in linguistic fabrications" ("Roth/CounterRoth: Postmodernism, the Masculine Subject, and *Sabbath's Theater*," *Arizona Quarterly* 54.3 (1998): 119; see also her "Return to *The Breast:* The Body, the Masculine Subject, and Philip Roth," *Twentieth Century Literature* 45.3 (1999): 317–36, and "This Obsessive Reinvention of the Real: Speculative Narrative in Philip Roth's *The Counterlife*," *Modern Fiction Studies* 37.2 (1991): 197–215. On the idea that the post-Auschwitz self is postmodern, see the preface to Dominick LaCapra's *Representing the Holocaust: History, Theory, Trauma* (Ithaca, NY: Cornell UP, 1994), where he acknowledges the function of the Holocaust as a "more or less covert point of rupture between the modern and the postmodern" (xi).

3. *Goodbye, Columbus* (New York: Bantam, 1959) 13.

4. Sidra DeKoven Ezrahi, *Booking Passage: Exile and Homecoming in the Modern Jewish Imagination* (Berkeley: U of California P, 2000) 229.

5. Quoting Thane Rosenbaum in conversation.

6. For Diaspora Jews, perhaps the most useful, recent, theoretical formulation that bears on the vexed subject of Jewish identity is Daniel and Jonathan Boyarin's: "We will suggest that a Jewish subject-position founded on generational connection and its attendant anamnestic responsibilities and pleasures affords the possibility of a flexible and non-hermetic critical identity" ("Diaspora: Generation and the Ground of Jewish Identity," *Critical Inquiry* 19.4 [1993]: 701). Neither genealogy nor geography, neither faith nor practice, but family and memory, their "responsibilities and pleasures," become, then, the ground of what we now think of as collective Jewish identity. One very interesting new spin on this issue for American Jews is Sidra DeKoven Ezrahi's, who contextualizes our difficulty in knowing what we belong to and how we manifest that connection by comparing our sense of identity with the possibilities of identity for Jews in Israel. Considering our literature, she argues that our fictions of identity are a "diasporic privilege, unmoored and fanciful" by comparison with the facts that ground identity in Israel, facts that are rooted in its "ingathering of the material, obligatory world" (224).

7. Preface to the *Lyrical Ballads,* 2nd ed. (1800).

8. *My Life as a Man* (New York: Holt, Rinehart, 1974) 240.

9. Ezrahi has pointed out that Roth's later work—from *The Counterlife* on—focuses sharply the problem faced by Jews who, after the destruction of the European Diaspora, could no longer accept their way of accommodating exile as a "provisional but viable Jewish condition, suspended between ancient memories of destruction and visions of redemption" (221). After the Holocaust, Ezrahi argues, it appeared that "the *galut,* or exile, could no longer furnish a normative model for the rehabilitation of Jewish life" (221). And after the Zionist creation of Israel, which furnished a new normative model for that rehabilitation, Roth's fictional "experiments in trying on alternative destinies" set themselves up in opposition to that new model. Thus, for Ezrahi, Roth's later novels differentiate between "exilic and 'autochthonous' forms of Judaism: as a mimetic culture or masked ball in *galut*" or as "a 'genuine' and 'real' culture in the sacred center" that was once, and has become again, Israel. In her view, "Zion and Exile resurface" in Roth's later work "as alternative organizing principles of the Jewish imagination" (235). And, one would add, as alternative principles of existence as well. My study breaks this complicated existential and theoretical Jewish problem into two parts, considering on one hand the way in which writers of the new wave process represent—from the perspective

of the Diaspora—the issue of returning to, or recreating, or reimagining "home." And on the other hand, this study takes up the problem in new wave writers of the Jewish self—fragmented, fluid, radically conflicted, ingeniously performative, tormented by memory—that emerges in Roth's earlier work.

10. But cf. Ezrahi's argument that the "vertiginous process of endless self-invention" apparent in Roth's *Zuckerman Trilogy* and *Counterlife* captures a peculiarly "diasporic" playfulness that *Operation Shylock* then opposes to the "Zionist pull of 'the real'" (224–25). Diasporism, in that later novel, amounts to "the privilege to 'swim in art,' to try out any role, any character, without paying the consequences of fixed identity" (228), consequences that Israelis, of course, have to pay as they become "the center of gravity for the drifting, ex-centric, diasporic imagination" (231).

11. Published too late (1993) to be considered a forerunner of new wave writings, this book—as Michael Rothberg has argued—develops, as Ezrahi also points out, "binary oppositions" in characters "many of which focus on questions of individual and collective identity" (*Traumatic Realism: The Demands of Holocaust Representation* [Minneapolis: U of Minnesota P, 2000] 195). According to Rothberg, Roth's later work juxtaposes the essentially incoherent identity of American Jews with the stable identity of the Israeli writer and survivor, Aharon Appelfeld, in order to "anchor" (200) Zuckerman by differentiation or to "modulate" his "self-hatred" (190) by addressing "the spatially and temporally displaced effect on Jewish-American identity of the extermination of European Jewry" (193).

12. "Imagining Jews," *Reading Myself and Others* (New York: Farrar, Straus and Giroux, 1975) 229.

13. *The Temple of Culture: Assimilation and Anti-Semitism in Literary Anglo-America* (Oxford, UK: Oxford UP) 205.

14. Lonoff is a combination of Salinger, Malamud, and several New York Jewish intellectuals (Freedman 205–06).

15. *The Ghost Writer*, in *Zuckerman Bound: A Trilogy and Epilogue* (New York: Farrar, Straus, and Giroux, 1985) 121.

16. Debra Shostak has argued that "embodiment for Roth's male characters is largely focused on their sexuality and, almost inevitably, on the capacity of the penis as literal organ to achieve the symbolic power of the phallus" ("Roth/CounterRoth" 120).

17. But David Monaghan, in *"The Great American Novel* and *My Life as a Man*: An Assessment of Philip Roth's Achievement" (*The International Fiction Review* 2 [1975]: 113–20) argues that there is a "consistent" vision, which he calls "the theme of failure of commitment" (113).

18. In "Fathers and Sons in History: Philip Roth's *The Counterlife*," Matthew Wilson notes that the novel "enacts the contestation of 'history'

as a master narrative with the heterogeneity of 'histories'" (*Prooftexts* 11.1 [1991]: 42).

19. *The Anatomy Lesson* (New York: Farrar, Straus and Giroux, 1983) 445–46. Remembering that American writers like Henry James, T. S. Eliot, Ernest Hemingway, and F. Scott Fitzgerald, among others, deliberately moved away from home and family to become writers, one wonders whether Roth's lament is peculiar to American Jews.

20. From a social point of view, this effort at reconnection probably serves as what Michael Rothberg has called in another context "a metaphor for the emergence in the Jewish community of a new understanding of 'the Holocaust' in the late 1960's, an understanding that testifies to the spatially and temporally displaced effect on Jewish-American identity of the extermination of European Jewry" (*Traumatic Realism* 193).

21. But Michael Rothberg has argued that recollection of the Holocaust is recommended to Nathan by Judge Wapter as an "antidote" to Nathan's "self-hatred" (191).

22. In the second part of "'I Always Wanted You To Admire My Fasting'; or, Looking at Kafka" (*Reading Myself and Others* 247–70).

23. Ezrahi speaks of Roth's "nostalgic geography" that makes Eastern and Central Europe the "ultimate reference for the authentic Jew" (232). But nostalgia actually yields to tragic insight when Roth discovers that what Europe offers cannot be carried home to America.

24. But see Emily Miller Budick's "Acknowledging the Holocaust in Contemporary American Fiction and Criticism," *Breaking Crystal: Writing and Memory after Auschwitz*, ed. Efraim Sicher (Urbana: U of Illinois P, 1998) 329–43. Budick argues that Anne "gives voice to an anguish that Zuckerman's novel cannot quite contain. . . . [S]he indeed ghostwrites or haunts his text and speaks through it" (339).

25. "Epilogue," *The Prague Orgy*, in *Zuckerman Bound: A Trilogy and Epilogue*.

26. But cf. Ezrahi, who believes that "the culture of nostalgia is manifest in American Jewish writing ranging from the more sentimental to the more ironic, eclectic efforts at recovery and projection" (228). Chapter 10, on "home," deals more fully with the problem that Roth's discovery raises for American Jewish writers of the new wave.

27. Shostak believes that Roth "clearly accepts the psychoanalytic proposition that the place to look for the source of subjectivity is in desire" ("Roth/CounterRoth" 120).

28. *The Counterlife* (New York: Farrar, Straus and Giroux, 1986) 311.

29. Shostak, "'This Obsessive Reinvention of the Real'" 199.

30. "An Interview with Philip Roth," *Reading Philip Roth* 12.

31. Aharon Appelfeld noticed years ago that "the stranger brings out the Jew in Roth" ("The Artist as a Jewish Writer," *Reading Philip Roth* 15).

2. Writing the Pathos of Belatedness

1. Efraim Sicher ("The Holocaust in the Postmodernist Era," *Breaking Crystal: Writing and Memory after Auschwitz*, ed. Efraim Sicher [Urbana: U of Illinois P, 1998] 298–99) reminds us that George Steiner was the first to point out that "We come *after*. We know now that a man can read Goethe or Rilke in the evening, that he can play Bach and Schubert, and go to his day's work at Auschwitz in the morning" (*Language and Silence: Essays on Language, Literature, and the Inhuman* [New York: Atheneum, 1967] ix). Unlike Sicher, I am considering here only the children of survivors and not the "generation contemporaneous" with them who "may share many of their psychological, ideological, and theological concerns" (Introduction, *Breaking Crystal* 7).

2. Eva Fogelman, who originated and led one of the first groups in which children of survivors explored their legacy, observes that until the publication of Helen Epstein's *New York Times* piece on 19 June 1977, and her subsequent book, *Children of the Holocaust: Conversations with Sons and Daughters of Survivors* (New York: Putnam, 1979), there was little awareness among these individuals that they shared distinctive characteristics ("Group Belonging and Mourning as Factors in Resilience in Second Generation of Holocaust Survivors," *Psychoanalytic Review* 85.4 [1998]: 537).

3. Thane Rosenbaum, *Second Hand Smoke* (New York: St. Martin's P, 1999).

4. Tompkins argues that popular novels need to be seen "as doing a certain kind of cultural work within a specific historical situation" for they provide "society with a means of thinking about itself, defining certain aspects of a social reality which the authors and their readers shared, dramatizing its conflicts, and recommending solutions. It is the notion of literary texts as doing work, expressing and shaping the social context that produced them, that I wish to substitute finally for the critical perspective that sees them as attempts to achieve a timeless, universal ideal of truth and formal coherence" (*Sensational Designs*, [Oxford, UK: Oxford UP, 1985] 200).

5. *Writing and Rewriting the Holocaust* (Bloomington, Ind.: Indiana UP, 1990) 3.

6. Alvin Rosenfeld, "Exploring the Dark Underside of Survival," *Forward*, 28 May 1999, 12.

7. As I have argued elsewhere ("Traumatic Memory and American Jewish Writers: One Generation After the Holocaust," *Modern Jewish Studies* 11.3–4 [1999]: 188–97), the "work of mourning" left to those who come "after" a collective and historical—rather than a purely personal—loss comes clearest in the scholarship of historians like Saul Friedlander,

Dominick LaCapra, and Eric Santner, who learned from two early scholars of postwar German psychology, Alexander and Margarete Mitscherlich the usefulness of carrying insights from psychoanalytic literature
over to social and cultural phenomena and the importance of acknowledging that "internal acceptance of loss must be struggled for, learned,
and accomplished. This is why," the Mitscherlichs point out, "in psychoanalysis we speak of the *work* of mourning" [my emphasis].

8. I've borrowed this term from Aaron Hass, *The Aftermath: Living
with the Holocaust* (Cambridge, UK: Cambridge UP, 1995).

9. Like Michael Rothberg, I want to define "traumatic event" here as
"an event that was not fully experienced at the time of its occurrence
and that thus returns to haunt the psyches of its victims" (*Traumatic Realism: The Demands of Holocaust Representation* [Minneapolis: U of Minnesota P, 2000] 12).

10. Freud's story of the child who masters the absence of his mother
by playing a game in which he first discards and then retrieves an object
provides a clear example of repetition as psychologists understand it.
The point of the game is to make the passive experience of loss active, to
"master" it by making it happen (see his "Remembering, Repeating and
Working Through"). This tendency to repeat a certain action as a means
of gaining control over whatever has caused great pain appears often in
postmodern theoretical discourses; Eric Santner has observed that one
notices in it a repetitive "metaphorics of loss and impoverishment . . . of
shattering, rupture, mutilation, fragmentation . . . of fissures, wounds,
rifts, gaps and abysses" (*Stranded Objects: Mourning, Memory, and Film
in Postwar Germany* [Ithaca, NY: Cornell UP, 1990] 7).

11. Peter Novick's *The Holocaust in American Life* (New York: Houghton Mifflin, 1999) does as good a job as any other work of documenting
the proliferation of Holocaust texts, courses, and performances in popular culture.

12. See, for example, Yehuda Bauer's "Jewish Resistance—Myth or
Reality?" and "Unarmed Resistance and Other Responses" in his *Re-
thinking the Holocaust* (New Haven, CT: Yale UP, 2001) 119–66.

13. Atina Grossman, "Victims, Villains, and Survivors: Gendered
Perceptions and Self-Perceptions of Jewish Displaced Persons in Occu-
pied Postwar Germany," *Sexuality and German Fascism,* spec. issue of the
Journal of the History of Sexuality 11.1–2 (2002): 291–318.

14. In 1988, William G. Niederland recalled introducing the term
"survivor syndrome" into the professional literature in 1961; his article
on the "The Clinical Aftereffects of the Holocaust in Survivors and
Their Offspring" (in *The Psychological Perspectives of the Holocaust and of
Its Aftermath,* ed. Randolph L. Braham [New York: Columbia UP, 1988]
45–52) summarizes his findings on that syndrome.

15. "Lifelong Reporting Trip," *Second Generation Voices: Reflections by Children of Holocaust Survivors and Perpetrators,* ed. Alan L. Berger and Naomi Berger (Syracuse, NY: Syracuse UP) 81.

16. Efraim Sicher argues that "telling the story is a form of working through trauma, which ideally ends with the separation of the second generation from the dead and their connection to a real past, to a family and people in which they are a living link, transmitting a heritage to future generations. It is storytelling above all that shapes collective and personal memory in that transmission, and the way the story is told, the issue of narrativity itself, therefore must be central to any discussion of the situation of the post-Holocaust generation, which is positioned between history and memory and is removed from the experience by fifty years and more" (Introduction, *Breaking Crystal* 13).

17. Dan Bar-On, who has studied the second generation in Israel and in Europe, explains that their parents, the survivors "had their own reasons for repressing and silencing what they had gone through, including the feeling of guilt about family members who perished, the difficulty of handling the images of horror and the pain of separation, and the helplessness in dealing with these feelings in the new, very different, Israeli reality. The survivors wanted to forget and make others forget, and they tried to save their children from having to face such difficult memories" ("Transgenerational Aftereffects of the Holocaust in Israel: Three Generations," *Breaking Crystal* 99).

But Ellen Fine, in an essay on the post-Holocaust generation in the Diaspora, explains that "despite their reluctance to talk, the parents transmitted their experience through indirect references such as glances, fragments of conversation among themselves and other survivors, emotional responses to current events, the display of old photographs, and other forms of non-verbal communication" ("Transmission of Memory: The Post-Holocaust Generation in the Diaspora," *Breaking Crystal* 191).

18. *Displaced Persons: Growing Up American after the Holocaust* (New York: Scribner, 2001) 341.

19. Lina Reitman-Dobi recalls that her "mother never sat down to deliver a detailed account of her childhood itinerary. Over the years, information about her childhood and the effects of the war came in scattered pieces. They still do" ("Once Removed," *Second Generation Voices* 17).

20. In a similar way, Lina Reitman-Dobi remembers her mother referring to her father's war medals from a "country that later tries to kill him" as if "it had been written by someone for a serendipitous effect. My mother depersonalized a lot of things this way," she observes ("Once Removed" 23–24). Asher Z. Milbauer recalls that his parents' "most gruesome" stories "were punctuated by humor, an occasional

chuckle, and even laughter, all of a soothing and caressing quality" ("Teaching to Remember," *Second Generation Voices* 39).

21. Sidra DeKoven Ezrahi in *Booking Passage: Exile and Homecoming in the Modern Jewish Imagination* (Berkeley: U of California P, 2000) observes that "after 1945 the mandate to remember takes on deadly earnestness for Jewish writers; every act of recollection becomes a gesture of re-collection, of rescue, measured . . . by its function as one more defense against oblivion" (205). In this process, she argues, "the endemic American quest for a lost—an irrecoverable—community" (215) will produce a "culture of nostalgia . . . in American Jewish writing ranging from the more sentimental to the more ironic, eclectic efforts at recovery and projection" (228).

22. Counting the immigrants themselves—and not their American-born children—as first generation Americans, Norman Podhoretz ("The Last Time I Saw London," *Commentary*, January 2001, 36–43) cites a "sociological 'law' (richly confirmed in the ethnic and religious worlds around us today) that was propounded by Marcus Hansen in the 1950's about immigrants to America: what the second generation wishes to forget, the third wishes to remember" (38). The present study counts the children of survivors as the "second generation" after the Holocaust and, in most cases, as "first generation" Americans. But they conform, in their "wish to remember," to their cohort who belong to what Podhoretz would call "third generation" Americans.

23. *The War After: Living with the Holocaust* (London: Heinemann, 1996) 17.

24. For Lisa Reitman-Dobi, too, the parental past was laundered and the children were expected to "appreciate the rich childhood that had been denied" to her mother, without mourning its loss ("Once Removed" 18–19). Instead, she remembers, "I felt sad. I felt sad for my mother, sad for everyone, and then guilty for feeling sad" (19).

25. One must bear three caveats in mind when considering the generalizations supported by these memoirs. First, as Joseph Berger reminds us at the outset of his memoir, one ought not to understand the characters of these parent/survivors as constructed only by the Holocaust. His mother, he learned, "was shaped in large part by the years before the war. And I was shaped by those years as well. Her mother's death when she was not quite six robbed me of a piece of my mother. Her father's decision to send her away from home at fourteen so she could earn her own way sent me out into the world in ways that I was never ready for. . . . Her panicked distraction has become my panicked distraction; her grief has, in some small measure, become my grief; her laughter, my laughter, whether I like it or not" (*Displaced Persons* 20). For the purposes of this study, the confluence of feeling between parent

and child is of primary significance. But one needs to remember the shaping influence of the parental past that predates the war as well as recognize the powerful role of the Holocaust in the lives of these parents and children.

Second, individual variations among the children of survivors are probably as important as what they have in common. Anne Karpf recognizes that many of the difficulties she experienced were particular to her—that her sister had a different configuration of problems—and that there were as many different kinds of survivor families as survivors. She notes that "there were also other traumatised families who had similar difficulties to us—the families of alcoholics, or drug addicts, for instance." But she points out as well that "if survivor families shared many problems with non-survivor families, in us these were often peculiarly intense and in my own case made many common solutions unavailable. Certainly my fear of annihilation was quite unlike anything expressed by my peers and bore no relation to my actual experiences" (142–43).

And, third, many studies confirm that, as Eva Fogelman reports, "there are no significant differences between children of survivors and a controlled cohort group on mental illness indices, symptoms, psychiatric disorders" ("Group Belonging and Mourning" 538).

26. Lisa Reitman-Dobi also believes that her mother "had basic living confused with being in perpetual motion. The only reason to stop moving was fatigue and even that was not an acceptable state of affairs" ("Once Removed" 22).

27. But Sara Horowitz understands this process differently. "The memory work of children of survivors," she argues, "struggles to disrupt the canonicity of Holocaust representation by inscribing its own versions onto the past and rediscovering its disruptive effects in themselves" ("Auto/Biography and Fiction after Auschwitz: Probing the Boundaries of Second-Generation Aesthetics," *Breaking Crystal* 291–92).

28. Julie Salamon notes the effect on herself of her mother's determination to think "positive" after her liberation: "When I heard my mother's description of the food at Auschwitz, I understood why my closest friend never believes me when I compliment her on a meal. I understood why I was brought up to think that there were two designations for food: 'delicious' and 'less delicious'" (*The Net of Dreams: A Family's Search for a Rightful Place* [New York: Random, 1996] 120).

29. Similarly, Lisa Reitman-Dobi notes retrospectively that her mother was unable to "relate" to her child's normal childhood. "When children were catty at school, she groped for what to say to me. Because her standard of childhood pain was conditioned by abstracted trauma, genuine commiseration with me was virtually impossible. . . . I didn't

know what to make of it. Her pain was worse, so mine was ridiculously small?" ("Once Removed" 27).

30. Sara Horowitz believes that "the second-generation writer feels the biographical and psychological imprint of the events of the Holocaust as immediate and present. At the same time, the experiential and temporal distance creates a blankness, a cognitive gap at odds with a psychological knowing" ("Auto/Biography and Fiction after Auschwitz" 290).

31. Efraim Sicher observes that "narrative is a way of making sense, of putting one's life in order, doubly difficult after the Holocaust left blanks and disorder . . ." (Introduction, *Breaking Crystal* 6).

32. Eva Fogelman explains that "American Jews did not want to be near the survivors because they were victims. It made *them* look bad." She notes that "guilt for not rescuing or helping in other ways" may also have contributed to Americans' avoidance of survivors and their stories ("Group Belonging and Mourning" 539).

33. Sara Horowitz observes that " second-generation writers anchor their aesthetic representations in research rather than in memory, as they trace a trauma both remembered and not remembered, transmitted and not transmitted" ("Auto/Biography and Fiction after Auschwitz" 278).

34. The name and the phrase "all her lost children" call up, of course, Jeremiah's image of mother Rachel, whose "cry is heard in Ramah / Wailing, bitter weeping/ Rachel weeping for her children. / She refuses to be comforted / For her children who are gone" (Jeremiah 31:15).

35. The critical introduction to part 3 of the Bergers' *Second Generation Voices* and Naomi Berger's own essay, "Coming Full Circle," offer several different ways of describing these journeys back to Europe: they appear as "rituals of remembrance," as "pilgrimages," and as confrontations with "walled-off areas deep in [the] being" of the one who goes "home" again (91, 109).

36. Asher Z. Milbauer notes that his parents' experience of Europe led them to instill in their children an "awareness of being different" that might help them "deal with the pain we would inevitably experience when rejected by what they perceived [as] an inhospitable foster home instead of a native land" ("Teaching to Remember" 43). But Julie Salamon's *Net of Dreams* makes explicit the sense of Europe as "home" — or at least as a way to get "home." When she decides to go to Poland to revisit Auschwitz during the making of Spielberg's "Schindler's List," she confesses that she "really didn't care whether his movie worked or not. I just thought it might help me find my way home" (9).

37. Cf. Ezrahi, chapters 8 and 9. Efraim Sicher senses more ambiguity in our attitudes toward Europe: "we are all touched by the fire in one

way or other, and our confrontation with our cultural roots in Europe is burdened with mixed feelings" (Introduction, *Breaking Crystal* 14).

38. *Lost in Translation: A Life in a New Life* (New York: Dutton, 1989) 6.

39. But cf. Alice Yaeger Kaplan's reading of this work, which emphasizes the unreality of Hoffman's nostalgic re-presentation of her childhood home.

40. I have traced in detail Helen Epstein's return to Europe in my discussion of her memoir: *Where She Came From* ("Traumatic Memory and American Jewish Writers"). In her essay, "Returning" she records the visit to a ruined Jewish cemetery in which she rejects the notion that Europe is home (*Second Generation Voices* 125, 127); Naomi Berger records a similar moment when she turns back from a cemetery she had wanted to visit but found locked against her ("Coming Full Circle," *Second Generation Voices* 109). Perhaps Melvin Bukiet's is the most extreme form of rejection: "There is nothing here for me," he writes, when he recalls visiting the village his family lived in; "It is not that the evil is more personal here than at Auschwitz, but that it is unexpected" [note well, the present tense]; the people who live there now have even forgotten what it was like to hate Jews ("Memory Macht Frei," *Second Generation Voices* 136–38).

Michal Govrin, however, enlarges the significance of the return to Europe by likening it to "the journey every child makes to the regions of before he was born, to the unknown past of his parents, to the secret of his birth" ("The Journey to Poland," *Second Generation Voices* 141).

41. "Is This Picasso, or Is It the Jews?" *Tikkun* (1997) 41.

42. In Freud's shadow, we enjoy a significant body of scholarly literature on traumatic memory and mourning. In 1966 two German psychoanalysts first called attention to Germany's inability to mourn its own unmastered past. They meant by "mastering" a "sequence of steps in self-knowledge" (Mitscherlich 14). Freud called these "remembering, repeating, working through." Each of those terms has become crucial to later scholars in this field. But it is the last one, "working through," that speaks most directly to the kind of cultural work second-generation writers are doing. When memory of trauma is repressed or contaminated, as Lawrence Langer has shown us, and when the repetitive acting out of losses we cannot bear to remember turns sterile, as Dominick LaCapra has argued, then working through becomes crucial to mourning. For him the term means "acquiring some perspective" on traumatic experience (*Representing the Holocaust: History, Theory, Trauma* [Ithaca, NY: Cornell UP, 1994] 200); it calls for an effort to achieve critical distance (200), to modify experience by interpretation (209), to make ever more specific what was lost, and to feel, again, the anguish of losing (215). This is the work of mourning, he explains, in which even the

carnivalesque may play a part. If we would master this traumatic past, he warns, we must be prepared to "read scars," for whatever is "not confronted critically does not disappear; it tends to return as the repressed" (126; all of the above material is drawn from my essay, "Traumatic Memory and American Jewish Writers"). Emily Miller Budick also notes that "mourning, according to Freud, serves an important function in the life of the individual. As Saul Friedlander and Dominick LaCapra have pointed out, the psychic function of mourning might be no less important for a community or a people or a nation" ("Acknowledging the Holocaust in Contemporary American Fiction and Criticism," *Breaking Crystal* 331).

Dan Bar-On summarizes changing interpretations of the phrase "working through": It "was developed in relation to individual therapy. It was used to explain the laborious psychological process, demanded over and above a one-time 'insight,' as the individual confronts the contents of repressed childhood trauma. . . . Even though the concept was developed by Freud to describe the process between patient and therapist, it was widened over the years to cope with social traumatic experiences and . . . post-traumatic stress disorder. . . . The original goal of the process of working through—'letting go' of the influence of the repressed content—was later replaced by a more modest goal—the ability to 'live with' the painful traumatic event" ("Transgenerational Aftereffects of the Holocaust in Israel" 96).

Although one can never overlook the individual context in which "working through" takes place in the writings of the second generation, the collective, cultural application of that term—as LaCapra and Friedlander use it—is more directly pertinent to what I think of as the "cultural work" performed by these texts.

43. *The Modern Jewish Canon: A Journey through Language and Culture* [New York: Free P, 2000] 218–19. See also Susan Rubin Suleiman's discussion of Holocaust memoirs written in a "stepmother" language ("Monuments in a Foreign Tongue: On Reading Holocaust Memoirs by Emigrants," *Exile and Creativity: Signposts, Travelers, Outsiders, Backward Glances,* ed. Susan Rubin Suleiman [Durham, NC: Duke UP, 1998] 397–417). Suleiman was born in Budapest in 1939.

44. Though Alan Berger objects to the metaphor (Introduction, *Second Generation Voices* 6), it persists in much writing by and about the second generation. Wendy Joy Kuppermann, for example, recalls that when she heard her father describe the ravaged beauty of a girl who "survived" the war, she "could not take away her father's deep pain so she just took his hand. They were knit together into the very same scarred keloid thread of the warp" ("The Far Country Memoirs," *Second Generation Voices* 61). I am particularly interested in the ways that

metaphor comes when a writer finds the voice sufficient to tell this old pain. Nava Semel twists the metaphor of the scar just enough to enlarge its reference. Recalling her first attempts to tell long-silenced family stories, she writes: "Not young. I ran in the scorched field where a meteor had passed. Everything that had once grown here turned to ashes and was burned up. I sit at the margin of the crater left by the blow to the planet and ask how it came. From what corner in what orbit, and if in the next rotation, it will strike again, lying in wait behind us" ("Intersoul Flanking: Writing about the Holocaust," *Second Generation Voices* 71).

45. *Why History Matters: Life and Thought* (New York: Oxford UP, 1997) 39.

46. *Budapest Diary: In Search of the Motherbook* (Lincoln: U of Nebraska P, 1996) 46.

47. "A Yiddish Writer Who Writes in French," *Second Generation Voices* 230.

48. "On the Yiddish Question," *Second Generation Voices* 233.

49. Robert Alter has developed at length the particular properties of "The Jewish Voice," *Commentary*, October 1995, 39–45.

50. One student of second-generation poets and novelists in Israel sees in their work primarily a "transgenerational transfer of the survivors' syndrome" (Hanna Yaoz, "Inherited Fear," *Breaking Crystal* 161). Their poetry, she believes, becomes "fantastic" because "what the Nazis did deviated from any former reality and pushed the imagination to the absurd"; therefore, "when we speak of the Holocaust the fantastic *is* real" (164).

51. *Where She Came From: A Daughter's Search for Her Mother's History* (Boston: Little, Brown, 1997) 10.

52. For a sense of the importance of "reparation" in the process of mourning and the different ways in which it has been understood by theorists see n.9 in my "Traumatic Memory and American Jewish Writers" 194–95.

53. Though Freud and others imagine that memory serves the process of mourning, Eugene L. Pogany observes that mourning works "to access and preserve memory—to lighten grief so that memory could . . . be kept alive and carried on" ("Path to Kaddish: Prologue to a Son's Spiritual Autobiography," *Second Generation Voices* 185).

3. Voice and Mourning in the Aftermath

1. This anxiety has a distinguished history. In 1949 Theodor Adorno said that "after Auschwitz, to write a poem is barbaric." He republished the sentence in 1951, and in 1962 he explained that: "Through the aesthetic principle of stylization . . . an unimaginable fate still seems as if it

had some meaning; it becomes transfigured, with something of the horror removed" (John Felstiner, "Translating Paul Celan's 'Todesfuge': Rhythm and Repetition as Metaphor," *Probing the Limits of Representation: Nazism and the Final Solution*, ed. Saul Friedlander [Cambridge, MA: Harvard UP] 242).

Sidra DeKoven Ezrahi notes that Adorno returned again and again to his original statement, probing the contradiction that "the abundance of real suffering tolerates no forgetting . . . [that] this suffering . . . demands the continued existence of art [even as] . . . it prohibits it. It is now virtually in art alone that suffering can still find its own voice, consolation, without immediately being betrayed by it" ("The Grave in the Air: Unbound Metaphors in Post-Holocaust Poetry," *Probing the Limits of Representation* 260). The Jewish Museum exhibit of March 2002 provoked the most recent critical responses from Walter Reich, "Appropriating the Holocaust" (*New York Times*, 15 Mar. 2002: A23) and Michael Kimmelman, "Evil, the Nazis and Shock Value" (*New York Times*, 15 Mar. 2002: E33, 35). Andrew Levy has written on the ways in which Holocaust images are being exploited within the international corporate culture ("Play Will Make You Free: Reprising 'The Triumph of the Will,'" *The Americanization of the Holocaust*, ed. Hilene Flanzbaum [Baltimore: Johns Hopkins UP, 1999] 211–24). Sidra DeKoven Ezrahi foresaw this exploitation of Holocaust imagery (in "Revisioning the Past: The Changing Legacy of the Holocaust in Hebrew Literature," *Salmagundi* 66 [Winter 1985/Spring 1986]: 246). Steven Aschheim has also predicted that "National Socialism and the atrocities its adherents committed will continue to play foundational roles [in contemporary Israeli and Diaspora culture] but will increasingly do so not only in problematic but also in consciously problematizing ways. More and more the subject will be torn out of its known, predictable contexts and undergo critical 'defamiliarization.' The controversies around its proper interpretation, appropriate lessons, and commemoration will generate its eventual cultural centrality and vitality" ("Nazism and the Holocaust in Contemporary Culture," *In Times of Crisis: Essays on European Culture, Germans, and Jews* [Madison: U of Wisconsin P, 2001] 53).

2. Marianne Hirsch notes that "Adorno's radical suspicion has haunted writing for the last forty years" ("Family Pictures: *Maus*, Mourning, and Post-Memory," *Discourse* 15.2 [1992]: 9). Efraim Sicher, for example, is concerned about "the distorting images of the Holocaust in popular culture . . . which . . . may be working against memory or appropriating the Holocaust to political agendas and cultural values quite removed from history or the original victims" ("The Scandal of the Holocaust," *The European Legacy* 6.5 [2001] 639–41). Lawrence Langer, in "Preempting the Holocaust" (*Preempting the Holocaust* [New

Haven, CT: Yale UP, 1998] 1–22, shares this concern. Eli Wiesel has said that "when knowledge becomes imagination it is as damaging as when imagination assumes the authority of knowledge" (qtd. in Berger *Children of Job: American Second-Generation Witnesses to the Holocaust* [Albany: SUNY P, 1997] 18). Sara Horowitz has considered the critical case against imaginative work on the Holocaust in "Auto/Biography and Fiction after Auschwitz: Probing the Boundaries of Second-Generation Aesthetics" (*Breaking Crystal: Writing and Memory after Auschwitz*, ed. Efraim Sicher [Urbana: U of Illinois P, 1998] 276–96).

3. Cynthia Ozick has written: "In theory, I'm with Theodor Adorno's famous dictum: after Auschwitz, no more poetry. And yet my writing has touched on the Holocaust again and again. I cannot *not* write about it. It rises up and claims my furies" ("Roundtable Discussion," *Writing and the Holocaust*, ed. Berel Lang [New York: Holmes and Meier, 1988] 284). Alan Mintz notes that "today the Holocaust is pervasive" in American culture (*Popular Culture and the Shaping of Holocaust Memory in America* [Seattle: U of Washington P, 2002] 3). Michael Rothberg also notes "the Holocaust's intensified presence in contemporary culture" (*Traumatic Realism: The Demands of Holocaust Representation* ([Minneapolis: U of Minnesota P, 2000] 184).

4. In "Notes toward a Holocaust Fiction," *Accidents of Influence: Writing as a Woman and a Jew in America* (Albany: SUNY P, 1992) 107.

5. See Hirsch's *Family Frames: Photography, Narrative, and Postmemory* (Cambridge, MA: Harvard UP, 1997). The term suggests a phenomenon of "transmitted, borrowed, or second-generation memory" that has been passed unconsciously to children and grandchildren by parents who often could not speak of their experiences (Marianne Hirsch and Susan Rubin Suleiman, "Material Memory: Holocaust Testimony in Post-Holocaust Art," *Shaping Losses: Cultural Memory and the Holocaust*, ed. Julia Epstein and Lori Hope Lefkovitz [Urbana: U of Illinois P, 2001] 89). To explain the persistence of unspoken memory in survivors of trauma who conducted, afterward, apparently normal lives, Hirsch and Suleiman note that "students of traumatic memory have proposed a model of dissociation, based on the work of Pierre Janet, as an alternative to Freud's model of repression to represent the processing of trauma. The traumatic material is split off, intact, and persists on a parallel track to consciousness and the present but is still unavailable to narrative recall and assimilation. Such splitting is, in effect, a kind of juxtaposition because the traumatic experience exists, unintegrated and next to everyday living" (100). For more clinical data, see Arlene Steinberg, "Holocaust Survivors and Their Children: A Review of the Clinical Literature," *Healing Their Wounds: Psychotherapy with Holocaust Survivors and Their Families*, ed. Paul Marcus and Alan Rosenberg (New

York: Prager, 1989) 23–48; Milton E. Jucovy, "Therapeutic Work with Survivors and Their Children: Recurrent Themes and Problems," *Healing Their Wounds* 51–66; and Paul Marcus and Alan Rosenberg, "Treatment Issues with Survivors and Their Offspring: An Interview with Anna Ornstein," *Healing Their Wounds* 105–16. As early as 1978 Henry Krystal reviewed the psychoanalytic literature, beginning with Freud, on trauma and affects (*The Psychoanalytic Study of the Child*, vol. 33 (New Haven, CT: Yale UP, 1978) 81–116.

6. Melvin Bukiet, Introduction, *Nothing Makes You Free: Writings by Descendents of Jewish Holocaust Survivors*, ed. Melvin Bukiet (New York: Norton, 2002) 16.

7. But some good critics, like Andrew Furman, consider "second-generation fiction . . . Holocaust fiction" (*Contemporary Jewish American Writers and the Multicultural Dilemma: The Return of the Exiled* [Syracuse, NY: Syracuse UP, 2000] 63). The problem with the idea that second-generation writing is Holocaust writing becomes clear when one finds a critic as good as Ruth Franklin (in "Identity Theft: True Memory, False Memory, and the Holocaust") arguing that second-generation writers "elevate their own childhood traumas above and even beyond the sufferings of their parents" [*New Republic*, 31 May 2004, 31]). When one realizes that the subject of second-generation work is the aftermath, not the Holocaust, the ground for such comparisons simply disappears.

8. We have now a significant body of clinical research on the passing of this bitter legacy from parents to children. See, for example, Martin Bergmann's "Recurrent Problems in the Treatment of Survivors and Their Children," (*Generations of the Holocaust*, ed. Martin S. Bergmann and Milton E. Jucovy [New York: Basic Books, 1982] 247–66) or *Healing Their Wounds*. See also the work of Dan Bar-On, "Transgenerational Aftereffects of the Holocaust in Israel: Three Generations," *Breaking Crystal* 91–118.

9. Alexander and Margarete Mitscherlich, *The Inability to Mourn: Principles of Collective Behavior*, trans. Beverley R. Placzek (New York: Grove, 1975) 14.

10. "Remembering, Repeating, and Working Through," vol. 12, *The Standard Edition of the Complete Psychological Works of Sigmund Freud*, trans. and ed. James Strachey (London: Hogarth P, 1981) 145.

11. As Lawrence Langer has demonstrated in his *Holocaust Testimonies: The Ruins of Memory* (New Haven, CT: Yale UP, 1991).

12. According to Dominick LaCapra, *Representing the Holocaust: History, Theory, Trauma* (Ithaca, NY: Cornell UP, 1994) 200, 209.

13. According to Eric Santner in "History Beyond the Pleasure Principle: Some Thoughts on the Representation of Trauma," *Probing the Limits of Representation* 147. Michael Rothberg defines a "traumatic

event . . . according to recent clinical and theoretical perspectives . . . [as] an event that was not fully experienced at the time of its occurrence and that thus repeatedly returns to haunt the psyches of its victims" (*Traumatic Realism* 12). "Fully experienced," for these theorists, means that the feelings evoked by the event could not at the time be fully felt because of the extreme incoherence or incomprehensibility of the event, or because of the state of shock induced by trauma in the one who experienced it (133–40).

14. LaCapra, "Representing the Holocaust," *Probing the Limits of Representation* 126. I am quoting liberally throughout this paragraph from an earlier version of this argument that I published in 1999 ("Traumatic Memory and American Jewish Writers: One Generation After the Holocaust," *Modern Jewish Studies* 11.3–4 [1999]: 188–97). Claire Kahane has recently added another function to the work of mourning described by the theorists I have quoted. Kahane suggests that when we mourn we both hold and let go of what we have loved and lost; the "ego itself is altered, taking on bits and pieces of the lost object and of our relationship to it" ("Geographies of Loss," *Shaping Losses* 50). But because all of our relationships are ambivalent, the hostility felt toward the lost beloved may turn mourning into "melancholia," an "attachment to the experience of loss and to its perpetual recurrence" (50). In her view, writers work through this ambivalence by forging "through representation a new relation to the lost object" (50). See also Saul Friedlander's "Trauma, Memory, and Transference," *Holocaust Remembrance: The Shapes of Memory*, ed. Geoffrey Hartman (Oxford, UK: Blackwell, 1994) which argues that "working through," for historians, means being aware of both the strong emotional impact and the numbing effect of work on the Holocaust and "rendering as truthful an account as documents and testimonials will allow, *without giving in to the temptation of closure*" (260–61; Friedlander's emphasis).

15. According to Eric Santner in *Stranded Objects: Mourning, Memory, and Film in Postwar Germany* (Ithaca, NY: Cornell UP, 1990) 53.

16. "Manners, Morals, and the Novel," *The Liberal Imagination: Essays on Literature and Society* (1950; New York: Harcourt Brace, Jovanovich, 1978) 194.

17. *The County of Birches* (Vancouver, BC: Douglas and McIntyre, 1998) 32.

18. Cheryl Pearl Sucher's *The Rescue of Memory* (1997; New York: Berkley, 1998) offers comparable insights into the differing resonances of embodied male and female parents in work by second-generation women writers. The narrator's father in this novel is warmly embodied in the physical gestures of affection he both gives to and receives from his daughter: she "squeezes his hand" (80); he pinches her neck (156);

she rests her head, frightened, on the "soft leather of . . . [his] shoe" (158); he holds her fast, to calm himself as they both look for the first time at her mother lying inert in the hospital (171). Her aunt remembers him in his youth as "strong . . . like a bull" (132). Though his daughter knows he is deeply scarred by the war and by his wife's illness, "nothing about his appearance revealed anything of what he had been through" (207). For women writers, a father's body seems to retain vitality and warmth despite their awareness that it conceals the residue of suffering.

But the mother's body tells a different story. Crippled in maturity by a brain fever she contracted first in Auschwitz, she is transformed by suffering. A photograph of her at nineteen shows a woman "standing up straight . . . beautiful and happy," nestling into the "cove" of her lover's neck (196). But at forty, one arm and leg withered, unable to walk without assistance, her body is "scarred . . . strafed by the blunt armor of knee high braces . . . her eyes webbed by defeat. . . . her voice . . . distorted by fatigue. . . . dampened by melancholy . . . no longer melodic and whimsical" (181). In this transformation all agency and desire are driven from the damaged body of the survivor-mother. Only at the novel's end, does the mother's voice, captured on tape while the daughter grew up, restore a sense of her vitality and the fullness of her love.

19. Michael Andre Bernstein, a historian, would probably call this "backshadowing": "a kind of retroactive foreshadowing in which the shared knowledge of the outcome of a series of events by narrator and listener is used to judge the participants in those events *as though they too should have known what was to come*" (*Foregone Conclusions: Against Apocalyptic History* [Berkeley: U of California P, 1994] 16; Bernstein's emphasis). But in Bukiet's work there is no judgment and certainly no blame.

20. *Stories of an Imaginary Childhood* (Evanston, IL: Northwestern UP, 1992).

21. These evocations of the Holocaust were noticed first by Lawrence L. Langer (in "Home, Before Dark," rev. of *Stories of an Imaginary Childhood, Tikkun* 9.6 [1994]: 75, 79).

22. But Ruth R. Wisse suggests there are other reasons behind American Jewish writers' attempts to reconstruct a European past; she argues that those who "feel the historic, moral, and religious weight of Judaism, and want to represent it in literature, have had to ship their characters out of town . . . to an unlikely *shtetl*, to Israel . . .[,] to other times and other climes, in search of pan-Jewish fictional atmospheres" (from a 1976 *Commentary* piece, qtd. by Andrew Furman in *Contemporary Jewish American Writers and the Multicultural Dilemma* 42).

23. Andrew Furman (*Contemporary Jewish American Writers and the Multicultural Dilemma* 43–47) elaborates on the ways in which the emergence of artistic voice in Bukiet's narrator subverts communal values and rituals.

24. It's just possible that the image of the artist as snake recalls Primo Levi's description of one survivor as "inhumanly cunning and incomprehensible like the Serpent in Genesis" (*Survival in Auschwitz* [1960; New York: Collier Books, 1993] 100).

25. *After* (New York: St. Martin's P, 1996) 17.

26. Alan L. Berger, however, believes that "Bukiet views memory in salvific terms. It is nothing less than the path to achieving a *tikkun atzmi*" (*Children of Job* 73). Andrew Furman also argues that Bukiet's imagination is "theological."

27. Marianne Hirsch notes, on the contrary, that the form of Spiegelman's text raises the question "how different media—comics, photographs, narrative, testimony—can interact with each other to produce a more permeable and multiple text that may recast the problematics of Holocaust representation and definitively eradicate any clear-cut distinction between the documentary and the aesthetic" ("Family Pictures" 11). But James E. Young suggests that imaginative and historical work may be distinctive, but complementary: "Together the facts of history and their memory exist side by side, mutually dependent for sustenance and meaning" (*At Memory's Edge: After-Images of the Holocaust in Contemporary Art and Architecture* [New Haven, CT: Yale UP, 2000] 39).

28. Marianne Hirsch has commented on the "self-reflexivity that . . . pervades" this text ("Family Pictures" 12). Because Spiegelman objects to the classification of *Maus* as "fiction" ("A Problem of Taxonomy," letter, *New York Times Book Review,* 29 December 1991: 3), it is important to note that in his view the story of the Holocaust in this work, though it is a work of "art," is not invented but "true." But James E. Young understands that "by using mice masks, the artist . . . asks us not to believe what we see. They are masks drawing attention to themselves as such, never inviting us to mistake the memory of events for the events themselves" (*At Memory's Edge* 32). See Sara Horowitz's essay, for a fuller discussion of the generic issues Spiegelman raises. She concludes: "Such a reconstruction of the Holocaust past is dangerous . . . yet at the same time this memory work is the only means to recover the traumatic past and so to mourn—one's parents' losses, as well as one's own" ("Auto/Biography and Fiction after Auschwitz" 292).

29. Michael Rothberg comments on the "stylistic rupture with the rest of the work" that "reopens the wound of the mother's suicide" (*Traumatic Realism* 213).

30. Hirsch notes that he "keeps his wife's memory alive through the pictures of her he has all over his desk" ("Family Pictures" 19).

31. Rothberg notes Vladek's "inability to mourn her death" (*Traumatic Realism* 211). Hamida Bosmajian explains: "Vladek does not ever tell how he felt during and after the Holocaust; he denies feeling, and that may have been one of his crucial failings in his relation with Anja" ("The Orphaned Voice in Art Spiegelman's *Maus* I and II," *Literature and Psychology* 44:1–2 (1998): 226–27). Artie's drawings in "Prisoner of the Hell Planet" show Vladek "profoundly overcome by grief," but he does not verbalize it and ultimately he protects himself against feeling it by destroying his dead wife's journal.

32. *Maus: A Survivor's Tale* (New York: Pantheon, 1986) 4–5.

33. *Elijah Visible* (New York: St. Martin's P, 1996).

34. But Andrew Furman argues that "the unbridgeable chasm dividing memory from imagination in *Elijah Visible* represents Adam Posner's greatest burden as a second-generation survivor in America" (*Contemporary Jewish American Writers and the Multicultural Dilemma* 70).

35. *Second Hand Smoke* (New York: St. Martin's P, 1999) 145.

36. Alvin Rosenfeld (*Forward*, 28 May 1999, 11) noticed that Mila is "a character who clearly possesses Mr. Rosenbaum's imagination and who carries well beyond stereotype and idealization to expose some of the darker undersides of survival."

37. The idea is not new; in Nathaniel Hawthorne's story "Rappaccini's Daughter" a scientist who cultivates poisonous plants deliberately exposes his daughter to them—so that she becomes lethal to suitors, but invulnerable to poison.

38. Although Norma Rosen "cringed" in 1992 at the thoughtless comparison of subways to cattle cars, she recognized that holocaust images would "embark, as they must, on their second life" ("The Second Life of Holocaust Imagery," *Accidents of Influence: Writing as a Woman and a Jew in America* [Albany: SUNY P, 1992] 52, 53).

39. Like at least one exhibit in the Jewish Museum show of March 2002.

40. *The Golems of Gotham* (New York: HarperCollins, 2002) 11–12.

41. Enid Shomer, "A Child's Private Holocaust," *Moment* 21.5 (1996): 91.

4. Recalling "Home" from Exile

1. *Booking Passage: Exile and Homecoming in the Modern Jewish Imagination* (Berkeley: U of California P, 2000) 15.

2. "Writing and the Unmaking of the Self," *Contemporary Literature* 29 (1988): 438.

3. In "Writing and the Unmaking of the Self." As I pointed out in chapter 1, n.2, Debra Shostak has also noted Roth's continuing problematizing of subjectivity. Roth addressed this issue in earlier works as well, notably in the Zuckerman trilogy.

4. In using this word, I follow the lead of Gerard Manley Hopkins, who wrote that "Each mortal thing does one thing and the same: / Deals out that being indoors each one dwells / Selves—goes itself; *myself* it speaks and spells" ("As Kingfishers Catch Fire, Dragonflies Draw Flame," lines 5–7).

5. See chapter 2, "Leaving Home and Mother" in my *Writing Mothers, Writing Daughters: Tracing the Maternal in Stories by American Jewish Women* (Urbana: U of Illinois P, 1996).

6. But in 1976 Ruth R. Wisse argued that American Jewish writers were setting their fictions in Europe because the Jewish atmosphere in America was thinning out ("American Jewish Writing, Act II," *Commentary*, July 1976, 40–45). Ezrahi has also argued that for American Jews the journey back to Europe becomes a search for "authenticity" (220) or "normative models" (221).

7. The ironic transformation of Europe from the site of exile to lost homeland is, in Ezrahi's reading, a product of the Holocaust: "what was destroyed," she explains, "becomes over time an authentic original that can be represented but not recaptured. . . . [T]he Holocaust may have turned the European exile from a place in which Home is imagined to a 'real' home that can only be recalled from somewhere else and reconstructed from its shards; retrospectively, that is, the destruction seems to have territorialized exile as a lost home" (17). For American Jews who are still at home in exile, Europe provides a paradigm for that complicated state of being, and it is as well the literal home of many earlier generations of Jews.

8. Ezrahi describes such journeys as pilgrimages to a site that has become "a substitution for Jerusalem as the ruined shrine" (17). But this chapter will argue that for American Jewish women writers of the new wave, Europe is less "shrine" than actual place of family origin, of ordeal, and in some cases of extermination.

9. Memory of the past, as Yosef Yerushalmi has noted, has always been a "central component of Jewish experience" (*Zakhor: Jewish History and Jewish Memory* [Seattle: U of Washington P, 1982] xiv) reinforced not only by daily prayers that command remembrance but also by major festivals that punctuate the ritual year by recalling the collective past. As noted in ch. 2 (n. 22), this imperative to remember has taken on a profound importance for Jewish writers since World War II.

10. But in the European and British bildungsroman, or in the classical hero-journey described by Joseph Campbell, or even in Roth's *Counterlife,* whose protagonists leave home for the sake of ambition or desire, estrangement from home appears to be freely chosen.

11. *In My Mother's House: A Daughter's Story* (New Haven, CT: Ticknor and Fields, 1983) 7.

12. See, for example, Charlotte Baum, Paula Hyman, and Sonya Michel, *The Jewish Woman in America* (New York: NAL, 1977) 3–16, Susan Glenn, *Daughters of the Shtetl: Life and Labor in the Immigrant Generation* (Ithaca, NY: Cornell UP, 1990) 8, and Sydney Stahl Weinberg, *The World of Our Mothers: The Lives of Jewish Immigrant Women* (Chapel Hill: U of North Carolina P, 1988) 6, 9, 14.

13. According to Allan Nadler, the Gaon of Vilna was "the most accomplished Talmudic scholar in European Jewish History" (*The Faith of the Mithnagdim* [Baltimore: Johns Hopkins UP, 1997] 127).

14. I use the verb "storying" in my *Writing Mothers, Writing Daughters* to describe the ways in which women characteristically transform experience into narrative.

15. "Past Lives: Postmemories in Exile," *Exile and Creativity: Signposts, Travelers, Outsiders, Backward Glances,* ed. Susan Rubin Suleiman (Durham, NC: Duke UP, 1998) 418.

16. *The Poetics of Space,* trans. Maria Jolas (Boston: Beacon, 1969) xv.

17. *Why History Matters: Life and Thought* (New York: Oxford UP, 1997) 5.

18. *Jews and Feminism: The Ambivalent Search for Home* (New York: Routledge, 1997) 24.

19. *Budapest Diary: In Search of the Motherbook* (Lincoln: U of Nebraska P, 1996) 229.

20. "Living on Top," *A Place Called Home: Twenty Writing Women Remember,* ed. Mickey Pearlman (New York: St. Martin's P, 1996) 146.

21. Dominick LaCapra develops out of Freud the necessary insight into the manner in which writing of this sort functions in the process of mourning (see my "Traumatic Memory and American Jewish Writers: One Generation After the Holocaust," *Modern Jewish Studies* 11. 3–4 [1999]: 188–97). "Remembering, repeating, working through" are all crucial parts of this process, but Suleiman's and Epstein's work focuses particularly on the stage of "working through" by enabling perspective on traumatic experience, by helping the writer to acquire critical distance, by adding interpretation to experience, and by making more specific what was lost so that one might feel again the anguish of losing (200).

22. This idea is worked out in greater detail in my "Traumatic Memory and American Jewish Writers."

23. Alice Yaeger Kaplan, "On Language Memoir," *Displacements: Cultural Identities in Question*, ed. Angelica Bammer (Bloomington: Indiana UP, 1994) 63.

24. *Mazel* (New York: Viking, 1995) 16.

25. In earlier, immigrant writers like Mary Antin and Anzia Yezierska this triad of mother and sisters, silenced and/or subverted, develops similar insights into the wasting of women's gifts within traditional European Jewish culture before the war; see my chapter "Translating Immigrant Women: Writing the Manifold Self," *Writing Mothers, Writing Daughters* 19–47. The difference between immigrant writings and the ones in question here is partly, as Kim Chernin's memoir makes clear, the pervasive sense of loss in postwar writings that either recall or reimagine the shtetl. After the Holocaust, in other words, writers mourn the destruction of the culture that silenced women even as they mourn the loss of women's voices and stories in that culture.

26. *The River Midnight* (Toronto: Knopf Canada, 1999) 26.

27. It's important to note that he has been rendered impotent by traditional fears of women's seductiveness and by a traditional devaluation of male lust, for this novel insists that the shtetl constricts the behavior of men as well as women.

28. This desire to restore individual women to their home in a collective finds expression as well in E. M. Broner's *A Weave of Women* (New York: Holt, Rinehart and Winston, 1978) and Kim Chernin's *The Flame Bearers* (New York: Random, 1986).

29. *Hiding Places: A Father and His Sons Retrace Their Family's Escape from the Holocaust* (New York: Simon and Schuster, 2000) 44.

30. *Reluctant Return: A Survivor's Journey to an Austrian Town* (Bloomington: Indiana UP, 1999) 92.

31. *Out of Egypt: A Memoir* (New York: Riverhead, 1996) 49.

32. A less ambivalent sense that what used to be home is now thoroughly darkened by corruption, venality, and brutality—the only qualities that—characterizes the postwar, post Communist eastern Europe of Gary Shteyngart's comic novel *The Russian Debutante's Handbook* (New York: Riverhead, 2002). Like the world of Bukiet's *After*, from which every noble idea of the past has been erased, Shteyngart's eastern Europe is empty of everything that nostalgia would wish to recall.

33. *False Papers* (New York: Farrar, Straus and Giroux, 2000) 61–62.

34. Roger J. Porter observes that Aciman is "'home' only when he is not home, 'found' only when he is in a state of loss" ("Autobiography, Exile, Home: The Egyptian Memoirs of Gini Alhadeff, André Aciman, and Edward Said" in *Biography* 24.1 [2000]: 307). Kim Bendheim notes that Aciman "has made himself a home in our imaginations by articulating the impossibility of ever finding a home" ("For an Emigré Writer,

We Are All Exiles: André Aciman Talks about Nostalgia, Memory and Loss," *Forward*, 4 Aug. 2000, 11).

35. Aciman has observed that "Judaism is founded on the idea of remembering, and re-remembering, and remembering that you should not forget—that's what makes us Jewish, I think. You may not believe in God, but if you believe in that, you are still Jewish" (Douglas Century, "Aciman's Exodus," *Forward*, 3 Feb. 1995, 1).

36. In *Contemporary Jewish American Writers and the Multicultural Dilemma: The Return of the Exiled* (Syracuse, NY: Syracuse UP, 2000), Andrew Furman suggests that "the issue of memory and its tenuousness" is particularly important to Stern because he has taken it upon himself to "reinscribe . . . into collective memory" the immigrant neighborhood and culture that his work depicts (158–59). Stern says that his earlier work "had taken place in a kind of Jewish limbo; they were stories looking for a home. This vanished ghetto community rose out of the past like the lost city of Atlantis. It seemed an ideal setting for me to plunk down my stories, at least for a while" (Douglas Century, "Stern's Mythic Memphis: Dreaming Up a Shtetl in Tennessee," *Forward*, 25 Mar. 1994, 1).

37. "The Book of Mordecai," *Lazar Malkin Enters Heaven* (New York: Viking, 1986) 174.

38. Andrew Furman argues that for Stern memory also has the power to "redeem" the past by retrieving it (145).

39. In his essay "After the Law" (*Tikkun* 12.6 [1997]: 47–48) Stern describes himself as one of the "children of the children of the immigrants, so divorced from tradition and community that they can't even recall the story" of forest, fire, and prayer that originated with the Baal Shem Tov. Like others in this generation of Jewish writers, Stern sees himself as a victim of a "chronic spiritual homelessness." But like the hero of another kind of old Jewish story, he is also a trickster into whose lap a renegade immigrant boy drops a stolen Torah scroll that Stern hugs to his chest as he runs away.

40. "Bruno's Metamorphosis," *The Wedding Jester* (St. Paul, MN: Graywolf, 1999) 80.

41. Toward this sense of the past, Morris Dickstein suggests that Stern feels a "cooly detached piety" ("Dybbuks in Dixie," *New York Times*, 1 Mar. 1987) sec. 7, p. 11.

42. Furman notes some of the ways in which this story both resembles and differs from Philip Roth's "Eli, the Fanatic."

43. *Everything Is Illuminated* (Boston: Houghton Mifflin, 2002) 154–55.

44. *The Far Euphrates* (New York: Riverhead, 1997) 4.

45. *The Illuminated Soul* (New York: Riverhead, 2002) 66.

46. According to *The Torah: A Modern Commentary*, ed. W. Gunther Plaut (New York: Union of American Hebrew Congregations, 1981) 1079.

47. From *The Tale of Genji,* though Joseph's dream locates it within Midrash.

5. Portnoy's Successors

1. For some contemporary scholars the human body often symbolizes precarious social boundaries. When cultural anthropologist Mary Douglas began to investigate the rituals of purity that grow up around the idea of cleaning or avoiding dirt, she discovered that because we live "in a chaos of shifting impressions," we construct a stable world in our minds; we build a pattern that helps us to accept some perceptions and reject others that do not seem to fit the pattern; and the ones we reject become "dirt." As time passes and experiences pile up, she points out, "we make a greater and greater investment in our system of labels. So a conservative bias is built in. It gives us confidence" (1966; *Purity and Danger: An Analysis of the Concepts of Pollution and Taboo,* 2nd ed. [London: Routledge, 1984] 35–36). But the price of that confidence is the exclusion of much that exists in the world of experience and that we recognize as potentially destructive to existing patterns (94). The line or boundary that we assume between perceptions that fit our pattern and those that do not becomes fraught with danger. In many human cultures, the body becomes a model whose boundaries "represent any boundaries which are threatened or precarious" (114). Rituals concerning its products and its margins, its wholeness or its brokenness, suggest that it functions as a "symbol of society." For example, because "the ancient Israelites were always . . . a hard-pressed minority," for them "all the bodily issues were polluting. . . . The threatened boundaries of their body politic would be well mirrored in their care for the integrity, unity and purity of the physical body" (124).

Howard Eilberg-Schwartz cites Douglas in a different context, suggesting that Jewish preoccupation with the body reflects an awareness of the conflicts it generates for their social system ("The Problem of the Body for the People of the Book," *People of the Body: Jews and Judaism from an Embodied Perspective,* ed. Howard Eilberg-Schwartz [Albany: SUNY P, 1992] 17).

2. In *The Bonds of Love: Psychoanalysis, Feminism, and the Problem of Domination* (New York: Pantheon, 1988) Jessica Benjamin quotes Freud: "The repudiation of femininity can be nothing else than a biological fact, a part of the great riddle of sex" (160). Accepting "the repudiation of femininity as 'bedrock,'" she continues, "psychoanalysis has normalized it, glossing over its grave consequences not only for theory, but also for the fate of relationship between men and women" (160).

3. According to Nancy Chodorow, "Gender Relation and Difference in Psychoanalytic Perspective," *The Future of Difference*, ed. Hester Eisenstein and Alice Jardine (Boston: G. K. Hall, 1980) 3.

4. Daniel Boyarin in *Unheroic Conduct: The Rise of Heterosexuality and the Invention of the Jewish Man* (Berkeley: U of California P, 1997) theorizes that "the exclusion of women from the study of Torah" produced "a social system within which a group of men (the Rabbis) held power over the actual practices and pleasures of female bodies"(154).

5. See Sander Gilman's *The Jew's Body* (New York: Routledge, 1991), Daniel Boyarin's *Unheroic Conduct*, and chapter 4 ("The Countertype") in George Mosse's *The Image of Man: The Creation of Modern Masculinity* (New York: Oxford UP, 1996).

6. See John M. Hoberman's study of Otto Weininger's *Sex and Character* in "Otto Weininger and the Critique of Jewish Masculinity," *Jews and Gender: Responses to Otto Weininger*, ed. Nancy A. Harrowitz and Barbara Hymans (Philadelphia: Temple UP, 1995) 141–54, for a discussion of these generalizations about Jewish men.

7. Hoberman, "Otto Weininger" 146.

8. Hoberman, "Otto Weininger" 145.

9. Boyarin, *Unheroic Conduct* 20.

10. From Lori Lefkovitz's "Coats and Tales," *A Mensch among Men: Explorations in Jewish Masculinity*, ed. Harry Brod (Freedom, CA: Crossing, 1988) 19.

11. Cf. Boyarin, *Unheroic Conduct* 277, quoting Mosse: "'Zionists and assimilationists shared the same ideal of manliness.' . . . The project of these Zionists . . . was to transform Jewish men into the type of male that they admired, namely, the ideal 'Aryan' male."

12. See Paul Breines's *Tough Jews: Political Fantasies and the Moral Dilemma of American Jewry* (New York: Basic, 1990) 12. It's interesting to consider also the sense of manliness that emerges from Black American literature in which "manhood comes to stand for the crucial spiritual commodity that one must maintain in the face of oppression in order to avoid losing a sense of self-worth" (Richard Yarborough, "Race Violence, and Manhood: The Masculine Ideal in Frederick Douglass's 'The Heroic Slave,'" *Haunted Bodies: Gender and Southern Texts*, ed. Anne Goodwyn Jones and Susan V. Donaldson [Charlottesville: UP of Virginia, 1997] 160).

13. "Imaging the Jew," *Reading Myself and Others* (New York: Farrar, Straus and Giroux, 1975) 224.

14. *The Counterlife* (New York: Farrar, Straus and Giroux, 1986) 138.

15. "Goodbye, Columbus," *Goodbye, Columbus* (1959; New York: Bantam, 1976) 71.

16. *Damaged Goods* (Sag Harbor, NY: Permanent, 1984) 28.

17. *Fugitive Pieces* (Toronto: McClelland and Stewart, 1996) 12.

18. *A Blessing on the Moon* (Chapel Hill, NC: Algonquin, 1997) 11.

19. *Second Hand Smoke* (New York: St. Martin's P, 1999) 10.

20. *The Golems of Gotham* (New York: HarperCollins, 2002) 35.

21. As I have pointed out (in "Traumatic Memory and American Jewish Writers: One Generation After the Holocaust," *Modern Jewish Studies* 11.3–4 [1999] 188–89), to post-Freudian historiographers like Dominick LaCapra the work of mourning requires not only the labor of making specific what has been lost but also the ability to feel again the anguish of losing (*Representing the Holocaust: History, Theory, Trauma* [Ithaca, NY: Cornell UP, 1994] 215).

22. Efraim Sicher notes that "in Terry Eagleton's reassessment of Adorno's *Negative Dialectics* Auschwitz did not invalidate the aesthetic project . . . but it did change the aesthetics of pleasure. The body signified suffering, not pleasure: the body condemned to a living death beyond endurance" ("The Holocaust in the Postmodernist Era," *Breaking Crystal: Writing and Memory after Auschwitz*, ed. Efraim Sicher [Urbana: U of Illinois P, 1998] 301). In tracking the gender reversals that accompany Holocaust atrocities, Sara Horowitz identifies in Emanuel Ringelblum's ghetto diary a "recurrent image of the Jewish man turned 'wifely' by extreme circumstances," an image that "reinforces the extent of atrocity and the thoroughness with which it has pervaded one's intimate life" ("Gender, Genocide, and Jewish Memory," *Prooftexts* 20.1–2 [2000]: 172). She sets this image within the context of rabbinical images of Jewish male slaves in Egypt who are depicted with "characteristics attributed most often to the female"; "these rabbinic readings of slavery," she suggests, "depict a Jewish masculinity that is effectively unmanned by the traumas of history" (169).

23. Peter Stallybrass and Allon White, *The Politics and Poetics of Transgression* (London: Methuen, 1986).

24. See my "Traumatic Memory and American Jewish Writers" 188–89.

25. One character who appears in all of Rosenbaum's fictions, Rabbi Vered, embodies in a different but equally disturbing way the transformative effects of the Holocaust's legacy. Vered is a survivor of Auschwitz, a yeshiva boy turned playboy, a scholar transformed into a womanizer, a believer who will no longer defer to the possibility of God. His popularity with his large congregation suggests that contemporary American Jews identify with and feel the effects of his losses even though they themselves have not undergone his experience.

26. *After* (New York: St. Martin's P, 1996) 302–03.

27. Furman observes that the moment of this baby's birth bursts upon the eye like a flash "of light from this canvas of seemingly

inexorable darkness" (*Contemporary Jewish American Writers and the Multicultural Dilemma: The Return of the Exiled* [Syracuse, NY: Syracuse UP, 2000] 57).

28. As I point out in "Traumatic Memory and American Jewish Writers," theorists believe this work awaits not only Jews but also Germans (188–89).

29. *Dancing on Tishu B'Av* (New York: St. Martin's P, 1990) 2.

30. *The Far Euphrates* (New York: Riverhead, 1997) 128.

31. From a psychoanalytic point of view, Jessica Benjamin has pointed out that the father is a "magical mirror that reflects the self as it wants to be—the ideal in which the child wants to recognize himself" (*Bonds of Love* 100). From the beginning, she argues, "fathers represent what is outside and different—they mediate the wider world" (102); "the father is always the way into the world . . . [,] the liberator" (103).

6. Becoming Rubies

1. See my review of two recent studies of Holocaust literature "The Burden of Memory," *Forward*, 6 Feb. 1998, 1, 10.

2. Daniel Boyarin, *Intertextuality and the Reading of Midrash* (Bloomington: Indiana UP, 1990) 14.

3. Alicia Suskin Ostriker, *Feminist Revision and the Bible* (Cambridge, MA: Blackwell, 1993) 28.

4. David Biale, *Eros and the Jew: From Biblical Israel to Contemporary America* (New York: Basic Books, 1992) 12.

5. Tikva Frymer-Kensky, *In the Wake of the Goddesses: Women, Culture and the Biblical Transformation of Pagan Myth* (New York: Free P, 1992) 121. This scholar argues that women's position in biblical society is "clearly subordinate to the men"; that woman's sexuality is controlled by men; that woman's property rights are severely limited" (119). Some men, she agrees, "were in positions of power with an active role in history. Women were not" (123). But there is "nothing distinctively 'female' about the way that women are portrayed in the Bible" (120).

6. Ilana Pardes quoting Cassuto in *Countertraditions in the Bible: A Feminist Approach* (Cambridge, MA: Harvard UP, 1992) 44.

7. *Of Woman Born* (1976; New York: Bantam, 1977) 52.

8. This literature is composed of several different bodies of commentary on biblical texts compiled and redacted largely between the third and the sixth century of the common era, though some of the commentary was composed as late as the early middle ages.

9. *Purity and Danger: An Analysis of the Concepts of Pollution and Taboo*, 2nd ed. (London: Routledge, 1984) 4.

10. "The Problem of the Body for the People of the Book," *People of the Body: Jews and Judaism from an Embodied Perspective,* ed. Howard Eilberg-Schwartz (Albany: SUNY P, 1992) 27.

11. Judith Baskin quoting Jacob Neusner (*Midrashic Women: Formations of the Feminine in Rabbinic Literature* [Hanover, NH: UP of New England, 2002] 30): "in the patriarchal world of rabbinic Judaism man is normal and woman is abnormal, since she is always capable of upsetting the rabbis' ordered program for reality."

12. Baskin: ". . . it is important to recognize that the majority of the rabbis distinguished between procreation as an active male role . . . and bearing children as the female's designated passive purpose" (119). Again, "for the rabbis, procreation is a masculine act of potency quite different from the feminine role of bearing and birthing the fruit of male seed" (126).

13. Baskin quoting Michael Satlow (30): "rabbinic literature portrays women not only as sexually attractive to men, but also as more sexually avid and as less able to control their overwhelming desires."

14. Baskin: ". . . significant voices within rabbinic literature believe that the [menstruating woman] herself can be dangerous. The linkage of the menstruating woman, and hence all women, with peril and death for men is an ancient belief, which is deeply embedded in biblical and rabbinic thinking" (28).

15. *Rereading the Rabbis: A Woman's Voice* (Boulder, CO: Westview P, 1998) 4.

16. *Unheroic Conduct: The Rise of Heterosexuality and the Invention of the Jewish Man* (Berkeley: U of California P, 1997) 154.

17. Rochelle L. Millen notices also the effects of women's exemption from "time-specified mitzvoth" or commandments, like the commandment to participate in regular communal prayer: "The principle of women's exemption from time-specified mitzvoth, perhaps more than any other, has over the centuries determined the status of women in *halakhah* and the sociocultural locus of women in Jewish society. It is this principle that establishes and/or confirms women as outside the public domain and on the periphery of the religious, intellectual, and ritualistic aspects governing that domain" (*Women, Birth, and Death in Jewish Law and Practice* [Hanover, NH: UP of New England, 2004] 26).

18. Baskin observes that "with few exceptions, female voices are not heard in rabbinic literature. When they are, they are usually mediated through male assumptions about women's lesser intellectual, spiritual, and moral capacities. . . . Neither women's religious rituals, which undoubtedly existed, nor female understandings of their lives, experiences, and spirituality are retrievable in any significant way from rabbinic Judaism's male-directed writings which became so pivotal for ensuing patterns of Jewish life" (3).

19. Susan Glenn, *Daughters of the Shetl: Life and Labor in the Immigrant Generation* (Ithaca, NY: Cornell UP, 1990) 8.

20. Shulamit S. Magnus has recently brought to light, in the writing of Pauline Wengeroff, the first woman's voice in the canon of European Jewish enlightenment. Male writers enlightened during the *Haskalah* looked carefully at women and the family. In their view, women were "manipulative, overpowering, abusive mothers-in-law, into whose the clutches the future *maskilim* [enlightened ones] fall when, as child-husbands, they go to live in their in-law's homes. Wives are fertile traps, people with whom they share no meaningful relationship yet who will, unless resisted, anchor the *maskilim* in the suffocating world of tradition and familial responsibility" (*Jewish Emancipation in a German City: Cologne, 1798–1871* [Stanford, CA: Stanford UP, 1997] 182–83).

21. Paula Hyman, *Gender and Assimilation in Modern Jewish History* (Seattle: U of Washington P, 1995) 54.

22. *A Price below Rubies: Jewish Women as Rebels and Radicals* (Cambridge, MA: Harvard UP, 1993) 2.

23. "Zlatke," *Found Treasures: Stories by Yiddish Women Writers*, ed. Frieda Forman (Toronto: Second Story P, 1994) 121.

24. Modern theorists make clear, of course, the existence in Western culture of what Foucault called "received gender norms" that associate such qualities as "determination, cool emotional discipline, mastery" with the slender, flat bodies of boys rather than the roundnesses of young women (Sandra Lee Bartky, "Foucault, Femininity, and the Modernization of Patriarchal Power," *Feminism and Foucault: Paths of Resistance*, ed. Lee Quinby and Irene Diamond [Boston: Northeastern UP, 1988] 61, 62, 65).

25. For a fuller discussion of these and other writers of the seventies see my *Writing Mothers, Writing Daughters: Tracing the Maternal in Stories by American Jewish Women* (Urbana: U of Illinois P, 1996).

26. *The Romance Reader* (New York: Riverhead, 1995) 22.

27. *Giving Up America* (New York: Riverhead, 1998) 174–75.

28. It's important that one not overread biographically the rebellions and defections of Abraham's protagonists. One interviewer notes that although Abraham "no longer follows the Hasidic lifestyle . . . [,] Hasidic philosophy is still very much an 'internalized' part of her life. 'It's not a garment you put on,' she said, quoting James Joyce, who, when asked if he would ever return to Dublin, responded by inquiring whether he had ever left" (Sandee Brawarsky, "In Profile: Pearl Abraham," *Publishers Weekly*, 17 Aug. 1998, S28–S29).

29. *Eve's Apple* (New York: Random, 1997) 165.

30. Among the contemporary feminists who have studied the effects of the media on women's self images, Sandra Lee Bartky notes that "mass-circulation women's magazines run articles on dieting in

virtually every issue" ("Foucault, Femininity, and the Modernization of Patriarchal Power" 65); "It is not only her natural appetite or unreconstructed contours that pose a danger to woman: the very expressions of her face can subvert the disciplinary project of bodily perfection. An expressive face lines and creases more readily than an inexpressive one. Hence, if women are unable to suppress strong emotions, they can at least learn to inhibit the tendency of the face to register them" (67); "a woman's skin must be soft, supple, hairless, and smooth; ideally, it should betray no sign of wear, experience, age, or deep thought. Hair must be removed not only from the face but from large surfaces of the body as well . . ." (69); "the body by which a woman feels herself judged and which by rigorous discipline she must try to assume is the body of early adolescence, slight and unformed, a body lacking flesh or substance, a body in whose very contours the image of immaturity has been inscribed. . . . [A]n infantilized face must accompany her infantilized body, a face that never ages or furrows its brow in thought. The face of the ideally feminine woman must never display the marks of character, wisdom, and experience that we so admire in men" (73). Kim Chernin believes that this emphasis in fashion, which "expresses a shift from the voluptuous to the ascetic in women," reflects a "fear of women's power" that arose as a reaction to the feminist movement of the '60s (*The Obsession: Reflections on the Tyranny of Slenderness* [New York: Harper and Row, 1981] 98).

31. But the disease appears frequently and has attracted considerable attention among Jews. See, for example, Danielle Haas's "When the Woman of Valor Has Anorexia," *Jerusalem Report*, 5 July 1999, 28–32: "The pressures to be beautiful and marry well take a grave physical toll in the Orthodox world. One study in New York shows that almost two-thirds of Orthodox girls are at risk of developing anorexia and bulimia" (28).

32. Susan Bordo, "The Body and the Reproduction of Femininity: Feminist Appropriation of Foucault," *Gender, Body, Knowledge*, ed. Alison Jaggar and Susan Bordo (New Brunswick, NJ: Rutgers UP, 1989) 19.

33. In *Of Woman Born* Adrienne Rich observes that "motherhood . . . has a history, it has an ideology, it is more fundamental than tribalism or nationalism. . . . Throughout patriarchal mythology, dream-symbolism, theology, language, two ideas flow side by side: one, that the female body is impure, corrupt, the site of discharges, bleedings, dangerous to masculinity, a source of moral and physical contamination, 'the devil's gateway.' On the other hand, as mother the woman is beneficent, sacred, pure, asexual, nourishing; and the physical potential for motherhood . . . is her single destiny and justification in life" (15).

34. Bartky recalls Foucault's argument that the "constant foraging for sexual secrets and hidden stories" by professional interrogators in the nineteenth century "actually *created* new sexual secrets—and eroticized the acts of interrogation and confession, too" ("Foucault, Femininity, and the Modernization of Patriarchal Power" 91).

35. In an interview, Rosen suggests "there's a Jewish precedent for my narrator's behavior . . . [:] the intense fascination the Rabbis had with the female body." Rosen's study of Talmud has led him to believe that "at the center of much rabbinic speculation is the mystery of the female body—a deep fascination with it, a desire to contain, describe, define and regulate its functionings . . ." ("Talking about the Book and the Body," *Forward*, 16 May 1997, 19).

36. Susan Bordo ("Anorexia Nervosa: Psychopathology as the Crystallization of Culture," *Philosophical Forum* 17.1–2 [1986]: 73–103) assumes that "the body, far from being some fundamentally stable, a cultural constant to which we must *contrast* all culturally relative and institutional forms, is constantly 'in the grip,' as Foucault puts it, of cultural practices" (91). Femininity in particular, according to Foucault, as Sandra Lee Bartky reminds us, is an artifice ("Foucault, Femininity, and the Modernization of Patriarchal Power" 64) an achievement, "a mode of enacting . . . received gender norms" that are part of a discipline that "invades the body . . . [,] seeks to regulate its very forces and operations," and render it "docile" (61, 62).

37. Contemporary theorists, following Foucault, have taught us to see that the "constant probing and interrogation" of distressed women in the nineteenth century by doctors, psychiatrists and others not only *created* secrets where none had existed before, but also "eroticized the acts of interrogation and confession" (Bordo, "Anorexia Nervosa: Psychopathology as the Crystallization of Culture," *Feminism and Foucault: Reflections on Resistance,* ed. Irene Diamond and Lee Quimby [Boston: Northeastern UP, 1988] 90–91.)

38. Andrew Furman persuasively identifies as a "predominant theme" in Goldstein's work one such binary: the "tension between Orthodox Judaism and secular feminism" (*Contemporary Jewish American Writers and the Multicultural Dilemma* [Syracuse, NY: Syracuse UP, 2000] 83). I want to suggest here that for Goldstein the problem of binary thinking embraces the "Judaism/feminism" dichotomy but develops and subverts other dichotomies as well.

39. In her introduction to *The Future of Difference* (ed. Hester Eisenstein and Alice Jardine [Boston: G. K. Hall, 1980]) Hester Eisenstein explains: "The theme of 'difference' has been integral to modern feminist thought from at least the time of the publication of Simone de Beauvoir's *The Second Sex* and, in particular, since the rebirth of the

women's movement in the late 1960's. . . . An important task of feminist thinking . . . was to demonstrate that the differences between women and men had been exaggerated, and that they could be *reduced* . . ." (xv–xxiv).

40. *The Mind-Body Problem* (New York: Random, 1983) 55.

41. *The Dark Sister* (New York: Viking, 1991) 60.

42. See "The Abominations of Leviticus" in Douglas's *Purity and Danger.*

43. A similar epiphany occurs to the medium at a séance (254), during which William and others will recognize in the medium's tearing of her dress and undergarments to show the flesh of her belly "a projection from the repressed disturbances within" (141). There's an interesting parallel here with the cultural and political functions of female flesh in gigantic women characters in southern American women's writing (Patricia Yaeger, "Beyond the Hummingbird: Southern Women Writers and the Southern Gargantua," *Haunted Bodies: Gender and Southern Texts,* ed. Anne Goodwyn Jones and Susan V. Donaldson [Charlottesville: UP of Virginia, 1997] 287–318).

44. *Properties of Light: A Novel of Love, Betrayal, and Quantum Physics* (Boston: Houghton Mifflin, 2000) 3.

45. According to Dennis Slattery, Goldstein's work appears to conform to the trajectory of much contemporary theoretical work on the body. In his view, "in studies today. . . . the body is no longer portrayed simply as a template for social organization, nor as a biological black box cut off from 'mind,' and nature/culture and mind/body dualities are self-consciously interrogated" (*The Wounded Body: Remembering the Markings of Flesh* [Albany: SUNY P] 12). Like several Israeli novelists, Goldstein interrogates as well what Anne Golomb Hoffman calls "the product of established oppositions between male and female" ("Embodiments: An Introduction," *Prooftexts* 20.1–2: 9). Hoffman also points out what this chapter in general demonstrates: that "within the texts and histories that constitute Jewish tradition, we find the body of the woman as a marked other" (5).

46. "Carried from the Couch on the Wings of Enchantment: Writers on Writing" *New York Times,* 16 Dec. 2002: E1.

7. Midrash as Undertow

1. *The Far Euphrates* (New York: Riverhead, 1997) 136.

2. In "Poetry, Midrash, and Feminism" Steven P. Schneider noted that contemporary Jewish American poets were using poems "to create commentaries on the Jewish Bible." He called this "impulse . . . midrashic"(*Tikkun* 16.4 [2001]: 61).

3. In the new *Jewish Study Bible* (ed. Adele Berlin and Marc Zvi Brettler [New York: Oxford UP, 2004]) David Stern explains that "Midrash is the specific name for the activity of biblical interpretation as practiced by the Rabbis of the land of Israel in the first five centuries of the common era" (1863).

4. "Midrash and Allegory," *The Literary Guide to the Bible,* ed. Robert Alter and Frank Kermode (Cambridge, MA: Harvard UP, 1987) 626.

5. This concern with the effect of ancient sources on contemporary conduct appears also in more recent, Western, writers. In 1970, psychoanalyst and scholar Harry Slochower noted that novelists and poets often found in ancient myths symbolic values still pertinent to their own cultures; he called the fictional reanimation of those myths "mythopoesis" (*Mythopoesis: Mythic Patterns in the Literary Classics* [Detroit: Wayne State UP, 1970]). Dostoevsky, Malraux, Dante and Cervantes, among others, he argued, "looked back," giving literary form to myths that had once organized the values of their time, in order to carry those values forward.

6. *Regarding the Pain of Others* (New York: Farrar, Straus and Giroux, 2003) 86; Sontag's emphasis.

7. *The Collective Memory,* trans. Francis J. Ditter and Vida Yazdi Ditter (New York: Harper and Row, 1980) 80.

8. One recent critic, however, defines the "central tension of this literature" simply as an "ongoing process of defining Jewish American identity through intimate conversation with a Jewish textual tradition" (Tresa Grauer, "The Changing Same," *Mapping Jewish Identities,* ed. Laurence J. Silberstein [New York: New York UP, 2000] 38).

9. Ronald Hayman, *Thomas Mann: A Biography* (New York: Scribner, 1995) 424.

10. In a later work Mann justified the liberties he had taken with the scriptural narrative by allowing a character who represented Goethe to define "religious symbolism" as "a cultural treasure-house, wherein we have a perfect right to dip when we need to use the familiar image to make visible and tangible some general aspect of spirit (qtd. in Anthony Heilbut's *Thomas Mann: Eros and Literature* [New York: Knopf, 1996] 552–53).

11. *Biblical Women Unbound: Counter-Tales* (Philadelphia: Jewish Publication Society, 1996) x, xi, xiv. The Hebrew word "midrash" means "to search out," and according to James L. Kugel the original Biblical exegetes, all male, focused their interpretive energies on "what one might call surface irregularities in the text . . . [,] *problems*"; "the text's irregularity," he said, "is the grain of sand which so irritates the midrashic oyster that he constructs a pearl around it" ("Two Introductions to Midrash," *Midrash and Literature,* ed. Geoffrey H. Hartman and

Sanford Budick [New Haven, CT: Yale UP, 1986] 92). This work belongs to a recent stream of scholarly efforts both to describe the nature of classical midrash and to analyze its influences on contemporary theory and writing. See, for example, Daniel Boyarin's *Intertextuality and the Reading of Midrash* (Bloomington: Indiana UP, 1994); Gerald Bruns's "Midrash and Allegory"; Michael Fishbane's *The Exegetical Tradition* (Cambridge, MA: Harvard UP, 1998); Susan Handelman's *The Slayers of Moses* (Albany: SUNY P, 1982); Geoffrey Hartman's "Midrash as Law and Literature," *Journal of Religion* 74:3 (1994): 338–55; James Kugel's *Early Biblical Literature* (Philadelphia: Westminster P, 1986); David Stern's *Midrash and Theory* (Evanston, IL: Northwestern UP, 1996); and David Weiss Halivni's *Pshat and Drash: Plain and Applied Meaning in Rabbinic Exegesis* (New York: Oxford UP, 1991).

12. *Out of the Garden: Women Writers on the Bible,* ed. Christina Büchmann and Celina Spiegel (New York: Fawcett Columbine, 1994) and *Reading Ruth: Contemporary Women Reclaim a Sacred Story,* ed. Judith A. Kates and Gail Twersky Reimer (New York: Ballantine Books, 1994).

13. Daphne Merkin, "The Women in the Balcony: On Rereading the 'Song of Songs,'" *Out of the Garden* 250.

14. Norma Rosen, "Rebekah and Isaac: A Marriage Made in Heaven," *Out of the Garden* 23.

15. Michelle A. Friedman, "The Labor of Remembrance," *Mapping Jewish Identities* 97–121. Friedman describes this labor in terms that recall Halbwachs's and Sontag's emphasis on the need to make remembered moments meaningful: "The labor of remembrance," she writes, "requires one to wrestle with what it means to remember and how it is possible to remember what has come to be considered an incomprehensible history; it involves articulating oneself in relation to this history without erasing its 'messiness' and complexities" (97).

16. It's tempting to align this effort in contemporary personal essays with what Joseph Heinemann describes as *"Aggadah,"* a literary form that originated in the Second Temple period after the conquest of Palestine by Alexander the Great; it represented "an attempt to develop new methods of exegesis designed to yield new understandings of Scripture for a time of crisis and a period of conflict, with foreign cultural influence pressing from without and sectarian agitation from within" ("The Nature of the Aggadah," *Midrash and Literature* 42).

17. *Intertextuality and the Reading of Midrash* 14.

18. Boyarin cites in this regard the work of Gerald Bruns, who explains that exegetes recognize that within the Bible "later texts . . . throw . . . light on the earlier, even as they always stand in the light of what precedes and follows them" (16). Geoffrey Hartman

also suggests that the Bible "is a fusion of heterogeneous stories or types of discourse." But it is an uneasy "fusion," in which friction among its constituent elements persists (Introduction, *Midrash and Literature* 13), in which the evidence of a narrative sedimentation . . . has not entirely settled" (11).

19. Reported by Sandee Brawarsky in "Fathers, Sons and God," *Jewish Week*, 22 Dec. 2000: 39.

20. *Sacrifice* (New York: Metropolitan, 1999) 56.

21. *The Seventh Beggar* (New York: Riverhead, 2005) 333.

22. Karl Kerényi, *Mythology and Humanism: The Correspondence of Thomas Mann and Karl Kerényi,* trans. Alexander Gelley (Ithaca, NY: Cornell UP, 1975) 103.

23. Joseph Lowin has recognized the midrashic element in this story (*Cynthia Ozick* [Boston: Twayne, 1988] 70–73).

24. *The Pagan Rabbi and Other Stories* (New York: Schocken, 1976) 10.

25. Michael Fishbane traces the development of this biblical prohibition within the scriptures, *The Exegetical Tradition* 24.

26. "Bialik's Hint," *Metaphor and Memory: Essays* (New York: Knopf, 1989) 227.

27. In "Notes toward a New Yiddish" Ozick declared that as a Jew she was "an autodidact. . . . [M]y reading has become more and more urgent, though in narrower and narrower channels. . . . I read mainly to find out not what it is to be a Jew . . . but what it is to *think* as a Jew" (*Art and Ardor: Essays* [New York: Knopf, 1983] 157).

28. "Interpretation: Cynthia Ozick's Cannibal Galaxy," *Prooftexts* 6:3 (1986): 252.

29. "Notes toward a New Yiddish," *Art and Ardor* 238.

30. In *The Cannibal Galaxy,* as Naomi Sokoloff has pointed out, one character suggests the kind of "daring fusion" of cultural influences which might be possible for writers who could apply "midrash to [their] own scholarly work" ("Interpretation" 252).

31. "She: Portrait of the Essay as a Warm Body," *Quarrel and Quandary: Essays* (New York: Knopf, 2000) 187.

32. The strategy serves her even now, for her recent review of Updike's *The Early Stories, 1953–1975* (*New York Times,* 30 Nov. 2003: 8–9) proceeds in this way, explaining that "the past is not the same as history" by contrasting Updike's work with Saul Bellow's to show us how the absence from Updike's work of a "brooding and burdensome history . . . accounts for the luxuriance of their lyrical andantes" (9).

33. *Paradise Park* (New York: Dial, 2001) 25.

34. See, for example, Peter Kramer's "Ticket to 'Paradise': A Talk with Allegra Goodman," *Forward,* 5 Nov. 2001: 10.

35. "If It's Out There, It's In Here," rev. of *The Talmud and the Internet, New York Times Book Review,* 1 Oct. 2000: 12.

36. *The Talmud and the Internet: A Journey between Worlds* (New York: Farrar, Straus and Giroux, 2000) 13.

37. *Principles of Psychology,* vol. 2 (Mineola, NY: Dover, 1950) 488.

38. Jon D. Levenson, "Private Connections," rev. of *The Talmud and the Internet, Commentary,* December 2000, 69–70; Avrum Goodblatt, rev. of *The Talmud and the Internet, Judaism* 50.3 (2001): 372–73.

39. *Properties of Light: A Novel of Love, Betrayal, and Quantum Physics* (Boston: Houghton Mifflin, 2000) 8.

40. "Calmly We Walk through This April's Day," *Summer Knowledge: New and Selected Poems* (New York: New Directions, 1967) 66.

41. *The Illuminated Soul* (New York: Riverhead, 2002) 2.

42. In the richly layered imagery of the novel, these fabrics also call to mind, as I suggested in chapter 4, the colorful hangings that once accompanied the ark in the wilderness, and the textiles that adorned torah scrolls before they were collected from synagogues destroyed by the Nazis (231).

Index

Abel (biblical figure), 142
Abraham (biblical figure), 142, 179, 180–84
Abraham, Pearl, 173, 241n.28; *Giving Up America*, 153–55; *The Romance Reader*, 150–53; *The Seventh Beggar*, 184–86
Aciman, André, 105, 201, 234n.34; *False Papers*, 100–103; *Out of Egypt*, 96–102
"An Act of Defiance" (Rosenbaum), 65
Adams, Henry, 195, 205
Adorno, Theodor, 224n.1, 225n.2, 226n.3, 238n.22
African American literature, 237n.12
After (Bukiet), 9–11, 56–59, 70, 130–32, 234n.32
aftermath (of the Holocaust), 26–27, 47, 206; inability to write the story of, 59; as subject of second generation's fiction, 48–75, 227n.7. *See also* Holocaust; second generation
Aggadah (literary form), 246n.16
Agunah, 90, 91
Akedah, 142, 181–84
Aleichem, Sholem, 58, 147
Alexandria (Egypt), 96–102
Alter, Robert, 211n.5
ambivalence: of "home" imagery, 40–41, 52, 53–55, 93–99, 105–7; past

vs. present, in works about the Holocaust, 56; as reaction to Jewish women's exclusions, 83; toward Jewish tradition, 11, 12–13, 18, 21, 106–7; toward older models, 18. *See also* doubling
American Communist Party, 79–80, 83
American Jewish literature: definition of authors of, xiv; neglect of predecessors of, xi–xii; new wave of, defined, 6; scope of this study of, xiv. *See also* Holocaust; new wave writers; *specific authors and themes in*
anger. *See* rage
Anissimov, Myriam: "A Yiddish Writer Who Writes in French," 43
anorexia, 10, 142, 149, 155–62, 242n.31
Antin, Mary, 234n.25
antisemitism: in Bukiet's stories, 54, 56–59; contemporary, 206–7; in England, 36–37; in Europe, 40, 41, 56, 85, 106, 176–77. *See also* Germany: Nazism in; Holocaust
Appelfeld, Aharon, 214n.11, 215n.31
"The Apprentice" (Bukiet), 54
Art and Ardor (Ozick), 190
Aschheim, Steven, 225n.1
ashes imagery, 29, 73, 104, 174, 224n.44. *See also* fire imagery; smoke imagery

Asian cultures, 113–15
assimilation (of American Jews), 4–7,
    11–16, 18, 21, 31, 106–7, 210n.4
Auschwitz concentration camp, 16,
    229n.18; in Bukiet's *After,* 11; in
    Kalman's *Country of Birches,* 52;
    lessons learned in, 61, 66, 126,
    220n.28, 238n.22; memories of,
    30, 34, 63–64; in Rosenbaum's
    works, 64, 126. *See also* Holocaust
Austria, 94–96
autobiographies. *See* memoirs

Baal Shem Tov, 235n.39
Babel (biblical place), 185
Bachelard, Gaston, 82, 93
"backshadowing," 228n.19
Baghdad, 110
Bakhtin, Mikhail, 127–28
Bar-On, Dan, 218n.17, 223n.42
Bartky, Sandra Lee, 157, 241n.30,
    243nn.34, 36
Baskin, Judith, 146, 157, 240nn.11–
    13, 18
Beauvoir, Simone de, 243n.39
belatedness, 25–47. *See also* second
    generation
Belief. *See* God; Jewish tradition
Bellow, Saul, 7, 14, 16, 19, 44, 118–19,
    247n.32
Belsen concentration camp, 5
Bendheim, Kim, 234n.34
Benjamin, Jessica, 236n.2, 239n.31
Berger, Alan L., 223n.44, 230n.26
Berger, Joseph: *Displaced Persons,* 29,
    32, 33, 37–38, 219n.25, 221n.35
Berger, Naomi, 221n.35
Bernstein, Michael Andre, 228n.19
Biale, David, 142
"Bialik's Hint" (Ozick), 189
Bible, 142, 144; genealogy in, 143; in-
    tertextuality in, 181. *See also* "mid-
    rashic impulse"; *specific books and
    people in*
Biblical Women Unbound (N. Rosen),
    178, 180–81
binaries, 163–65, 190–91, 214n.11,

243n.38. *See also* doubling; gender;
    separation
bird imagery, 202–3
Blake, William, 170
A Blessing on the Moon (Skibell), 125
blindness. *See* vision imagery
"The Blue-Eyed Jew" (Bukiet), 55
body parts. *See* scars
Book of Daniel (biblical book), 174
"The Book of Mormon" (Stern), 102–3
Book of Numbers (biblical book), 113
Book of Ruth (biblical book), 143
books, 58
Bordo, Susan, 243n.36
Bosmajian, Hamida, 231n.31
Boyarin, Daniel, 144–45, 157, 181,
    213n.6, 237n.4
Boyarin, Jonathan, 213n.6
Broner, E. M., 10, 150, 234n.28
"Bruno's Metamorphosis" (Stern),
    103
Bruns, Gerald L., 175, 246n.18
Buchenwald concentration camp, 3
Budapest, 43, 85, 86–87
Budick, Emily Miller, 215n.24,
    223n.42
Bukiet, Melvin Jules, 133, 222n.40,
    230nn.23, 26; *After* by, 9–11, 56–
    59, 70, 130–32, 234n.32; "The
    Apprentice," 54; "The Blue-Eyed
    Jew," 55; "Levitation," 54; "New
    Words for Old," 55; "Nurseries,"
    54; "The Quilt and the Bicycle,"
    54, 55; "Sincerely Yours," 55; *Sto-
    ries of an Imaginary Childhood* by,
    53–56; "The Ventriloquist," 55;
    "Virtuoso," 54; "The Woman with
    a Dog," 55
Bund, 148
Burstein, Janet: mother of, xi–xii, 7.
    See also "Traumatic Memory and
    American Jewish Writing" (Bur-
    stein); *Writing Mothers, Writing
    Daughters* (Burstein)

Cain (biblical figure), 142
Call It Sleep (Roth), 123–24

Campbell, Joseph, 233n.10
The Cannibal Galaxy (Ozick), 188–89,
    247n.30
Carnival, 127–30
cattle car imagery, 8, 11, 16, 56, 58–59,
    64, 65, 67, 69, 72, 73
Celan, Paul, 7–8
Chernin, Kim, 234nn.25, 28, 242n.30;
    In My Mother's House, 78–81, 92;
    Obsession, 156
Chernin, Rose, 78–79, 83, 88, 89
Chesler, Phyllis, 10, 150
Chodorow, Nancy, 150
Christianity and Christians, 37, 94–96,
    106, 111, 136, 177, 188, 189, 192, 195
circumcision: blood associated with,
    145; in Friedmann's *Damaged
    Goods*, 121; lack of, in Raphael's
    Dancing on Tisha B'Av, 132; in Ro-
    senbaum's *Second Hand Smoke*, 70;
    in Roth's *Counterlife*, 10, 20–21,
    23, 24
Cohen, Shaye, 145
collective memory. *See* memory
    (collective)
concentration camps: liberation of, 4,
    27–28, 56, 59, 121, 130; as reducing
    people to objects, 30; seder set in,
    130–31; in Spiegelman's *Maus*, 60.
    See also Holocaust; survivors; *spe-
    cific concentration camps*
connectedness. *See* continuity (inter-
    connectedness); memory (collec-
    tive); reconnection
continuity (interconnectedness): as
    conflicted for male writers, 93; of
    rabbis' midrashic tradition, 144,
    175, 177, 179, 181, 195–96, 198, 199,
    239n.8; women writers' emphasis
    on, 77–78, 81, 84, 85, 90, 169–71.
    See also memory (collective); "mid-
    rashic impulse"; reconnection
cossacks, 79
The Counterlife (Roth), 233n.10;
    circumcision in, 10, 20–21, 23, 24;
    identity in, 16, 18, 19, 22–24, 77,
    213n.9, 214n.10; manliness in, 119

The Country of Birches (Kalman), 51–
    54, 57
cultural work: of new wave writings,
    212n.13; stories as performing, xiii,
    xiv, 6, 11–12, 25–26, 46–47, 49–50,
    52–53, 62, 87, 131–32, 176, 205–8,
    216n.4, 223n.42. *See also* memory
    (collective)
"culture," 209n.3
Czechoslovakia, 46, 222n.40

Dachau concentration camp, 3
Damaged Goods (Friedmann), 120–24,
    133, 134
"A Dancer" (Dropkin), 149, 158
Dancing on Tisha B'Av (Raphael),
    132–36
The Dark Sister (Goldstein), 165–71
DeLauretis, Teresa, 77
De Tocqueville, Alexis, 161–62
dialogue. *See* "midrashic impulse"
diaspora, 31; contemporary experi-
    ence of, 188–89; privileges of,
    213n.6, 214n.10. *See also* assimila-
    tion; exile and expulsion; multi-
    plicity (cultural)
Dickstein, Morris, 211nn.5, 6, 212n.13,
    235n.41
difference (cultural), 185–91, 195, 196,
    199, 204, 206–7, 243n.39. *See also*
    Enlightenment *(Haskalah)*; multi-
    plicity (cultural)
differentiation: by binary thinking,
    163, 166, 168–70; by ethnicity, 117–
    18; by gender, 122, 142–48, 156;
    by generation, 25–26, 48–51, 60,
    62–65, 68, 78, 80, 108–10
displaced persons, 28, 56
dissociation, 226n.5
Don Quixote (Cervantes), 198
doubling, 43–44, 90, 168; binaries
    as form of, 163–65, 168, 190–91,
    214n.11, 243n.38. *See also* am-
    bivalence; difference; memory
    (collective)
Douglas, Mary, 143, 166, 176, 236n.1
Dropkin, Celia: "A Dancer," 149, 158

Eagleton, Terry, 238n.22
Eden, 110–12, 136, 183
education. *See* knowledge
Egypt, 96–102, 201, 238n.22
Eilberg-Schwartz, Howard, 143, 145, 236n.1
Eisenstein, Hester, 243n.39
"Eli, the Fanatic" (Roth), ix, 4–6, 22, 34, 209n.1, 235n.42
Elijah Visible (Rosenbaum), 64, 66–67
embodiment: in carnivals, 128–30; as metaphor for society, 236n.1; new wave writers' emphasis on, 10, 52, 69, 71, 116–73, 175, 206, 214n.16, 236n.1, 244n.45. *See also* gender; ghost imagery; scars; sexuality; suicide
England, 36–37
English language: as altering experience undergone in another language, 42–44; efforts to transform, into language of a Jewish culture, 189; Jewish literature in, 8; as new home for refugees, 86, 87; as second generation's native tongue, 7
Enlightenment *(Haskalah):* as diminishing the power of rabbis, 147; life after, as offering seductions to observant Jews, 188–89, 192, 193, 196, 197, 204, 206; Nazism as threat to, 176–77; as opening the Jewish shtetl, 89, 90; women's voices of, 241n.20. *See also* assimilation; mythology; secularism
Epstein, Helen: on children of survivors, 216n.2; *Children of the Holocaust*, 29, 216n.2; on home, 81, 84–86; journey to Czechoslovakia by, 46, 222n.40; on silence surrounding Holocaust, 37; strategies of, to hear survivors' stories, 39; on survivors, 29–32, 34, 44, 45–46; *Where She Came From*, 222n.40, 224n.51; on "working through" trauma, 233n.21
Esau (biblical figure), 182, 184
essay: as a mixed literary form, xiv,

189–90; by new wave writers, xiv, 11, 99, 100, 178–81, 189–91, 193–97
"The Essay as a Warm Body" (Ozick), 191
estrangement: from European "home," 40, 93; in family relationships, 70, 74, 78–81, 84–86, 92, 182; menstruation as, from God, 145; and reconciliation, 78; women's, from Jewish tradition, 88, 89. *See also* continuity; separation; suicide
ethnicity: new wave writers' emphasis on, xiii–xiv, 6, 16–17, 23, 24, 82–84, 86, 90–92, 210n.4; as theme in immigrant Jewish literature, 17. *See also* Jews
Europe: efforts to imagine Jews' lives in pre-Holocaust, 6–7, 40–41, 50–55, 59, 60, 65, 68, 74–78, 87–93, 103–5, 214n.9, 229n.22, 232nn.6, 7–8, 234nn.25, 27; Holocaust as destroying Jews and Jewish culture in, 18, 81, 177, 178, 180, 234n.25; Holocaust as lens for looking at past in, 54, 55, 96; Jews' journeys to, 9, 39–40, 46–47, 78, 84, 221nn.35, 36, 222n.40, 232nn.7, 8; lack of nostalgia for Jewish past in, 40–41, 77, 82–84, 88, 107, 232n.8, 234n.32; longing for life in, before the Holocaust, 15, 222n.39; as a place of the terrifying past, 94–96; reconnection between American Jews and the past in, as essential to mourning, 5–6, 8, 39, 46–47, 132; research on, 78, 85, 87–88, 221n.33. *See also* exile and expulsion; Holocaust; home; reconnection; *specific places in*
Eve (biblical figure), 142, 143, 160, 161
Everything Is Illuminated (Foer), 107
Eve's Apple (J. Rosen), 155–62, 165
exile and expulsion: as American literary theme, 215n.19, 233n.10; Jews' experience of, 40, 81–82, 86, 97, 98, 136, 203–4, 213n.9; and language, 42–44; in Skibell's

Blessing on the Moon, 125. *See also* diaspora; Europe; Holocaust; home; homelessness

Exodus (Uris), 119

expulsion. *See* exile and expulsion

Ezrahi, Sidra DeKoven: on Adorno, 225n.1; on Jewish identity, 213n.6; on journeys to European "home," 232n.6; on nostalgia, 211n.7, 215n.26, 219n.21; on Roth, 213n.9, 214n.11, 215n.23; on stories about home, 76, 232n.7

False Papers (Aciman), 100–103

family, xi, xii, xiv–xv, 14–15, 18–19, 21–115, 123, 126, 134, 137, 141, 143, 147, 150–53, 155, 158, 160–66, 174, 179, 180, 183–85, 213n.6, 218nn.16–19, 220n.25, 226n.5, 231n.30

The Far Euphrates (Stollman), 107–12, 136–40, 174

femininity, 10, 243n.36; and males, 117, 120, 121, 236n.2, 238n.22; nurturing associated with, 158. *See also* gender

feminism: Bible from viewpoint of, 11, 178, 179–80; and body image, 156, 167–69, 242n.30; on gender, 117; as influence on author, xii; Jewish women's embrace of, 83, 243n.38; and marriage, 89–90, 150–55; and motherhood, 157–58. *See also* patriarchy; women

Fence imagery, 187

Ferber, Edna, 77

fiction: by American Jewish writers of the new wave, xiv, 48–75, 77, 78, 87–90, 92–93, 102–7, 150–73, 181–88, 191–92, 197–205; "midrashic impulse" in, 11, 174, 176–77, 182–89, 191–92, 197–205; by women writers in Yiddish, 10, 148–49; work of, 8, 27. *See also* stories

Fine, Ellen, 218n.17

Finkielkraut, Alain, 12–13, 23, 24, 210n.3

fire imagery, 69, 104, 199. *See also* ashes imagery; smoke imagery

first generation. *See* immigrants; survivors

Fishbane, Michael, 247n.25

Fitzgerald, F. Scott, 215n.19

Foer, Jonathan Safran: *Everything Is Illuminated*, 107

Fogelman, Eva, 216n.2, 220n.25, 221n.32

Foucault, Michel, 157, 243nn.34, 36–37

fragmentation: of survivors' stories, 29, 35–36, 45–46, 84, 218; of time, 64, 82, 198; vs. wholeness, 194–95. *See also* estrangement; exile and expulsion; separation; suicide

Frank, Anne: in Rosen's *Eve's Apple*, 160, 161; in Roth's *Ghost Writer*, 5, 19–20, 22, 215n.24

Franklin, Ruth, 227n.7

Freedman, Jonathan, 4, 19, 210n.3

French language, 43, 87

Freud, Sigmund, 36; on gender, 117, 236n.2; on mourning, 49–50, 70, 211n.6, 222n.42, 224n.53, 233n.21; Ozick on, 190–01; on repetition, 26, 49–50, 64, 70, 217n.10, 222n.42, 228n.13

Friedlander, Saul, 216n.7, 223n.42, 228n.14

Friedman, Michelle A., 246n.15

Friedmann, Thomas: *Damaged Goods*, 120–24, 133, 134

Frymer-Kensky, Tikva, 239n.5

Fugitive Pieces (Michaels), 124–25

Furman, Andrew: on assimilation, 210n.4; on memory, 235nn.36, 38; on new wave writing, 211nn.5, 6, 227n.7, 230n.23, 238n.27, 243n.38

fusion (Ozick's concept of), 189–90

Garden of Eden. *See* Eden

gas imagery, 73

gate imagery, 187

gender: issues of, in female writers of the new wave, 11, 77–93, 141–73,

gender *(continued)*
175, 206, 228n.18, 243nn.38–39,
244n.45; issues of, in male writers
of the new wave, 9–10, 116–40, 175,
206; and power, 114, 116, 117, 163,
170; reversals of, in Holocaust, 111,
136, 238n.22; separation by, in synagogues, 57, 134, 145–46. *See also*
femininity; "manliness"; men; patriarchy; women
Genesis (biblical book), 111–12, 185
German language, 42–43, 86–87, 91,
124
Germans, 34, 124
Germany: inability of, to mourn for
its past, 49, 222n.42, 239n.28; Nazism in, 27–29, 38, 40, 42, 48, 51, 56,
58, 60, 63, 65, 70, 81, 83, 86, 93, 95,
107, 111, 124, 126, 127, 130, 132,
134, 136, 160, 161, 176–77, 195,
200, 224n.50, 225n.1; occupation
of other countries by, 82; surren-
der of, in World War II, 4. *See also*
Germans; Holocaust
"The Ghost and Saul Bozoff" (Stern),
103–4
ghost imagery, 5, 19–20, 22, 215n.24
The Ghost Writer (Roth), 5, 6, 18, 19–20
Gitlin, Todd: *Sacrifice*, 182–84, 204
Giving Up America (Abraham), 153–55
glass (broken), 69, 73, 75
glasses imagery, 10, 11, 130. *See also*
vision imagery
God: connection to, in Stollman's
works, 137–40; disconnection
from, as theme in writings of the
new wave, 11, 37–74, 132; disconnection from, in Lerner's memoir,
83; disconnection from, in Roth's
works, 16; punishment from, 136,
139, 178–80, 183; testing by, 142;
visions of, 192
Goldstein, Rebecca, 204–5, 243n.38;
Dark Sister, 165–71; "Looking back
at Lot's Wife," 179–80; *Mazel*, 87–
90, 92; *Mind-Body Problem*, 163–65,
168; *Properties of Light*, 170–73,
197–99

The Golems of Gotham (Rosenbaum),
72–75, 129–30
"Goodbye, Columbus" (Roth), 4–6,
15–16, 31
Goodheart, Eugene, 77
Goodman, Allegra: *Paradise Park*,
191–92, 204
Govrin, Michal, 222n.40
Grossman, Atina, 28
"G'ula and Shulamit" (Potash), 149–
50, 158

Haas, Aaron, 216n.8
Hagar (biblical figure), 180–81
hair: absence of, 12, 21, 122, 153, 156,
157, 242n.30; imagery of, 11, 73,
74; pubic, 146, 157
Halbwachs, Maurice, 176, 246n.15
Hansen, Marcus, 211n.6, 219n.22
Hartman, Geoffrey, 246n.18
Haskalah. See Enlightenment
Hauptman, Judith, 144
Hawthorne, Nathaniel, 231n.37
healing (from Holocaust trauma),
112, 136; impossibility of, 64,
94–96, 125, 136–40; superficial,
135–36
Hebrew language, xi, 24, 58, 88, 111,
112, 133
Heinemann, Joseph, 246n.16
Hemingway, Ernest, 215n.19
Hershman, Marcie: "Living on
Top," 84
Hiding Places (Rose), 93–94
Hiroshima (Japan), 4
Hirsch, Marianne, 48, 81, 225n.2,
230nn.27, 28, 231n.30
Hoffman, Anne Golomb, 244n.45
Hoffman, Eva: *Lost in Translation*,
40–41, 43, 81
Hollander, John, 8, 209n.3
Holocaust: academic study of, 65, 73;
avoidance of, xi–xiii, 3, 5–9, 15–16,
31, 37, 49, 93–94, 221n.32; current
attention to, xiii, 3, 5, 6, 8, 217n.11;
denial of, 73; as destruction of Eu-
ropean Jewry and its culture, 18,
81, 177, 178, 180, 234n.25; impact

of, on contemporary writers, 82–
83; as a kind of home, 93; legacy
of, xii, 3, 7, 8, 15, 25–75, 125–29,
132–36, 207, 218n.17, 238n.25; as
a lens for looking at the European past, 54, 55, 96; as transforming people into victims, xii,
12, 27–29, 34, 122, 221n.32; "working through" the pain of, 39, 46–
47, 49–50, 206, 218n.16, 222n.42,
228n.14, 233n.21. *See also* aftermath; concentration camps; healing; imagery; innocents; looking
back; loss; malaise; memory (collective); mourning; moving on;
rage; scars; survivors; *Yiddishkeit*
home: American Jewish writers'
efforts to imagine Jews', in pre-
Holocaust Europe, 6–7, 40–41,
50–55, 59, 60, 65, 68, 74 78, 87–92,
103–5, 214n.9, 229n.22, 232nn.6,
7–8, 234nn.25, 27; drawings of, by
children living in war, 82; Eden as,
110–12; estrangement from European, 40, 93, 222n.40; exile as a
kind of, xiv, 55, 76–77, 197; as a
fully achieved self, 47, 77–78, 85;
Israel as, 95, 96; Judaism not, for
some Jewish women, 83; and language, 86–87, 93, 111–12; longing
for, 95, 96, 100–102, 107; meanings
of, among new wave writers, 9,
21, 76–115, 175, 206; memory as,
113–15; as ruined, 183; as site of
women's struggle and spirituality, 81. *See also* exile and expulsion; homelessness; journeys;
Yiddish language
homelessness, 113–15, 200–204,
235n.39. *See also* exile and expulsion; home
homosexuality, 10, 133–38
Hopkins, Gerard Manley, 232n.4
Horowitz, Sara, 219n.27, 221nn.30,
33, 226n.2, 230n.28, 238n.22
Howe, Irving, 211n.5
Hungarian language, 43, 85, 86–87
Hungary, 43, 51, 85, 86–87

Hurst, Fanny, 77
Hyman, Paula, 147

identity. *See* ethnicity; gender; Jews;
self; "selving"
The Illuminated Soul (Stollman), 112–
15, 200–205
imagery: of ashes, 29, 73, 104, 174,
224n.44; of birds, 202–3; of broken
glass, 69, 73, 75; of cattle cars, 8,
11, 16, 56, 58–59, 64, 65, 67, 69,
72, 73; of fences and gates, 187; of
fire, 104, 199; of gas, 73; of ghosts,
5, 11, 19–20, 22, 37–74, 101, 124–25,
129–31, 166, 215n.24; of glasses, 10,
11, 130; of hair, 8, 11, 73, 74; Holocaust, 8, 11, 48, 73, 187, 225n.1; of
mirrors, 16, 21, 26, 135, 148, 150,
153, 165, 168, 177, 206, 239n.31; of
showers, 11, 72, 73; of smoke, 11,
29, 71, 73; of snakes, 55, 230n.24;
of tattoos, 11, 32, 54, 65, 71–73,
126, 127; of teeth, 10, 11, 57, 130;
of violins, 74–75; of vision, 202,
203; of windows, xi, 206–8. *See
also* embodiment; gender
The Imaginary Jew (Finkielkraut), 12–
13, 23, 24
immigrants: "first generation" of, 4,
6, 7, 14, 16, 19, 44, 79, 81, 118–
19, 160–61, 219n.22; old country visions of, 56; pre-Holocaust,
234n.25; as Steve Stern's subject,
102–7; trauma suffered by, 18, 25,
26, 52, 53, 63, 79, 130–32, 229n.19.
See also survivors (of the Holocaust: first generation)
"Individuation." *See* differentiation
*In My Mother's House: A Daughter's
Story* (Chernin), 78–81, 92
innocents (suffering of), 33, 52, 105,
106, 136–37, 139. *See also* Holocaust
interconnectedness. *See* continuity
intertextuality. *See* "midrashic
impulse"
Isaac (biblical figure), 142, 179–84, 187
Ishmael (biblical figure), 180–82
Islam, 101

Israel: Helen Epstein in, 35; Jewish identity in, 213nn.6, 9, 214n.10; post-Holocaust commitment to, xi, 12, 23; as Weiss's home, 95, 96. *See also* Zionism

Jacob (biblical figure), 118, 182
James, Henry, 19, 20, 34, 215n.19; as character in novel, 166; Ozick on, 190, 191
James, William, 194; as character in novel, 166, 168, 169, 171
Janet, Pierre, 226n.5
Jeremiah (biblical figure), 221n.34
Jerusalem, 194
Jewish Museum exhibit of March 2002, 225n.1, 231n.39
Jewish tradition: assimilated Jews' ambivalent relation to, 11, 12–13, 18, 21, 106–7; binaries in, 166; and Enlightenment, 189; learning associated with, 58, 133; memory's valorization by, 26, 204, 232n.9, 235n.35; men's longing for connection to, 132–33; men's valorization by, 116, 117; new wave writers' relation to, 11, 57; rituals of, 101, 123, 129–33, 135, 136, 139, 140, 165; women and, 10, 79, 80, 83, 88–93, 106, 117, 133–34, 141–48, 151, 155–65, 169, 172–73, 177–78, 180, 237n.4, 240n.17, 244n.45; women's longing for connection to, 80, 81, 83, 180, 192. *See also* patriarchy
Jews: American, as assimilated, 4–7, 14–16, 31, 106–7, 210n.4; Chasidic, 150–54, 184–86, 241n.28; in England, 36–37; exile and expulsion experienced by, 40, 81–82, 86, 97, 98, 136, 203–4, 213n.9; as gendered, embodied creatures, xiv, 9–11, 116–73; "gentle" vs. "tough," 118–19, 126–27; male, as feminized, 117–18; meaning associated with being, 132–33; mixtures avoided by, 188, 198–99; Orthodox, 120–23, 133–34,

154, 163, 164, 242n.31, 243n.38; pogroms against, 79–80; Reform, 133; self-hatred among, 15, 35, 98, 124, 214n.11; stories of, as offering meaning, 131–32; as victims after the Holocaust, xii, 12, 27–29, 34, 122, 221n.32. *See also* diaspora; ethnicity; exile and expulsion; gender; Holocaust; Jewish tradition; "midrashic impulse"; new wave writers; self (identity)
Jews and Feminism (Leavitt), 83
Jochanan ben Zakkai, 194, 196
Jong, Erica, 150
Joseph and His Brothers (Mann), 176–77, 180, 181, 186–89, 198
Josephus, 196, 205
journeys: to Europe, 9, 39–40, 46–47, 78, 84, 221nn.35, 36, 222n.40, 232nn.7, 8; Jewish history as, 203–4; life as, 198; as theme in writings by new wave writers, 9, 56, 76, 81–84, 93–96, 101, 107, 108, 113, 126–27, 203–4
Joyce, James, 241n.28
Judaism. *See* Jewish tradition; rabbis

Kafka, Franz, 209n.3
Kahane, Claire, 228n.14
Kalman, Judith: *The Country of Birches*, 51–54, 57
Kaplan, Alice Yaeger, 86, 222n.39
Karpf, Anne: *The War After*, 9, 31–32, 35–37, 39, 44–45, 220n.25
Kermode, Frank, 193
Kiefer, Anselm, 73
Kimmelman, Michael, 225n.1
knowledge (education; scholarship): destruction of, 58, 131; devaluation of, 58; inadequacy of human, 202; Jewish tradition's association with, 58, 133; as a kind of home, 114; women's exclusion from, 79, 80, 83, 117, 144–47, 237n.4; women's obtaining of secular, 147–48. *See also* memory (collective); research

Krystal, Henry, 227n.5
Kugel, James L., 245n.11
Kuppermann, Wendy Joy, 223n.44

LaCapra, Dominick: on the Holocaust, 212n.2; on mourning,
  222n.42, 233n.21, 238n.21; on
  "reading the scars" left by the
  Holocaust, 10, 217n.7, 222n.42
Ladino poetry, 58
lager. See concentration camps
Laius (classical figure), 182
Langer, Lawrence, 26, 38, 222n.42,
  225n.2, 229n.20
language: acquisition of new, by
  Holocaust survivors, 28; altering
  of experience in one, by telling in
  another, 42–44, 47; doubling of
  selves through, 43–44, 87; and
  home, 86–87, 93, 111–12; recovery
  of native, 46, 87; in Roth's *Ghost
  Writer,* 20; as transformed by new
  wave writers, 7, 185, 198. *See also*
  silencing; translation; voice(s); *specific languages*
Lazar Malkin Enters Heaven (Stern),
  102–7
Leah (biblical figure), 143
Leavitt, Laura: *Jews and Feminism,* 83
Lerner, Gerda: *Why History Matters,*
  42–43, 81, 82–83, 86–87
Levi, Primo, 37, 230n.24
"Levitation" (Bukiet), 54
Levy, Andrew, 225n.1
"The Little Blue Snowman of Washington Heights" (Rosenbaum),
  67–68
"little secrets" (of the collective past),
  7–9, 76; family scars as result of,
  49, 121; from before the Holocaust,
  141–73; and "midrashic impulse,"
  175, 178, 184, 197; telling, 206–8;
  work of the mind as critical to
  revealing, 204–5. *See also* gender;
  Holocaust: legacy of; Jewish tradition; loss; mourning; rage; scars
looking back, 174–80, 198, 205, 245n.5.

See also memory (collective); "midrashic impulse"; moving on
"Looking Back at Lot's Wife" (Goldstein), 179–80
loss: acceptance of, 76, 84; of home,
  76–115, 234n.25; memory as consolation for, 115, 199–205, 224n.53;
  "midrashic impulse" as recuperating, 178–81, 196; of one's mother
  tongue, 42–43, 86–87; of past
  knowledge, 58, 131; as rooted in
  mortality, 184; of second generation's childhood, 65, 66–67; as
  theme in author's life, xii–xiii; as
  theme in Roth's works, 4–6, 21–
  22; as theme in works by new
  wave writers, xiii, 7, 8, 13, 42–45,
  49, 56–66, 94–96, 177, 178–81,
  193–94; translation as effort to
  recuperate, 193–94; of women's
  gifts through their exclusions, 89,
  234n.25; of Yiddish language, 12,
  22, 43–44. *See also* God; Holocaust;
  home; language; malaise; memory; mourning; scars
Lot's wife (Biblical figure), 179–80
Lowin, Joseph, 247n.23

Magnus, Shulamit S., 241n.20
malaise, 83, 111; among Jewish
  women, 144, 153; perception of,
  among Holocaust survivors, 28,
  34, 53; among post-Holocaust
  American Jews, 12, 15, 18, 34, 65,
  160–62
Malamud, Bernard, 7, 14, 16, 19, 44,
  118–19
"manliness": in African American literature, 237n.12; Holocaust as reshaping meaning of, for Jewish
  men, 9–10, 20–21, 57, 116–40. *See
  also* gender; scars; sexuality
Mann, Thomas: *Joseph and His Brothers,* 176–77, 180, 181, 186–89, 191,
  193, 195, 196, 198, 201–2
Maus: A Survivor's Tale (Spiegelman),
  59–66, 70, 71, 230n.27

Maus II (Spiegelman), 63
Mauthausen concentration camp,
    3, 58
Mazel (Goldstein), 88–90, 92
memoirs: by new wave writers, xiv,
    25–48, 77–87, 92–102; work of, 8
memory (collective): as consolation
    for loss, 115, 199–205, 224n.53; as
    depending on recovering and
    interpreting the Holocaust's leg-
    acy, 11, 69, 174–205, 219n.21; em-
    powering of, without healing or
    redeeming, 27, 69; failure of, 18–
    19, 73; fashioning of, xiv; as home,
    113–15; and identity, 213n.6; Jew-
    ish tradition's valorization of, 26,
    204, 232n.9, 235n.35; numbness as-
    sociated with, 29–31, 35, 52, 68,
    228n.14; as partly imagined, 88;
    past and future bound up in, 81,
    84, 174–205; process of, as a kind
    of journey home, 102–4; as re-
    pressed by trauma, 26, 38, 50,
    61, 64, 222n.42, 226n.5, 230n.28;
    "second-hand," among second
    generation, 25–26, 48, 64, 67–
    69, 74, 216n.3, 226n.5; as step in
    mourning, 49, 174; stories as in-
    structing, 176, 180, 184, 218n.16;
    as threatening assimilationists in
    Roth's "Eli, the Fanatic," 5. *See also*
    knowledge; memoirs; remanence;
    research; stories
men (Jewish): excluding of, from
    various European occupations,
    118; Holocaust as reshaping
    meaning of "manliness" for, 9–10,
    20–21, 57, 116–40, 228n.18; Jewish
    tradition's valorization of, 116,
    117; power of, over women's
    bodies, 144–45, 237n.4; and pro-
    creation, 143, 146, 159, 240n.12;
    women as threatening to, 144–
    47, 157, 240n.14, 241n.20, 242n.30,
    242n.33; writers, on home, 93–
    115. *See also* patriarchy; rabbis
menstruation, 144, 145–46, 157, 164,
    240n.14, 242n.33; and anorexia, 156

Metaphor and Memory (Ozick), 189
Michaels, Anne: *Fugitive Pieces*,
    124–25
"midrashic impulse": defined, 11,
    175, 244n.2, 245nn.3, 11; history
    of, 175; of new wave writers, 22,
    174–205
Milbauer, Asher Z., 218n.20, 221n.36
Millen, Rochelle L., 240n.17
The Mind-Body Problem (Goldstein),
    163–65, 168
Mintz, Alan, 226n.3
mirror imagery, 16, 21, 26, 135, 148,
    150, 153, 165, 168, 177, 206, 239n.31
Mitscherlich, Alexander and Marga-
    rete, 217n.7, 222n.42
"Moishe the Just" (Stern), 105–6
Monaghan, David, 214n.17
motherhood, 10; as a defining imper-
    ative for Jewish women, 142–43,
    158–59, 242n.33; and feminism,
    157–58; rabbinic views of pro-
    creation and, 143, 144, 146, 159;
    vs. sexuality, 149, 158
mourning (of losses sustained during
    the Holocaust): avoidance of, by
    American Jews, 4, 49, 65; avoid-
    ance of, by survivors, 61; difficulty
    of, 12; for lost languages, 42–44,
    86–87; need for, 162; reconnection
    between American Jews and the
    European past as essential to, 5–6,
    8, 39, 46–47, 132; by second gener-
    ation, 26–27, 42, 46–47, 49–50, 52–
    53, 59, 60–65, 68, 71–75, 127–30,
    174, 216n.7; steps in, 49–50, 62–63,
    174–75, 222n.42; strategies for, 74,
    84–85, 230n.28; as work, 216n.7,
    222n.42, 228n.14. *See also* repara-
    tion; "working through"
moving on, 13, 15, 174, 176, 178, 198,
    205, 218n.16. *See also* looking back;
    "midrashic impulse"
multiplicity (cultural), 186–89, 191,
    193, 195–98, 206. *See also* differ-
    ence; Enlightenment *(Haskalah)*
mutilation. *See* scars
My Life as a Man (Roth), 17–18, 20, 21

mythology: figures in pre-biblical, 142, 171, 172; pre-Holocaust world as reduced to, 9, 40; survivors' narratives as assuming role of, 36, 39; underlying Western culture, xii, 176–77, 186–89, 245n.5

Nachman of Bratslav, 184, 185
Nadler, Allan, 233n.13
narrative structure: fragmentary nature of survivors', 29, 35–36, 45–46, 84, 218; inadequacy of survivors', 34; Roth's, 21, 24; as a way of ordering experience, 221n.31; in works by new wave writers, 7, 60–61, 201–2. *See also* language; time
Nattel, Lilian: *The River Midnight*, 87, 88, 90–92
Nazis. *See* Germans; Holocaust
Neusner, Jacob, 240n.11
new wave writers: defined, 6, 211n.5; emphases of, 6–7, 50–52, 57, 76, 212n.13, 213n.9; fiction by, 48–75; on "home," 76–115; and identity, 16–17; on looking back and moving on, 174–205; memoirs by, 25–47; men's embodiment in works of, 116–40; Roth's legacy to, 14–24; women's embodiment in works of, 141–73
"New Words for Old" (Bukiet), 55
Niederland, William G., 217n.14
Norich, Anita: "On the Yiddish Question," 43–44
nostalgia, 6, 13, 31, 80, 211n.7; for immigrant past, 160, 215n.23, 222n.39; resistance to, about European Jewish past, 40–41, 77, 82–84, 88, 107, 232n.8, 234n.32
Novick, Peter, 3, 217n.11
numbness (as Holocaust legacy), 29–31, 35, 52, 68, 228n.14
"Nurseries" (Bukiet), 54

Oedipus (classical figure), 182
Olsen, Tillie: "Tell Me a Riddle," 14, 141

Operation Shylock (Roth), 19, 214nn.10, 11
Otwock (Poland), 38
Out of Egypt (Aciman), 96–102
Ozick, Cynthia, 11, 204, 226n.3; "Bialik's Hint," 189; *The Cannibal Galaxy*, 188–89, 247n.30; "The Essay as a Warm Body," 191; on links between fiction and essays, xiv, 189–90; *Metaphor and Memory*, 189; "The Pagan Rabbi," 187–88; polemic approach of, 190–91, 195, 199; *Quarrel and Quandary*, 191, 247n.31; "Remembering Maurice Samuel," 190; "Toward a New Yiddish," 189, 247n.27

"The Pagan Rabbi" (Ozick), 187–88
Paley, Grace, 14–15
"The Pants in the Family" (Rosenbaum), 65
Paradise Park (Goodman), 191–92
Pardes, Ilana, 142, 143
patriarchy (sexism), 82, 85, 116, 117, 122, 133, 141–44, 150–53, 163; contempt of women of, 117, 146, 148–50, 157. *See also* Jewish tradition: women and
Podhoretz, Norman, 219n.22
Pogany, Eugene L., 224n.53
Poland: Jews' feelings about, 40–41; in Rosenbaum's works, 11, 126–27; in Spiegelman's *Maus*, 60; survivors from, 38–39; visits to, 9, 46–47, 221n.36
polemics, 190–91, 195, 199
Polish language, 43, 91, 124
political activities (among women), 79–80, 83, 147–48
Porter, Roger J., 234n.34
Portnoy's Complaint (Roth), 118, 119
"postmemory," 48, 64, 67, 74, 226n.5. *See also* memory: "second-hand"
Potash, Rikuda: "G'ula and Shulamit," 149–50
Properties of Light (Goldstein), 170–73, 197–99

Quarrel and Quandary (Ozick), 191,
    247n.31
"The Quilt and the Bicycle" (Bukiet),
    54, 55

rabbis: *Haskalah* as diminishing
    power of, 147; midrashic tradition
    of, 144, 175, 177, 179, 181, 195–96,
    198, 199, 239n.8; and procreation,
    143, 144, 146, 159; in Rosenbaum's
    fiction, 238n.25; and women, 10,
    79, 80, 83, 88–93, 106, 117, 133–
    34, 141–48, 151, 155–65, 169, 172–
    73, 177–78, 180, 237n.4, 240n.17,
    244n.45; and women's bodies,
    144–45, 237n.4; and women's sex-
    uality, 143–47, 157, 162, 163–64,
    168, 172–73, 243
Rachel (biblical figure), 39, 76, 143,
    221n.34
rage: as Holocaust legacy, 7, 32–35,
    59–60, 62, 63, 66, 70, 130, 133, 134,
    136; women's, 80, 82–83, 85, 88.
    See also estrangement; suicide
Raphael, Lev: *Dancing on Tisha B'Av*,
    132–36
"Rappaccini's Daughter" (Haw-
    thorne), 231n.37
Rashi, 195
Raskin, Miriam: "Zlatke," 148–49, 158
Rebekah (Biblical figure), 179, 180, 187
reconnection (between American
    Jews and the European past): dif-
    ficulty of, 12, 22; as essential to
    mourning the Holocaust, 5–6, 8,
    39, 46–47; new wave writers' ges-
    tures of, 7, 8, 13, 76, 81, 82, 84–86,
    92–94, 127. *See also* continuity
redemption, 27, 73–74
refugees. *See* displaced persons;
    survivors
Reich, Walter, 225n.1
Reitman-Dobi, Lina, 218nn.19, 20,
    219n.24, 220nn.26, 29
relationships. *See* continuity; es-
    trangement; family; rage; sepa-
    ration; suicide

Reluctant Return (Weiss), 94–96
remanence, 100–102, 201
remembering. *See* memory (collec-
    tive); "postmemory"; remanence
"Remembering Maurice Samuel"
    (Ozick), 190
reparation, 46, 47
repetition: Freud on, 26, 49–50, 64, 70,
    217n.10, 222n.42, 228n.13; in Gold-
    stein's *Dark Sister*, 166; in Rosen-
    baum's *Second Hand Smoke*, 71
research, 78, 85, 87–88, 221n.33; as
    means of recovering voices, 36–
    42, 46
return of the repressed. *See* memory:
    as repressed by trauma; repetition
Rich, Adrienne, 10, 143, 167, 242n.33
Ringelblum, Emanuel, 238n.22
The River Midnight (Nattel), 90–92
The Romance Reader (Abraham), 150–53
"Romancing the Yahrtzeit Light" (Ro-
    senbaum), 65, 68–69, 129
Rose, Daniel Asa: *Hiding Places*, 93–94
Rosen, Jonathan, 11, 173, 204, 205;
    Eve's Apple, 155–62, 165; *The Tal-
    mud and the Internet*, 11, 193–97,
    199, 201–2, 243n.35
Rosen, Norma, 204; *Accidents of Influ-
    ence*, 48; *Biblical Women Unbound*,
    11, 178, 180–81, 197; on witnessing
    the Holocaust through imagina-
    tion, 8, 48, 231n.38
Rosenbaum, Thane, 11, 213n.5; "An
    Act of Defiance," 65; *Elijah Vis-
    ible*, 64, 66–67; *The Golems of
    Gotham*, 72–75, 129–30; "The Lit-
    tle Blue Snowman of Washing-
    ton Heights," 67–68; on new
    wave writers, 6, 211n.6; "The
    Pants in the Family," 65; "Ro-
    mancing the Yahrtzeit Light," 65,
    68–69, 129; on "second-hand
    memory," 216n.3; *Second Hand
    Smoke*, 66, 70–73, 125–30
Rosenfeld, Alvin, 231n.36
Rosensaft, Menachem Z., 211n.9
Roth, Henry: *Call It Sleep*, 123–24

Roth, Philip: *The Counterlife,* 10, 16, 18–24, 77, 119, 213n.9, 214n.10, 233n.10; "Eli, the Fanatic" by, xi, 4–6, 22, 34, 209n.1, 235n.41; *The Ghost Writer,* 5, 6, 18, 19–20; "Goodbye, Columbus," 4–6; identity in works by, 15–24, 31, 77, 116, 213n.9, 214nn.10–11, 232n.3; manliness in works by, 118–19; *My Life as a Man,* 17–18, 20, 21; *Operation Shylock,* 19, 214nn.10, 11; *Portnoy's Complaint,* 118, 119; postwar American life in works by, 4–6, 15–16, 31; sexuality in works by, 10, 19–20, 119, 129; voices in works by, 44; *The Zuckerman Trilogy,* 16, 214n.10
Rothberg, Michael, 214n.11, 215nn.20, 21, 217n.9, 226n.3, 227n.13; on Spiegelman's *Maus,* 230n.29, 231n.31
Russian language, 91
Ruth (biblical character), 143

Sacrifice (Gitlin), 182–84
Salamon, Julie: *The Net of Dreams,* 28, 220n.28, 221n.36
Samuel, Maurice, 190
Santner, Eric, 217nn.7, 10
Sarah (biblical figure), 142, 143, 181, 183
Satlow, Michael, 240n.13
scars: invisible, among second generation, 25, 26–27, 29, 33–34, 36, 37, 60–64, 71, 125–29, 134, 136; loss of native language as, 42–44; "reading" of, 47, 49, 50, 66, 70, 74, 124–25; ritual, as marking Jewish men, 10, 21; wounds under, 49, 56, 61, 66, 223n.44; in writings of new wave writers, 9–10, 51–52, 56–72, 95, 111, 124–26, 130, 132, 136. *See also* circumcision; healing; tattoo imagery
Schechner, Mark, 41
Schneider, Steven P., 244n.2
scholarship. *See* knowledge
Scholem, Gershom, 190
Schwartz, Delmore, 16, 199

second generation: and aggression, 33, 140; defined, 4, 7–8; emerging voices among, 36–47, 50, 53, 55, 56, 60, 61–64, 70, 71–72, 75, 230n.23; Holocaust's impact on, 8, 25–75, 125–29, 132–36, 218n.17; as looking back, 174, 211n.6, 219n.22; mourning by, 26–27, 42, 46–47, 49–50, 52–53, 59, 60–65, 68, 71–75, 127–30, 174, 216n.7; studies of, 216n.2; suffering of, as nothing compared to their parents', 33–35, 52, 65, 220n.29; suppression of voices among, 31–36. *See also* new wave writers; separation
Second Hand Smoke (Rosenbaum), 66, 70–73, 125–30
secularism: in Goodman's *Paradise Park,* 192; in Ozick's "Pagan Rabbi," 187–89. *See also* Enlightenment
seders, 73–74, 129–32
Seforim, Mendele Mocher, 58
self (identity): as double, 43; fully achieved, as a journey "home," 47, 77–78, 85; as a grave in which the past is buried, 43–44; hatred of one's, 15, 35, 98, 124, 214n.11; hiding from one's, 93–94; Holocaust's denial of Jews', 95; and "home" for women writers, 77–93; as "inside a sea of competing voices," 197; inventing a, 16, 214n.10; and language, 42–44; and memory, 213n.6; Roth's treatment of post-Holocaust, 15–19, 22–24, 31, 77, 116, 212n.2, 213n.9, 214nn.10–11, 232n.3; as seen through the lens of gender, 9, 116–73. *See also* "selving"
Self-hatred, 15, 35, 98, 124, 214n.11
"Selving," 77, 81, 83, 88, 89–90. *See also* Self (identity)
Semel, Nava, 224n.44
separation: consolation for, 205; difficulty of, between survivors and their children, 31–32, 35–36, 38, 44, 45–47, 64–65, 67–70, 133–35;

separation *(continued)*
  by gender and power, 114, 116, 117, 163, 170; by gender in synagogues, 57, 134, 145–46; between Jewish husbands and wives during menstruation, 145; of Orthodox male body, 121; between past and present, 59, 64, 105, 107, 108; psychological (dissociation), 226n.5; as theme in American Jewish writing, 17, 108–10. *See also* estrangement; exile and expulsion; suicide
The Seventh Beggar (Abraham), 184–86
sexism. *See* patriarchy
sexuality: in Bukiet's works, 55, 57, 131; female, and rabbis, 143–47, 157, 162, 163–64, 168, 172–73, 243; female, in new wave writings, 150–73; in Friedmann's *Damaged Goods*, 119–23; in Goldstein's *Properties of Light*, 171; in Kalman's *Country of Birches*, 53; vs. motherhood, 149, 158; in Nattel's *River Midnight*, 91; in new wave works, 129, 183; in Raphael's *Dancing on Tisha B'Av*, 133–36; in Roth's works, 10, 19–20, 119, 129; in Stollman's *Far Euphrates*, 137–38, 140; in women's writings in Yiddish, 148–50
Shepherd, Naomi, 147–48
Shevuoth, 123
Shostak, Debra, 212n.2, 214n.16, 215n.27, 232n.3
shower imagery, 11, 72, 73
shtetl. *See* home
Shteyngart, Gary: *The Russian Debutante*, 234n.32
Shulman, Alix Kates, 150
Sicher, Efraim, 216n.1, 218n.16, 221nn.31, 225n.2, 37, 238n.22
silencing (of women), 80, 83, 88, 89, 93, 142, 146–47, 151, 180, 234n.25, 240n.18
"Sincerely Yours" (Bukiet), 55
Skibell, Joseph: *A Blessing on the Moon*, 125

Slattery, Dennis, 244n.44
slavery, 238n.22
Slochower, Harry, 245n.5
smoke imagery, 11, 29, 71, 73
snake imagery, 55, 230n.24
Sokoloff, Naomi, 188–89, 247n.30
Sontag, Susan: *Regarding the Pain of Others*, 175–77, 246n.15
Spiegelman, Art: *Maus*, 59–66, 70, 71, 230n.27; *Maus II*, 63
Spielberg, Steven, 221n.36
spirituality, 81, 91–92. *See also* God; Jewish tradition
Steiner, George, 216n.1
Stern, David, 245n.3
Stern, Steve, 235n.36; "The Book of Mormon," 102–3; "Bruno's Metamorphosis," 103; "The Ghost and Saul Bozoff," 103–4; *Lazar Malkin Enters Heaven*, 102–7; "Moishe the Just," 105–6; "A String around the Moon," 105; "The Tail of a Kite," 106–7, 235n.42; *The Wedding Jester*, 103, 105, 106
Stollman, Aryeh Lev: *Far Euphrates* by, 107–12, 136–40, 174; *Illuminated Soul* by, 112–15, 200–205
stories: collective memory as instructed by, 176, 180, 184, 218n.16; cultural work performed by, xiii, xiv, 6, 11–12, 25–26, 46–47, 49–50, 52–53, 62, 87, 131–32, 176, 205–8, 216n.4, 223n.42; family, 31–36, 45–46; themes of, 76; as a way of ordering experience, 221n.31. *See also* essay; fiction; memoirs; memory (collective); narrative structure; "storying"; voice(s)
Stories of an Imaginary Childhood (Bukiet), 53–56
"storying," 81, 89. *See also* stories
"A String around the Moon" (Stern), 105
Sucher, Cheryl Pearl, 228n.18
suffering. *See* Holocaust; innocents; scars; suicide
suicide: Chernin's grandmother as threatening, 79; in Friedmann's

Damaged Goods, 120–24; in Gitlin's *Sacrifice,* 182, 183; in Goldstein's *Mazel,* 88–90, 92; n Rosen's *Eve's Apple,* 158, 159–60, 162; in Rosenbaum's work, 73–74, 129–30; in Spiegelman's *Maus,* 60–61, 63

Suleiman, Susan Rubin, 226n.5, 233n.21; *Budapest Diary,* 43, 81, 84–87; *Exile and Creativity,* 223n.43

survival (lessons of), 61, 66, 126, 220n.28, 238n.22. *See also* survivors

survivors (of the Holocaust: first generation): in Bukiet's works, 9–10, 56–59; difficulty of separation between, and their children, 31–32, 35–36, 38, 44, 45–47, 64–65, 67–70, 133–35; experience of, 18, 25, 26, 52, 53, 63, 79, 130–32, 229n.19; fragmentary nature of stories of, 29, 35–36, 45–46, 84, 218; in Gitlin's *Sacrifice,* 183; in Goldstein's works, 165; and "little secrets" of our collective past, 7–9; as objects, 28, 56; rage of, 7, 32–35, 59–60, 62, 63, 66, 70, 130, 133, 134, 136; reconstructing lives of, in memoirs, 27–47; rescue of, xi, 7; restoration of voices of, through their children's memoirs, 29, 46–47; in Roth's works, 5, 22, 34; silence of, 5, 29, 32, 36, 37, 59, 84, 85, 120, 121, 125, 133, 134, 136, 218n.17; silence surrounding, 37; as suffering from malaise, 28, 34, 53; suicide by, 60–61, 120–24; "syndrome" affecting, 217n.14, 224n.50; vitality of, 28, 32. *See also* Holocaust; immigrants; "little secrets"; loss; mourning; scars; second generation; separation

synagogues, 57, 134, 145–46

"The Tail of a Kite" (Stern), 106–7, 235n.42

The Tale of Genji (Murasaki), 115

The Talmud and the Internet (J. Rosen), 193–97, 199, 201–2

Tantrism, 170, 198

tattoo imagery: and emotional

numbness, 30; in works by new wave writers, 11, 32, 54, 65, 71–73, 126, 127

teeth imagery, 10, 11, 57, 130

"Tell Me a Riddle" (Olsen), 14, 141

third generation, 84, 235n.39

Tikkun (magazine), 6

time: as an echo chamber where voices connect, 181, 188, 198–99, 205; fragmentation of, 64, 82, 198; interlacing of, 90, 187. *See also* narrative structure

Tompkins, Jane, xiii, 6, 25–26, 87, 216n.4

Torah. *See* Bible; knowledge

"Toward a New Yiddish" (Ozick), 189, 247n.27

trains. *See* cattle car imagery

translation: as act of betrayal, 44; as recuperative strategy, 193–97

"traumatic event," 217n.9, 227n.13

"Traumatic Memory and American Jewish Writing" (Burstein), 87, 216n.7, 222n.40, 224n.52, 228n.14, 233nn.21–22, 238nn.21, 24, 239n.28

Trilling, Lionel, xiii, 50, 209n.3

Uris, Leon, 119

"The Ventriloquist" (Bukiet), 55

Victorian literature, xi, xii

Vilna Gaon, 79

violin imagery, 74–75

"Virtuoso" (Bukiet), 54

vision imagery, 202, 203. *See also* glasses imagery

voice(s): of characters of immigrant writers, 44; competing, 197; emerging of, among second generation, 36–47, 50, 53, 55, 56, 60, 61–64, 70, 71–72, 75, 230n.23; historical, 204; historical context as means to recovering, 36–42, 46; inner, 141; as living in essays, 190, 191; of people different from ourselves, 207–8; recovering of silenced, 29, 46–47, 88, 89, 180–81, 229n.18; silencing of women's, 80, 83, 88, 89, 93, 142,

voice(s) *(continued)*
146–47, 151, 180, 234n.25,
240n.18; suppression of second
generation's, 31–36; time's connecting of, 181, 188, 198–99, 205.
See also language

Warsaw, 38–39
Waugh, Patricia, 77
The Wedding Jester (Stern), 103, 105,
106
"The Wedding Jester" (Stern), 105
Weiss, David W.: *Reluctant Return*,
94–96
Wengeroff, Pauline, 241n.20
Western tradition. *See* Enlightenment
(Haskalah); mythology
Wharton, Edith, 190, 191
Why History Matters (Lerner), 86
Wiener Neustadt (Austria), 94–96
Wiesel, Eli, 226n.2
Wilson, Matthew, 214n.18
window imagery, xi, 206–8
Wisse, Ruth, 42, 211n.7, 229n.22,
232n.6
"womanliness." *See* femininity
"The Woman with a Dog" (Bukiet), 55
women: abuse of, 79; as contaminating to men, 144–47, 157, 240n.14,
242n.33; contempt for, in patriarchy, 117, 146, 148–50, 157; difficulty of connecting with other,
78–81; disabling of, in European
"home," 41–42; embodiment of,
122, 141–73, 229n.18; exclusions of
Jewish, 10, 79, 80, 83, 88–93, 106,
117, 133–34, 141–48, 151, 155–65,
169, 172–73, 177–78, 180, 237n.4,
240n.17, 244n.45; as inferior to
men, 144–45, 147, 157, 163, 169,
172; motherhood as imperative for
Jewish, 142–43, 158–59, 242n.33;
non-Jewish, 23, 64, 68–69, 154; as
passive in procreation, 143, 144,
146, 240n.12; political activities
among, 79–80, 83, 147–48; as
rebels, 88–92, 150–53, 160–61;

silencing of, 80, 83, 88, 89, 93, 142,
146–47, 151, 180, 234n.25, 240n.18;
solidarity among, 91–93; work of,
147; writers, "midrashic impulse"
among, 177–81, 187–89; writers, on
home, 77–93, 232n.8. *See also* femininity; feminism
Woolf, Leonard and Virginia, 190
Wordsworth, William, 17
"working through" (the pain of the
past), 39, 46–47, 49–50, 206, 218n.16,
222n.42, 228n.14, 233n.21. *See also*
mourning
World War II, 4. *See also* Holocaust
writers: cultural work performed by
stories written by, xiii, xiv, 6, 11–12,
25–26, 49–50, 52–53, 62, 87, 131–32,
176, 205–8, 216n.4, 223n.42; female,
on home, 77–93; male, on home,
93–115; power of, to transform the
residue of atrocity, 72–75, 84–85,
102–3; Roth's use of characters as,
17–23. *See also* essay; fiction; memoirs; new wave writers; *names of
specific writers*
Writing Mothers, Writing Daughters
(Burstein), 232n.5, 233n.14,
234n.25, 241n.25

Yeats, William Butler, 170
Yerushalmi, Yosef, 232n.9
Yezierska, Anzia, 234n.25
Yiddishkeit, 5, 12, 18
Yiddish language, 124; author's lack
of knowledge of, xi; as devalued
language, 91; Jews as having lost,
12, 22, 43–44; legacy of, 47; writers
in, 10, 58, 147, 148–49
Yiddish theater, 89
Yom Kippur, 91
Young, James E., 26, 230nn.27, 28

Zionism, xii, 118, 119, 148, 213n.9. *See
also* Israel
"Zlatke" (Raskin), 148–49, 158
The Zuckerman Trilogy (Roth), 16,
214n.10. *See also Ghost Writer*